Management for Professionals

For further volumes:
http://www.springer.com/series/10101

Bernd Heesen

Effective Strategy Execution

Improving Performance with Business Intelligence

Springer

Prof. Bernd Heesen
Hochschule Ansbach & Prescient
Residenzstr. 8
91522 Ansbach
Germany
bernd.heesen@prescient.pro

ISSN 2192-8096 e-ISSN 2192-810X
ISBN 978-3-642-43768-7 ISBN 978-3-642-19205-0 (eBook)
DOI 10.1007/978-3-642-19205-0
Springer Heidelberg Dordrecht London New York

Springer is part of Springer Science+Business Media (www.springer.com)

Acknowledgements

There have been many people who helped me tremendously to develop the ideas for this book over the past years. I would like to thank all of them for their time and contribution.

I am specifically thankful to the contributing authors for sharing their stories. I strongly believe in the significant added value. These real live stories help to demonstrate the practical relevance of the concepts and methods I present in my book.

Most of all, I would like to thank my daughters Annika, Julia, Katrina and Tiffany for their patience with me. I dedicated a significant amount of my time to conceptualize, plan and write this book and missed spending this time with you.

Last but not least, I would like to thank Christian Rauscher and the team at Springer for believing in my idea and supporting me with this publication.

And now I want to thank you for reading this book. I have not written this book because of the royalties. I have written it because I believe I can fill a gap and hope to share some valuable content. Sharing knowledge is my passion as professor, consultant and author. I hope you enjoy the read. Feel free to visit the website www.strategicbusinessintelligence.com for more information. I am very interested in your honest feedback. Share with me what you like and dislike. I am a true believer in feedback loops as the foundation for continuous learning and improvement.

Nuremberg/Germany, 2011 Bernd Heesen

Preface

Turbulent times create a threat for the survival of organizations while also offering new opportunities. Why do so many companies fail to adapt? How can companies create an environment in which their management receives alerts early enough to adjust their strategy execution before a business tsunami hits? Which communication infrastructure should be established to support the required changes in planning and execution on all affected organizational levels? What kind of IT infrastructure is needed to make this happen? This book presents many examples to demonstrate how an improved strategic management approach, leveraging established management concepts in conjunction with innovative technology solutions, can lead to improved results.

Even in nonturbulent times, strategy execution can only be effective if the strategy is understood by the actors; how else should they be able to support it. While vision and mission statements are typically nice to read, they rarely specify in detail what is intended to be accomplished by when and who will be accountable for making it happen. Often strategic goals, e.g., short-term and long-term financial objectives, are conflicting with each other; e.g., investments in research and development may lead to superior new products and revenue in future but lead to a reduced profit for this fiscal period. Without clearly defined strategic objectives management will find itself in dilemmas and will struggle to make the right strategic decisions. I have been in executive positions myself and experienced the negative effects this can have on the business. Opportunistic interests may also interfere with the interests of the organization. This effect can be moderated by reflecting the expected added value and potential side effects when evaluating the consequences of strategic decisions. I will introduce the concept of the **Value Scorecard**™,[1] a scorecard which is not only balanced but focuses on the attainment of maximum value, whatever the ultimate goal may be for an organization. Value can be measured differently depending on the kind of organization. For profit

[1] Value Scorecard™ is trademarked by Bernd Heesen/Prescient.

companies financial measures such as revenue growth, earnings per share, or return on sales might be used. Government organizations might measure value to be the quality of life of their citizens. A nonprofit organization collecting and distributing donations to people in need, like Aidmatrix (2010), might count the number of food servings or medical services provided as their measure of value to save a maximum number of lives. Improvement of these ultimate goals typically depends on improvements in supporting processes, which can be measured as well. Organizations such as Aidmatrix for example focus on improving their efficiency in operations to have minimal overhead cost so they are able to spend 96 cent per donated dollar on their humanitarian programs. Understanding the correlations between these key performance indicators, how one affects the other, can significantly help to better predict the impact of a decision on the overall goal. A for-profit organization for example benefits from understanding to what extent an improvement in customer satisfaction or brand value is expected to lead to increased sales. The Value Scorecard™ provides a framework to define the relevant elements of a strategy including the definition of measurable objectives and initiatives and to differentiate between those indicators which can be impacted directly and short term (leading indicators) or indirectly with a delay (lagging indicators). An example is the investment in a new quality improvement program in manufacturing which leads to an increase in manufacturing cost and the number of recognized errors in production (leading indicators) in the short term. Since malfunctions are recognized before the product is delivered to the customer, this leads to fewer customer complaints and returns and an improvement in customer satisfaction over time (lagging indicators). A number of cases in the book will help you to see how organizations have leveraged this kind of an understanding to improve the effectiveness of their strategy execution.

Strategies are rarely static since they need to be adjusted to accommodate changed circumstances. This means that strategy formulation and execution are continuous, permanent tasks, which impact decisions regarding the allocation of resources via the budgeting process, establishment of goals via the planning process, and the execution of the business and initiatives to reach the strategic goals. It is a management challenge to align all organizational members to pull in the same direction, toward the strategic objectives. The **Strategic Alignment Process™**[2] helps managers step by step to focus on the most critical tasks to accomplish this task. The basic foundation of this process is the knowledge that management time is scarce and delegation and empowerment should be leveraged to the extent possible.

Management in this sense is not limited to the executive level. Nowadays business decisions are made on all levels of the organizational hierarchy. Smaller teams are often used to be more reactive and flexible and business may be performed by profit centers, business divisions, and business units operating with much autarky and autonomy. Therefore, when I use the word management in this

[2] Strategic Alignment Process™ is trademarked by Bernd Heesen/Prescient.

book, my understanding is inclusive of everyone who is a decision maker within the organization.

A term of special importance, Management by Objectives (MBO), has been popularized by the management guru Peter Drucker in his book *The Practice of Management* (Drucker, 2006a) since 1954. Generations of management students have heard about this concept. But to which extent did they practice it? Thanks to the improvement of IT systems capabilities it can now be put into practice on a new scale. I consider this to be the revival of the Management by Objectives in the twenty-first century, which I refer to as **MBO 2.0™**.[3] Following the terminology of Web 2.0, this naming indicates the availability of new innovative applications facilitating interactive and collaborative dialogue within the organization and with external stakeholders.

The **World of Strategic Business Intelligence™**[4] is the conceptual foundation to align two worlds and perspectives that too often exist in isolation, business and IT. Many IT departments follow their own agendas not sufficiently understanding the requirements of their colleagues responsible to execute the business, whom they support. Yes, IT is a support function! Its existence is justified by adding more value than cost to the organization. The individuals executing the strategy should be able to establish performance targets for their unit and to measure and monitor it. Alerts should be triggered to make management aware of critical developments that need management attention, thereby facilitating an effective use of the scarce time of all decision makers. To be useful, this information needs to be captured and distributed to the decision makers with minimal delay using advanced IT solutions including broadcasting, alerts, or management cockpits, which are easy to use and help to visualize complex information, e.g., using color coding, trend indicators, and maps to display geolocation performance.

How can this be supported from an IT standpoint? While I do not intend to describe all technological details of relevance, I will share the basic architecture required to support these critical business needs. A solid overview will help managers responsible for strategy execution to develop a better understanding of what can be done and how much of an effort this may require on the IT and business side. In the end, new IT solutions are only beneficial to the organization if they are accepted by the users and used properly. A change management effort needs to accompany the introduction of new systems to explain the benefits and make end users understand what they can expect as well as any limitations, which may be resolved in future initiatives. Setting appropriate expectations and supporting all those affected by the change of processes, which may include the use of new systems, significantly improves the acceptance. Finally, I will share some state-of-the-art solutions of **Business Intelligence** or **Decision Support Systems** to allow you to envision how this could be potentially applied to the benefit of your organization.

[3] MBO 2.0™ is trademarked by Bernd Heesen/Prescient.

[4] World of Strategic Business Intelligence™ is trademarked by Bernd Heesen/Prescient.

Now, what is the value of concepts if they are not applied? I do not want to leave you just with a new framework for effective strategy execution but with new management tools which you can use right away. In a complex world management needs to remain in control, and to have visibility of all performance indicators in all their organizational entities worldwide with zero latency. Is it not enjoyable to use the remote control for the TV? Whenever you make up your mind about what you like to view, you just click on a button and you get what you want. I transferred this concept to management, which for obvious reasons is slightly more complex. But the idea should be the same. If an executive or manager has an information need, it should just be a click away. Now is this realistic? How realistic has been the idea from President Kennedy, that Americans should put their feet on the moon? One has to have a vision to work toward in order to get there. With this in mind, a new tool I invented is the **Strategic Alignment Remote Control™**[5] which supports the preparation and execution of a strategy. It allows to access all relevant information at all levels of the organization across the globe allowing the management team to focus their attention on the most relevant problems as well as opportunities.

Seven **Case Studies** from different industries across the globe provide examples of how the new concepts can be applied to improve organizational performance. They include companies such as Daimler, Würth, Tetra-Pak, Germany's Federal Employment Agency, City of Aix-Les-Bains in France, and Giesecke & Devrient. Additional examples from organizations such as Disney, Marriott, Volkswagen, Avis, FedEx, and Harrah's help to demonstrate how the application of these concepts adds unique value.

This book provides new ideas and practical advice for anyone responsible for strategy execution; it is about practically relevant concepts and how to apply them within the context of the real world. Effective Strategy Execution is intended for professionals as well as those who want to prepare themselves for their career, not just for executives. People do not become effective in strategy execution by reading books; they become effective by applying new, superior concepts in their own environment. This book provides the foundation individuals need to be effective members of their organizations as practitioners or consultants in the field of strategy formulation or execution.

I have helped many organizations on all continents during my consulting career. Improving the effectiveness of their organization was the core objective in all these cases. This required the organization to recognize their own suboptimal effectiveness in the first place! Without the capability of self-reflection improvements are rarely possible. Therefore, I want to encourage you to take the free **Strategy Execution Effectiveness Survey™**.[6] The survey will help you to assess your organizational effectiveness in regards to strategy execution. Right after completing the survey you will have access to a summary of all survey responses, which allows

[5] Strategic Alignment Remote Control™ is trademarked by Bernd Heesen/Prescient.

[6] Strategy Execution Effectiveness Survey™ is trademarked by Bernd Heesen/Prescient.

you to compare your performance with those of other organizations. In addition, you can download the compiled survey findings on the book website **http://www.strategicbusinessintelligence.com**. The compiled survey will outline best practices and provide recommendations for improvement. By entering the coupon code **u3b8fp** on the first page of the survey, you can request a more detailed industry specific survey analysis report.

Once the opportunities for improvement are uncovered, the only task left to be done is to leverage the opportunity! I hope that this book will encourage you to use your creativity and commitment to improve the effectiveness of your organization.

Contents

Chapter 1
Management Challenges in Dynamic Business Environments

Why do some organizations outperform others? Why are so many companies going out of business every year? Why do they have problems coping with challenges in the market? A prediction from Gartner indicates that more than 35% of the top 5,000 global companies will regularly fail to make insightful decisions about significant changes in their business and markets (Gartner, 2009a). This sounds alarming. Does this seem to reflect the current status quo? How can organizations potentially increase their chance of survival under these circumstances? I will try to address these and additional questions in the following introduction.

What is the life expectancy of an organization these days? How do the Fortune 500 weather the storms? Do they manage to have an increased likelihood to survive? They don't seem to do very well. One-third of the companies listed in the 1970 Fortune 500, for instance, had vanished by 1983. They were either acquired, merged, or broken to pieces (de Geus, 1997). The Economist published the result of a study which found that the life expectancy of a typical multinational firm lies between 40 and 50 years. For less exalted firms, life can be even shorter. The life expectancy of the average European and Japanese company was found to be less than 13 years (Economist, 1997).

Why is it difficult for companies to demonstrate sustainable high performance? Results based on the analysis of 2,000+ companies in 12 developed and emerging economies by Bain & Company found that only about one company in eight, or 12%, achieve sustained and profitable growth over a decade (Zook & Allen, 2010). What are the main factors for a positive performance in the long run? Companies that showed the best performance were those that took advantage of turbulent market conditions. They came up with new products and services, or a radically new business model, and were able to transform themselves quickly to adapt to changed market conditions. If the more successful companies leverage new opportunities created in turbulent markets, should turbulence be cherished, and are markets really more turbulent? Are business circumstances really more turbulent than they have been? Yes, Chris Zook and James Allen argue; turbulence has increased by a factor of more than three over the past three decades. They define turbulence in terms of major structural changes that require companies to change the

B. Heesen, *Effective Strategy Execution*, Management for Professionals,
DOI 10.1007/978-3-642-19205-0_1, © Springer-Verlag Berlin Heidelberg 2012

way in which they compete. They compared data collected in the 1970s with data from the early 2000s, not even reflecting on the financial crisis that started in 2008. Based on their definition, between 15 and 25% of industries were considered to be turbulent in the 1970s. Thirty years later, it had increased to between 65 and 75%.

If turbulent markets are becoming the standard and if successfully dealing with these circumstances leads to success, how can organizations prepare themselves, and how should they adjust the way they operate? Companies need to improve their responsiveness to changes in their environment, since competition in these market conditions is about speed. Decision times are getting shorter.

But which occurring changes do organizations need to be prepared to deal with? The following is a list of some of the current challenges: globalization, treating information as an asset, and finally, managing the complexity of all these challenges to make insightful strategic decisions before it is too late or hastier than those of competitors.

Globalization can help as well as hurt. Organizations can market their products globally, choose their suppliers, and recruit strategically from the lowest-cost countries. On one hand, this increases the options for your own organization; on the other hand, these options are available to your competitors as well, which means that you may have new competitors from abroad, offering their products and services in your markets. It is a threat if your competitors are smarter or quicker in leveraging the benefits of globalization, and your customers also compare products and services globally before placing an order. Utilizing the internet, business can be won or lost with a click, with new substitute offerings, or discount offerings by competitors. It is a challenge to remain aware of all relevant threats and opportunities, and this increases complexity for the management team.

Based on IBM's Global CEO Study 2010 for which 1,541 CEOs, general managers, and senior public sector leaders representing different sizes of organizations in 60 countries and 33 industries were interviewed, increasingly available information is one of the greatest business opportunities (IBM, 2010a). Companies should extract the maximum value from the information they have about their markets, customers, suppliers, employees, and competitors. Today, in a volatile world, competitive advantages have a shortened lifespan. For example, in June 2005, General Motors unveiled a new incentive plan to offer discounts on new car sales to the general public, which were previously only available to their employees (Davis, Miller, & Russell, 2006). This program, which was only available for 1 month originally, caused the steepest increase in sales in 19 years, and increased General Motor's market share. With this success, dealers asked for the program to be extended for another month. Shortly after the program was extended, their competitors, Ford and Chrysler, replicated the offer on their cars to eliminate the competitive advantage created by the program. The time span from starting the discount program until the moment the competition had become aware of the information, and then decided to copy the program, defined the lifespan of the competitive advantage. Timely information availability has now become a significant source of competitive advantage. Information should be treated as an invaluable asset.

Another finding of the IBM Global CEO Study 2010 (IBM, 2010a) was that 79% of CEOs anticipate business complexity to rise above the current level, and more than half of CEOs doubt their ability to manage it. Technology is also a contributing factor to complexity, developing interconnected applications and homogeneous reporting, based on a complex heterogeneous application systems infrastructure. They consider creativity in dealing with the dynamic business environment the most important skill, uncovering new trends, developing new business models and taking calculated risks and innovate how they lead and communicate. The study authors state that "with few exceptions, CEOs expect continued disruption in one form or another. The new economic environment, they agree, is substantially more volatile, much more uncertain, increasingly complex and structurally different" (IBM, 2010a, p. 14).

What can be done to deal with this challenging environment and prepare for the future? The study (IBM, 2010a) reveals that successful CEOs refashion their organizations to benefit from complexity by dealing with it adequately. Those organizations with above average success in their business, called Standouts in the study, pursue iterative, ongoing strategy development more than other organizations. This evolutionary approach of continuous strategy development is promising to be the most successful approach.

The results (IBM, 2010a) also show that CEOs feel their organizations are not to be able to transform available data into feasible action plans, let alone to detect emerging opportunities, despite the fact that they have plenty of data available in their databases. To gather new insights about trends and developments in the market in order to leverage available opportunities, they demand improved access to information. You cannot rely solely on your experience for new markets or regarding new technologies or trends, for which there exists no past experience. Gathering new information and distributing relevant pieces of information to the right individuals in the organization will be a key competence to aim for.

With all this going on, if this is a problem everyone has to deal with, along with the competition, why should the management care so much? No one can be expected to have all the solutions, right? Wrong! It is a tough time for managers and executives who are held accountable for the results of their business. The tenure of executives is becoming shorter these days, underperformance is not tolerated for long, and is one of the main reasons executives are forced to leave. This was the finding of an analysis of 10 consecutive years' worth of detailed data on CEO succession among the world's top 2,500 public companies (Favaro, Karlsson, & Neilson, 2010). The pressure to perform is increasing and executives have to develop viable plans as to how they intend to perform well. On the following pages I will address two of the key management challenges: dealing with complexity and the need for timely decision and execution.

1.1 Increased Complexity

What is complexity? Situations are perceived as complex if there is a high degree of uncertainty or if we just have no recipe for dealing with the situation. Given that executives perceive their environment as getting more and more complex, how one handles complexity may not only impact profitability, but also define the chances for survival. Organizations need to understand how their organization operates and where it can improve in order to compete successfully, and not only in the short term. Many factors are impacting a complex system consisting of a multitude of actors like customers, employees, competitors, partners, governments, and others. The science of cybernetics provides recommendations on how to better understand and deal with these complex and dynamic systems.

The term cybernetics (Cwarel Isaf Institute, 2010) was first used in 1834 by the French physicist André-Marie Amperé to describe the science of managing processes. Cybernetics (Wikipedia, 2011d) accepts that complexity is inherent in dynamic systems because their processes are often non-linear and therefore hard to observe and control. Cybernetics is the knowledge about how to apply regulation, control, and communication in complex systems. A feature specific to the way in which it can be applied to a business context, and involves the study of what things do and how they interact with one another, not just what they are, reflecting the dynamics rather than assuming a static state. This can be used as the foundation for finding problem resolutions.

How cybernetics can be applied in a business context was first introduced by Stafford Beer in the 1950s. Beer (Cwarel Isaf Institute, 2010) developed a set of methods and models to improve effectiveness in organizations:

- **The Law of Viability:** To be considered viable, an organization has to be capable of adapting to its constantly changing environment via learning from its experiences. The first and most important objective formulated by Beer is not profit maximization but survival. The benefit of this perspective is that is has a long-term orientation.
- **The Law of Requisite Variety**: Ashby's Law of Requisite Variety states that a complex system can only be dealt with by means that are equally complex. It does not simplify reality in the usual reductionist fashion. Instead the intent is to look at the reality from a level that is high enough to allow all factors that operate in complex systems to be separated out, and presented in a form in which they are clearly recognizable and comprehensible to anyone who is curious. This approach helps to build models with an appropriate level of complexity almost automatically.
- **Feedback Loops and Networks:** The origin of instability, chaotic development, and complexity lies in the fact that, as a result of their very nature, living and social systems have an open and dynamic character. They can be described by an approach that sees and organizes processes as circular: the end of a process is taken back to its beginning. The technical term for this is recursivity. In this way, loops become visible, and effective loops can be established. Once all the processes in a system have been closed on themselves or linked with one another, networks of interdependent loops become visible. These are typical for cybernetic models, and allow to view the situation, including its interdependencies.
- **The Viable System Model:** Conventional models of organizations, such as organizational charts, for example, are typically of a mechanistic and linear

nature. This kind of organization delegates much of the responsibility up the hierarchy instead of counting on personal responsibility. Employees, customers, partners, society, and other aspects of the world outside the organization, on which it depends and with which it interacts, are not sufficiently reflected. The Viable System Model focuses on the flows of information and knowledge. The contribution of individuals is of major importance. Between the bottom and the top of the hierarchy, there are systematic recursions or feedback which create a balance between the levels of the hierarchy, as the bottom and top learn from each other. A command-and-control type of leadership is replaced by an ordered pattern supplying the needed information at all levels of an organization to create effectiveness. Employees, customers, partners and society, or, in other words, all the aspects of the world outside the organization on which it depends and which it interacts with, are integrated, because they often have an enormous effect on the organization. Boosting intelligence also implies that employees on all levels are able to view the world from the perspective of their managers at all times. The ideal state is for everyone to know the points of view of everyone else sufficiently well to be able to orient their own behavior to the larger whole. In such a system, everyone can act self-organized, based on the information network, which enables effective co-operation. In this sense, a system can regulate itself and absorb a good amount of complexity within itself via self-organization. The managers only need to deal with what is left over. Schwaninger (2009) uses the term "residual variety" to describe this portion of the business, which management needs to take care of.

The Cwarel Isaf Institute (2010) compares the benefits of the Viable System Model to the medicine Aspirin, with five systemic and stabilizing effects, including the relief of pain, lowering of fever, checking of inflammation, prevention of heart attacks, and strengthening of immune reactions. The benefits of the Viable System Model are seen as similarly beneficial to organizations, by supporting the following tasks: doing things, coordinating, optimizing, observing, and drawing conclusions, and deciding on and keeping track of values and ensuring identity.

Cybernetics for regulation, control, and communication in complex systems can be applied in two different ways: first-order control as a mechanism to regulate and steer directly and second-order control as self-steering mechanisms of control. In **first-order control**, once a system is understood, the manager can interfere by taking corrective action, e.g., adjusting the temperature after looking at the thermometer, and recognizing a difference from the intended room temperature. One of the recognized effects might be that the temperature needs adjustment whenever external circumstances change, e.g., outside temperature, consuming time from the manager. A second disadvantage is the lack of permanent monitoring by the manager, who also has many other obligations, leading to a failure to adjust the temperature in time and leading to deviations, too warm or too cold, from the ideal room temperature. An example for a ***second-order control*** would be a thermostat, which permanently senses the room temperature and automatically adjusts the heating to always maintain a set temperature. The problem, controlling the room temperature, is identical. But understanding and reflecting the ineffectiveness of the described first-order control, requiring more management interaction, and still leading to a lower level of goal fulfillment, can lead to establishing the more effective second-order control of the system. The introduction of self-regulating systems can increase effectiveness significantly. I will describe the concept of Management by Objectives 2.0™ in Sect. 2.2, which also leverages a second-order control.

Now, how are companies expected to act in complex environments? Based on Schwaninger (2009), intelligent organizations act appropriately by adapting to changed circumstances, influencing their environment, potentially seek new milieus where they can survive, and making a positive net contribution to their viability.

Complexity, when dealt with appropriately, can even be turned into an advantage, as the following example of the three 2010 Nobel Prize winners in chemistry (Nobelprize.org, 2010) showcases. They were able to turn a toxin into a cure, the development of anti-inflammatory drugs, drugs against asthma, for antitumor activity. Professor Richard F. Heck, who has been working at the University of Delaware, Professor Ei-ichi Negishi from Purdue University, and Professor (emeritus) Akira Suzuki from Hokkaido University in Japan were rewarded by the Royal Swedish Academy of Sciences for their discovery of palladium-catalyzed cross couplings in organic synthesis. The discoveries by the three organic chemists had a significant impact not only in academic research but also in the development of new pharmaceuticals.

Pumiliotoxin (PTX) is one of several toxins found in the skin of poison dart frogs, for whom they serve as a chemical defense against predators. Pumiliotoxins affect the body because they interfere with muscle contraction in the heart and skeletal muscle. Converting this biological threat into a biological opportunity was possible by a detailed understanding of the loops and networks, including the production of the toxin, the reactions it caused in conjunction with knowledge networks related to diseases. Connecting and correlating these different sets of loops into a network enabled to find new and effective applications and processes.

One of the biggest management errors is the overemphasis of quarterly publicized profit, cost or revenue as a key performance indicator for the health of a business. Both these indicators are short-term indicators. To get a deeper understanding, it is important to know which factors impact the profit, revenue, or cost for the future. For instance, investing in research and development today will increase the cost now, but will establish the foundation for new products being introduced in the coming years, thereby contributing to extra revenue and market share. Cutting the cost today by reducing the headcount in customer service will improve the short-term profit, but might lead to reduced customer satisfaction in the long run, thereby contributing to an increased customer churn, and reduced revenue and profit in the coming years. While these scenarios may not apply the same way to all organizations, they demonstrate the need to create a deeper insight by developing a more complex set of performance indicators and an understanding of causal loops and networks. Analyzing the details and then synthesizing it to create a model reflecting the organizations' complex situation fulfills the requirements of the Law of Requisite Variety. I will introduce the concept of the **Value Scorecard™** in Sect. 3.2.1 to reflect the variety of performance measures. Such a model, including causal loops, can be utilized to test hypotheses, e.g., what happens to sales if the price is increased by $x\%$. Having prior knowledge about the price sensitivity of the different customer segments would allow to simulate different scenarios to determine the best price under the known circumstances. Marriott utilizes advanced analytics for price optimization, which I will describe in more detail in Sect. 3.2.2.1.

1.2 Timely Decision and Execution

Reacting faster to new customer trends, leveraging lower cost or higher-quality suppliers before competitors do are only two examples where speed can be the source for creating a competitive advantage. Other examples might be improving products or services or adding new innovative features to your products before the competition does, e.g., by reducing the product development cycles. An example might be to provide superior customer service based on quickly finding solutions to customers' problems, which can lead to an increase in customer loyalty. Another example might be to add an additional convenience for your customers before the competition does. Using the website to share product features or offering a customized made-to-order process to your customers, like Nike with *NIKEiD* (Nike, 2011) or adidas with *mi adidas* (Adidas group, 2011). Saving time is also relevant to your customers. Offering the chance to select, customize, and purchase a product with a couple of clicks from a convenient location of the customers' choosing might bring extra customers and revenue to your organization. Not offering the services available by your competitors may actually create a competitive disadvantage. At least it would be critical for you to have quick knowledge of what products and services are offered by your competition, e.g., understanding that your competitor is running a campaign with discounts to gain market share, which affects your business. Time lost before you are aware of these kind of relevant market factors create a delay in your response, giving your competition an advantage you might not want, or even creating a threat to the survival of your organization.

That speed in adapting to changes is relevant for the survival of organizations and species is undoubtful, especially if the environment changes faster than the organization can adapt. Raynor (2007) uses the example of the Cretaceous–Tertiary extinction event which caused the extinction of dinosaurs. The event dramatically changed the circumstances on our planet and dinosaurs, despite their dominant position on earth over a period of 135 million years, were not able to adapt quickly enough. Their capacity to adapt was too slow compared to the rate of change in their environment. Clearly organizations need to learn from this and establish flexible, adaptable structures which allow them to recognize and predict relevant changes, and adjust quickly in these turbulent times.

But are organizations sufficiently monitoring their environment to recognize and predict potential threats and opportunities early on? Accenture interviewed 600 executives in the United States, the United Kingdom, and Ireland to find that 22% of the respondents said their organizations do not use predictive analytics to predict how competitor activities, market trends, product/service developments, economic trends, or skill requirements might change. Based on Dave Rich, managing director of the Accenture Analytics Group, "The need for speed in decision-making is a key competitive differentiator, and lacking the insight into customers' preferences means mounting an expensive come-from-behind response. During previous downturns, companies that thrived used data-derived insights made by informed decision makers to produce lasting competitive advantage. We believe that predictive analytics will be the difference between the winners and losers in the next economic cycle" (Accenture, 2010). This statement confirms the relevance of timely availability of information.

Digital information is transmitted high speed, it can be instantly available at any place. If there is a competitive advantage to be had by being the fastest in having information and leveraging it in the business, and everyone is aware of it, then it will be tough to be the quickest. Any competitive advantage based on innovations will only last as long as the competition has gotten aware and developed a replica or a generic. Decisions have to be made and actions have to be taken fast in this dynamic business environment.

The value of information is actually decreasing over time, since any loss of time reduces the advantage which can be had over the competition. But it is not only relevant to have the information. One only gains a benefit by actually utilizing, making decisions based on it, and acting in accordance with the decision made. The delay caused by collecting data, analyzing the information, deciding, and finally executing what was decided goes along with a decrease in utility value as displayed in Fig. 1.1. An organization which acts quicker than their competition can gain a competitive advantage.

A maximization of the utility value can be reached by performing the following steps:

1. The most critical information needs are gathered.
2. The information recipients are identified.
3. The information sources are located.
4. The information is gathered and collected.
5. Suited communication channels are utilized to supply the information to the recipients.
6. Information systems are utilized to support a timely availability (pull) and distribution (push) of the information.
7. Information is analyzed, decisions are made reflecting the information, and actions are taken quickly.

How can you apply these steps and what is the most critical information? The decision makers should know what kind of information they need to make smart decisions. In the case of a retailer, it may be information about the buying behavior

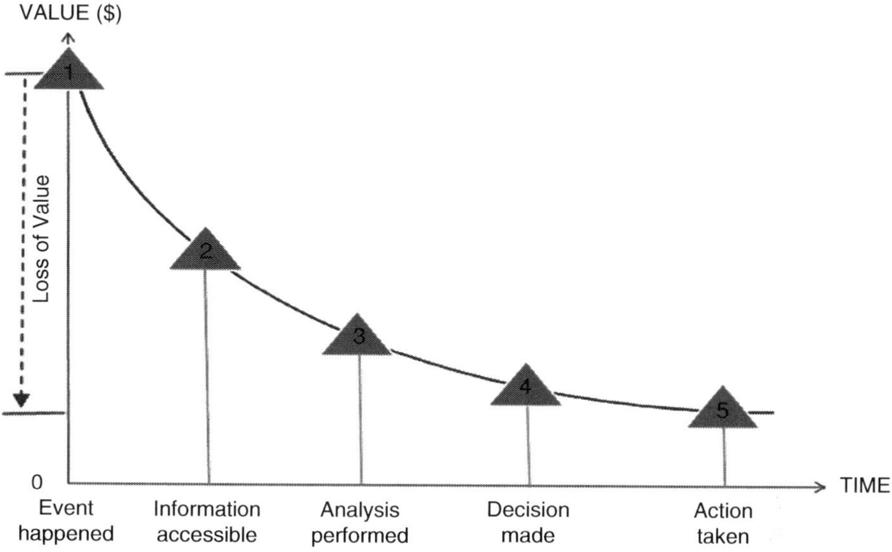

Fig. 1.1 Loss of value over time (adapted based on Hackathorn, 2003)

of their customers, recognizing patterns so that marketing campaigns, including discounts offered, are most effective, cross-selling is maximized, and customer churn is minimized.

This is exactly the business of Catalina Marketing (2010). Their data warehouse contains 3 years' worth of purchase history for 195 million U.S. customer loyalty program members at supermarkets, pharmacies, and other retailers, at total of more than 600 billion data records in a single database table. It is the largest loyalty database in the world and adds 300 million transaction records each week to its database. For retail customers in more than 24,000 U.S. and 8,000 international grocery, drug, and mass merchandiser stores, their transaction data from the cash register can be analyzed in real-time, triggering the printout of a unique set of coupons based on their shopping history and demographics for each individual. The coupons are printed out together with the receipt right at check-out. These high-impact promotions and advertisements are hand-delivered to shoppers at the point of sale, with an average promotional response rate of 6.3%, one of the highest in the industry. The shopper-driven advertising results in an increasing awareness by 16% points and recall by 24% points, as Catalina proudly announces on their website. No doubt, they have one of the largest online decision support business intelligence systems in the world. This information is not only used to analyze past behavior but also to predict future behavior, e.g., predicting customer churn before it happens. Eric Williams (May, 2009), chief information officer at Catalina, explains that they evaluated the transactions of customers who had not visited for a while in comparison to those that still shopped. They found an item that, if the customer had bought it and then stopped buying it often led to the customer stopping to buy in the store at all. The item that made the difference was fluid milk. With this predictive analytical information at hand, it was possible to evaluate this product in more detail and potentially to make sure fluid mild would always be fresh. Having this kind of information allows to execute the business more effectively.

Another example where information helps to improve business results is online marketing. If you have shopped at Amazon (Amazon, 2011), you might be familiar with product recommendations. While you look at one product you also receive recommendations to purchase additional products in the sections "frequently bought together" and "customers who bought this item also bought," which are based on analytics using data mining tools.

Similarly, online advertisers leverage the users on websites to improve the effectiveness of their advertisements. They create hundreds of versions of an ad using different fonts, colors, pictures, and evaluate the number of clicks each of those versions attracts. This way, they find the design which is most effective for a targeted audience. What is the impact of this kind of information utilization for the business? Tim Hanlon, executive vice president of VivaKi Ventures, the investment unit of Publicis Group, voices his opinion this way: "The question is, how do we combine creative energy, which is a manual and sort of qualitative exercise, with the raw processing power of computing, which is all about quantitative data? I think it's clear that the traditional process of agencies is clearly not going to survive the digital era without significant changes" (Clifford, 2008).

The rising importance of current information availability is also manifested in the commitment of organizations to establish adequate business intelligence infrastructures, including data warehousing. A survey conducted by the Data Warehousing Institute (Data Warehousing Institute, 2011) in 2009 found that 46% of the responding organizations intend to replace their data warehouse platform within the next 3 years (Henschen, 2010). Is this a reflection that the current infrastructure is insufficient? The following section will discuss challenges organizations will need to master to improve their chance for success.

1.3 The Challenges with Strategy Execution

Bruce Henderson, founder of the Boston Consulting Group, once stated, "All competitors who persist over time must maintain a unique advantage by differentiation over all others. Managing that differentiation is the essence of long-term business strategy" (Stern & Deimler, 2006, p. 1). To create such a competitive advantage, organizations not only invest time and effort to define a strategy but, more importantly they mobilize their complete organization to work on reaching their defined goals. Without effective strategy execution, the best strategy will not be of any value.

Now the question at hand is: How effective are organizations in executing their strategy? Harris Interactive surveyed 23,000 individuals with their instrument called the Execution Quotient (xQ) Questionnaire to measure the ability of an organization to focus and execute what they defined as their key objectives

(Covey, 2004). Surprisingly, they found that hardly anyone even measures progress on their most important goals and only 10% of the respondents reported that they have a clear, accurate, visible scoreboard to monitor progress toward reaching the strategic objectives. They also found the following:

- Only 39% felt that people are committed to the organization's direction.
- Only 37% had a clear understanding of what their organization is trying to achieve and why.
- Only 22% felt that all workers focused on organizational goals.
- Only 20% were enthusiastic about their team's and organization's goals.
- Only 20% said they had a clear "line of sight" between tasks and their team's and organization's goals.
- Only 17% felt their organization fosters open communication that is respectful of differing opinions that result in new and better ideas.
- Only 13% felt that people take individual initiative and responsibility for results.
- Only 10% felt that their organization holds people accountable for results.
- Only 10% felt that success measures are tracked accurately and openly.
- Only 10% felt that people have clear, measurable, deadline driven work goals.

Summarizing the key findings of this study, about two thirds have no clear understanding of what their organization's strategic goal is and how it is measured. About 80% have no clear "line of sight" between their tasks and their team's and organization's goals. About 90% have no clear, measurable, deadline driven work goals. The study did not evaluate how many of the organizations had an effective strategy execution. Implicitly though, it does not seem very likely that the strategy execution was successful in most of the participants' organizations under these circumstances.

Do these findings come as a surprise or do you feel as if you have been working under similar conditions yourself before? Let us take a look at some more case studies on the effectiveness of strategy execution to develop a better understanding of whether this result can be seen as somewhat representative.

A comprehensive review of 28 research studies evaluating the success and failure of business strategy implementations found that between 28 and 90% of strategy implementations fail (Candido & Santos, 2008).

What can be the reason that so many organizations not only fail to be effective in their strategy implementation but even fail completely? Pfeffer and Sutton (2000) argue that there is a gap between knowing what should be done and actually doing it. They report that even managers who know what needs to be done are often uninformed about the actual progress. Research findings from Kaplan and Norton (2001) confirm that 92% of the surveyed organizations don't report on their strategic lead indicators. They found additional reasons which may contribute to an ineffective strategy execution. The research showed that 85% of the surveyed companies' management team spends less than 1 h a month discussing their strategy, and 60% do not link strategy with budgeting. Not allocating resources according to the strategic goals seems like a problem which can be avoided. Allocating funds based on the established priorities should be possible.

many organizations actually follow a defined process to execute their strategy. A survey of 143 performance management professionals performed by the Balanced Scorecard Collaborative (Palladium, 2010) in 2006 found that only 54% of respondents had a formal process to manage strategy execution (Kaplan & Norton, 2008). The majority of those that followed a formal strategy execution process were outperforming their peer group of companies. So, having a formal strategy execution system seems to pay off, and increase the chance for success by a factor of 200–300% within the surveyed group.

Those organizations that measure their performance and the effects of their strategic actions do not only benefit from learning from the performance feedback, but the introduction of performance measurement systems also helps to clarify and communicate what matters to the organization.

Despite these obvious benefits, many scorecard implementations fail because of an inappropriate design of the measurement system, e.g., not measuring what is perceived as most relevant, or because it is rejected by those that feel threatened. As Neely and Bourne state, "Far too often people can recollect examples where senior management has used measurement data to score points over other managers and illustrate why they are failing to perform. In such organizations, especially where there is a culture of blame, measurement becomes almost impossible because nobody really wants measurement data to become available" (Neely & Bourne, 2000). If the performance management system cannot be avoided, one of the reactions of the affected individual may be playing games with numbers by focusing on meeting the measurable objective, but failing to deliver what is really critical for the business. A well-known example is that of call centers when employees are measured by the average time to answer a call. They might be picking up the phone and hang up before ever speaking to the person on the other line, just to make sure the call is answered within the expected time. Another way for them to reach short call times is to forward callers to other call center functions or providing them with a different number to call, which is supposedy responsible for theparticular issue. Who has not met with this experience? Isn't it interesting to see how an incorrectly implemented measurement system might be the cause for bad customer service? This is even more interesting, since the intention might have been to improve customer service.

Implementations of scorecards also frequently fail because of a lack of IT-infrastructure to provide correct calculation and timely availability of performance indicators. Sometimes data are not available, at other times, the quality of the data is insufficient, or the data are widely spread across the organization in unrelated databases, e.g., finance data in an ERP system, customer data in a Customer Relationship Management system owned by the sales department, and many more databases or Excel sheets being maintained without central oversight and knowledge. This kind of nonintegrated infrastructure does not support integrated evaluations and thereby limits the organizational capability to report organizational performance in a reliable way. Theoretically, it is possible to use these sources of data and calculate performance figures, but the amount of time, effort, and cost required is prohibitive if the infrastructure is not appropriate. Even if the information is brought together, the information consolidation in such a scenario will take extra time and not provide the management with required facts in time and on demand. A solid IT infrastructure is needed to support the collection, calculation, and distribution of the data which the management expects to have immediate access to. This is a dedicated effort and requires adequate support from the management team in regards to funding and time. This lack of understanding and support from the top management to establish a solid IT-infrastructure is one more reason for the failure of scorecard implementations. After all, what is the value of having defined measures originally, but not establishing the infrastructure, so they can never be used? This book intends to help clarify some of the core requirements and challenges when establishing such an infrastructure for a scorecard in the Chap. 3.

Given the fact that budgets are always limited, one needs to be focused on the efficiency of a scorecard implementation. The trick is to find the right balance of measuring as little as possible, but, at the same time, to make sure to measure everything that matters. In the end, the benefits of the initiative need to outweigh costs for the organization. This needs to be in the forefront of the minds of everyone involved. Validating to what extent the provided information is utilized, once it is made available, can help to create support for further initiatives, or to find out which reports and performance indicators are rarely used, and can be eliminated to reduce the continuing effort and cost to provide the information. A great example of how this can be done is provided in the case study in Sect. 6.1. The concept of the Business Intelligence Value Scorecard is presented to measure the contribution of their Business Intelligence initiative for the organization.

Clearly, if the organization's success can be improved by implementing a strategy execution system which allows to measure performance, then one needs to find out how to get this done efficiently.

Do you believe that some of these problems may also apply to your organization? The starting point for improvement is a rigorous self-assessment to see which of the outlined barriers (see Fig. 1.2) might also be a hurdle in your organization. The result of such an analysis might lead to uncover opportunities for improvement. I encourage you to take the free **Strategy Execution Effectiveness Survey™**. The survey will help you to assess your organizational effectiveness in regards to strategy execution (see details in the Preface), and to see how your organization performs in comparison to other organizations.

Executives and managers need to make sure all activities within the organization help to reach the strategic objectives. A couple of obstacles have to be overcome to create strategic alignment of organizational efforts. Organizations strive to be effective not only in the short term. Sustainable alignment leading to an effective strategy execution should help to reach the set objectives. This may require long breath from management, similar to a marathon race. Like in sports, time is of the essence in business as well, especially during turbulent periods. The objective, therefore, is to establish a competitive advantage by reaching alignment quicker than the competition. The time displayed in Fig. 1.2 is the world record in marathon at the time of publication. What the main obstacles are, and how to overcome these

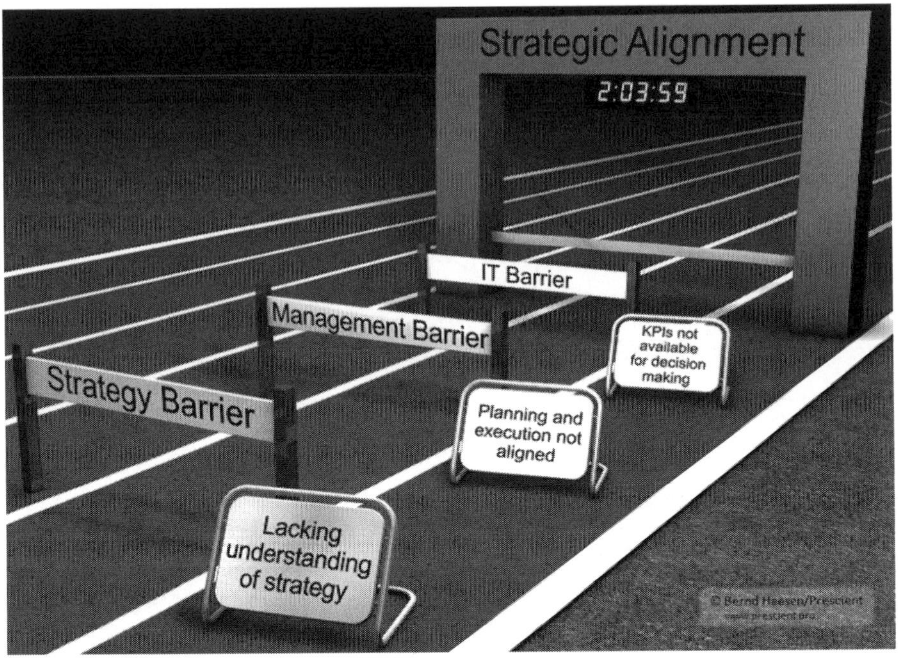

Fig. 1.2 Barriers to strategic alignment (©Bernd Heesen/Prescient. Used with permission)

three hurdles towards strategic alignment in record time shall be discussed in the following text.

1.3.1 Strategy Barrier

The first hurdle towards strategic alignment is the Strategy Barrier. Organizations that are not able to communicate their strategy to their organizational members, cannot expect them to be pulling in the same direction. Inefficiencies in strategy execution cannot be avoided in such a situation.

The earlier mentioned study from Harris Interactive had found that only 37% of the 23,000 individuals surveyed had a clear understanding of what their organization is trying to achieve. Another study performed by Clifford (2001) in 2001 found that only 20% of middle managers felt that they were really "in tune" with their organization. This lack of understanding of the strategic direction of the organization was even leading employees to become cynical or burnt out. Kaplan and Norton (2001) found, based on their research, that on average only 5% of a company's employees understand their organization's strategy.

It is obvious that employees who do not understand their own organization's strategy cannot help to execute the strategy effectively.

1.3.2 Management Barrier

After the first hurdle is overcome, and employees understand the organization's strategy, they could all start pulling in the same direction, towards accomplishing the strategic objectives. But do they do so?

As indicated, only 20% felt that they had a clear "line of sight" between their tasks and their team's and organization's goals; only 22% felt that all workers focused on organizational goals; only 39% felt that people are committed to the organization's direction, and only 10% felt that their organization holds people accountable for results. This represents the Management Barrier which needs to be overcome by creating an alignment via the coordination of efforts and encouraging cooperation from employees.

Coordination means that the strategic objectives of each individual subunit need to be defined in alignment with the overall organizational objectives, and resources need to be allocated accordingly. The definition of what is important to an organization and how to measure it requires a shared understanding of the so-called Key Performance Indicators, short-term as well as long-term, financial as well as non-financial, leading as well as lagging ones. A separate chapter, Sect. 3.2, will address this topic. Establishing a solid measurement system and using a budgeting process which reflects the importance of funding the most critical initiatives to reach the strategic objectives facilitates the coordination of all organizational efforts. A national survey of a cross section of 203 executives in the United States, conducted by Schiemann & Associates, Inc. (Lingle & Schiemann, 1996) confirmed that measurement plays a crucial role in translating strategy into results. Their findings indicate that the top companies in their respective industries distinguish themselves by having agreed-upon measures that managers understand, balancing financial and nonfinancial measures, and linking their strategic key performance indicators to the operational ones. They also update their strategic scorecard regularly and make sure they communicate performance results to all employees. But is this kind of behavior the norm for the majority of organizations?

The results of a study of HR and IT managers conducted by Kaplan and Norton (2005) seems to indicate the opposite. It revealed that the strategies of 67% of subunit or departmental plans were not aligned with the corporate strategies and plans. This misalignment in planning also included the allocation of budgets; 60% of organizations did not link their financial budgets to their strategic priorities. The same applied to incentive programs and compensation packages, which were not aligned with the strategic objectives for 70% of middle managers and more than 90% of frontline employees. An earlier study (Kaplan & Norton, 2001) had found that this even applies to senior managers; only 51% of senior managers in the United States and 31% in the United Kingdom had their personal goals linked to strategy.

Even the best strategy cannot be executed effectively under the above circumstances. In the end, the execution is done by the frontline workers, who deal directly with the customers at least as much as with the executives. Lawrence

MacGregor Serven refers to an experience, everyone can relate to: "Just think about your last trip to McDonald's or the last time you called the Microsoft help line. It was the local store manager or the technical support analyst who fulfilled your customer needs, not the CEO. How does that person know what to do, day in and day out, to implement the company's strategy? There can be an enormous gap between what top executives want to have happen and what actually does happen" (MacGregor Serven, 1999, p. 10).

Cooperation is needed. The question is how do we get employees to actually help us execute the strategy. Ultimately they perform business processes. For this aligning to work, employees need to be committed to the organizational goals, which might be supported by adequate incentive structures. Certainly the individual goals should be aligned with organizational objectives. Without any doubt, employees also need to have the required resources and skills to perform the tasks if execution is to be effective.

This is easier said than done. One of the problems with incentive programs linked to strategic objectives has been found to be the fact that the strategic objectives shift over time, especially in turbulent markets. A compensation model, which needs to be designed, communicated, and calculated, based on information on performance measures being tracked during the evaluation period, cannot be adjusted as quickly as a strategy might need to be fixed based on new circumstances. An example of the consequences of an incentive system which was not adjusted in sync with the adjustment of the strategy is presented in the case study in Sect. 6.7.

Establishing incentive systems which are linked to the strategic objectives may even be counterproductive, if the measures are not objective. An example would be to tie compensation to customer satisfaction, if the measure can be influenced by those being measured, e.g., if sales or service staff influence their clients by educating them about the significance of a favorable response to the satisfaction survey for their employment and compensation. While it may be easier to measure customer satisfaction as an attitude, it may be far more valuable, because it is a more meaningful evaluation of satisfaction with positive effects on the business, to measure the actual behavior of customers like repeat purchases or referrals of new customers over time. Obviously this may be measurable only with significant delay, depending on the average interval to be expected for a repeat purchase.

It is also much debated if incentives are more efficient if related to individual or team performance. While team-based incentives may encourage improved cooperation within the team, it can also lead to the free-rider problem, where those not contributing benefit from the initiative of those contributing. This can encourage a reduction in contributions. As Kaplan and Norton stated, "several empirical studies indicate that the economists' free-rider problem could be less serious than purported, that individuals may be more influenced by peer pressures and social relationships than by individual merit pay" (Kaplan & Norton, 2001, pp. 266–270).

Another issue with tying incentives to the strategic objectives is the availability of reliable data which tracks the performance of individuals or groups, and their contribution to the objectives, which leads over to the next barrier, the IT Barrier.

1.3.3 IT Barrier

How important is the availability of reliable and current information on the performance of the organization? Is this only a requirement invented by software manufacturers and consulting organizations who want to sell their products and services, or is this a real business need?

The national survey of a cross section of 203 executives in the United States, conducted by Schiemann & Associates, Inc. (Lingle & Schiemann, 1996) found significant differences in performance between organizations called measurement-managed companies and those characterized as non-measurement managed companies. Measurement-managed companies were those in which management reviewed performance measures regularly in three or more of six identified, primary performance areas based on agreed-upon key performance indicators. Table 1.1 displays significant gaps between those organizations with established measurement systems and those where performance measurement is not executed comprehensively.

The companies where performance measurement is part of the culture are obviously more effective in communicating their strategy. This is not surprising. Those responsible for measuring need to define what is measured and how it is measured in the first place, and this requires a shared understanding within the organization. When establishing the strategic objectives in such an organization, it will not be accepted

Table 1.1 Advantages of measurement-managed organizations[a]

	Measurement-managed organizations (%)	Non-measurement-managed organizations (%)	Gap (%)
Effective communication of strategy from top to bottom	60	8	52
Strong teamwork and cooperation among the management team	85	38	47
Agreement among top management on the business strategy	90	47	43
Last major cultural or operational change judged to be very or moderately successful	97	55	42
Information shared openly and candidly	71	30	41
At least three performance areas linked to compensation	47	9	38
Reported to be financially ranked in the top third of their industry	83	52	31
Perceived as an industry leader over the past 3 years	74	44	30
Extent to which employees self-monitored their own performance against agreed-upon standards	42	16	26

[a]Lingle and Schiemann (1996)

as sufficient just to make broad statements about future goals but, instead, it will be expected from management to define measurable objectives. The organizational dialog which is stimulated when discussing how the strategic objectives can be reached, and what the measurable contributions of individual organizational units should be to reach them, helps to foster a shared understanding of what matters to the organization. This leads to an improved agreement on the strategy.

Measurement-managed organizations are required to establish an environment where information about performance is available and can be utilized by employees directly for the purpose of self-monitoring. Performance information needed for self-monitoring therefore is shared openly. In the end these companies have a significantly improved likelihood to belong to the top third of their industry. So, it seems, the establishment of a measurement infrastructure as the foundation for a measurement management organization does not seem to be a story invented by software developers or consultants. Lingle and Schiemann (1996) summarize the competitive advantage created by establishing a measurement culture such that measurement-managed companies tend to anticipate the future more precisely and are likely to remain in a leadership position in rapidly changing environments. Basically, the study allows the conclusion that good measurement is essential for good management.

To enable good measurement and availability of this information for improved self-monitoring and decision making at all levels, the organization requires an infrastructure utilizing information technology. Data need to be captured, integrated, analyzed, and then shared with those making business decisions on all levels. Systems with this kind of functionality are what is known as a data warehouse or business intelligence infrastructure.

Do organizations already readily utilize such systems? An online survey of 254 executives at companies with more than US$ 500 million revenue conducted by the consulting firm Accenture (2008b) found that more than half of the organizations don't have a consistently updated enterprise-wide analytical capability, and two-thirds believe that they need to improve their analytical capability. One of the specifically mentioned challenges were their limited IT capabilities, as indicated by 39% of the executives. Accenture (2010) performed an additional research in 2009 based on interviews with 600 executives in the United States, the United Kingdom, and Ireland. The findings are that data silos and outdated information technology hinder organizations to gain relevant insights based on the data they have, and thereby leads to suboptimal business decisions. Isolated data were reported as a problem by 45% of the respondents, and 40% described their IT infrastructure to be not suited to support enterprise-wide analytics, while 51% felt that better analytics could help to improve their business. Participants mentioned that it would be important to improve the quality of the data in regards to consistency, accuracy, and completeness in order to really leverage it for improved analytics, and as a valuable information for decision makers. In addition to evaluating past performance the highest priority for the future, mentioned by more than two third of the participants, was to develop analytical capabilities which help to predict developments and the consequences of actions and decisions. A prerequisite for such advanced analytics is an understanding of cause and effect relationships, or at least correlations between key performance indicators, which can be gathered via data mining. An example of the successful application of data mining is presented as part of the case study in Sect. 6.4, where data mining is used to help predict and increase the likelihood of cross-selling certain products.

In future, it will be critical to have early access to information on the business and its environment, where major threats and opportunities may arise. How to prepare adequately will be presented in Chap. 3. In dynamic environments, the execution of the strategy cannot just rely on business diagnoses related to performance as a postmortem or a record of what already happened. Instead, analyses should be performed on the following three levels: past, current, and future. How to utilize the corresponding applications in organizations will be introduced in Chap. 4.

Chapter 2
The Strategic Alignment Process

In a dynamic environment, a new management philosophy is required, one with a recipe for dealing with complexity and creating a learning organization which can swiftly make decisions and is agile enough to implement and execute what was decided.

As indicated in the previous chapter, a couple of obstacles have to be overcome. Independent of the industry and the specific strategy, which may change as circumstances require, a competitive advantage on the meta level is to prepare the organization with the capacity to quickly align with new strategies faster than the competition, creating an adaptable, agile, and flexible learning organization. The core skills required will be: 1. Recognizing relevant changes, 2. Developing a capability to predict the impact of external changes on the organization, 3. Measuring, analyzing, and finally, understanding the direct and indirect effects of initiatives on the performance of the organization, 4. Decision making without unnecessary delay, and 5. Executing swiftly what was decided. Following this management process helps to develop the capacity to survive in turbulent times and, if this process is performed well, it is a sustainable foundation to establish a competitive advantage and maximum value creation. As displayed in Fig. 2.1, an effective strategy execution does not only depend on a well developed strategy, but also requires the complete organization to be aligned with this strategy.

What is it that managers actually need to do to effectively execute their strategy? Obviously, they need to have a clearly-defined strategy in the first place: this is the core, the foundation for their business success. What else matters? The challenges of strategy execution were already discussed in Sect. 1.3. I have developed a model called the **World of Strategic Business Intelligence™** to visualize the most relevant aspects for an effective strategy execution, with strategy being the core.

B. Heesen, *Effective Strategy Execution*, Management for Professionals,
DOI 10.1007/978-3-642-19205-0_2, © Springer-Verlag Berlin Heidelberg 2012

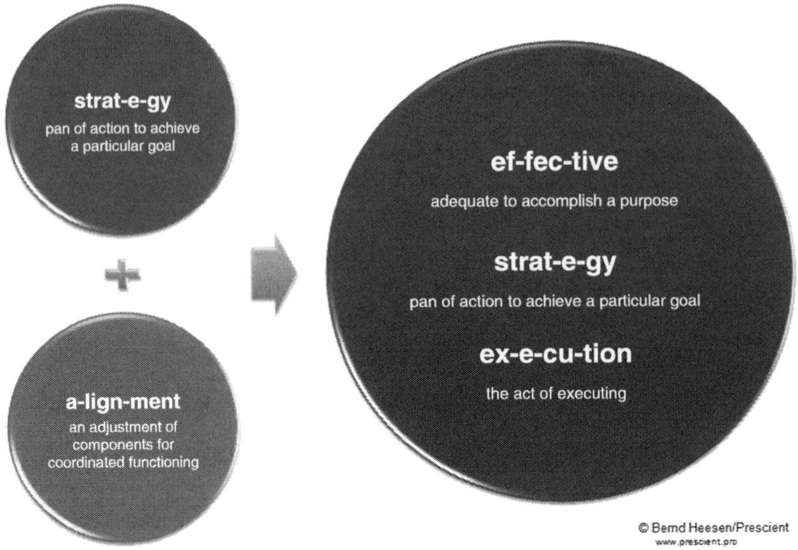

Fig. 2.1 Effective strategy execution (©Bernd Heesen/Prescient. Used with permission)

2.1 World of Strategic Business Intelligence

The World of Strategic Business Intelligence™ (see Fig. 2.2) allows an inside perspective on what matters most. Taking a superficial look at what is visible on the surface is often not sufficient to understand how a business operates and performs. I separated two perspectives which co-exist in organizations, the Business-Perspective and the IT-Perspective. Together, they address the urgent challenges of an effective strategy execution. The business perspective covers the hurdles discussed in Sect. 1.3.1 as well as Sect. 1.3.2, while the information technology perspective deals with the issues described in Sect. 1.3.3.

The arrows outline the dependencies of the different layers in the World of Strategic Business Intelligence™, recommending the correct sequence in which strategy execution should be managed. Starting with the strategy and keeping in mind that you can't manage what you can't measure, the logical next step is to define performance indicators and establish strategic objectives, which are measurable. There is no point, though, in defining objectives if they are not measured. For that purpose, you need data. Because data can originate from many different sources and be in different formats, the data needs to be integrated and harmonized in so-called information models supported by an IT infrastructure, which I will present in Chap. 3. There is no benefit of collecting information if it is not utilized. Value creation, therefore, lies in communicating the relevant information to the respective stakeholders. Stakeholders from the business perspective include groups like customers, investors, business partners, and employees with responsibility for the effective execution of specific internal operations. Information needs differ

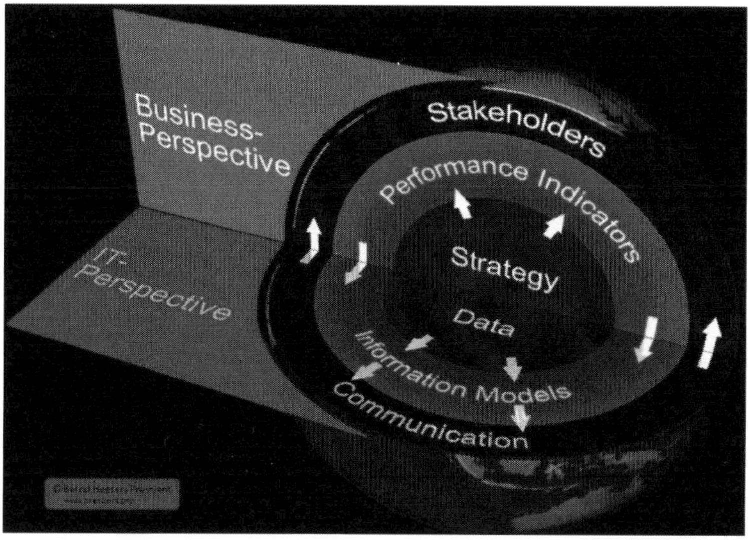

Fig. 2.2 World of strategic business intelligence™ (©Bernd Heesen/Prescient. Used with permission)

significantly and should be assessed early in the process since the availability of the information depends on suitable information models and data sources. This World of Strategic Business Intelligence™ visualizes the networks of interdependencies as typical for cybernetic models, something lacking in some of the literature focusing only on the business perspective or only on the information technology perspective. It illustrates the dependency of business on data, information models, and communication, traditional as well as new, and innovative communication channels or technologies. It also shows that the utilized performance indicators depend on the information needs of the stakeholders on one side, but also depend on the intended strategy. Since you can't measure what you can't describe, information models can only be developed based on a precise definition and description of performance indicators. How to do this properly will be explained in Sect. 3.2. Information can only be communicated if the facts are available, which, in turn, requires the existence of respective information models. Effective communication needs to match the needs of the information recipients, called 'stakeholders' in the model. How often is information made available, but is of little use? The problem is not that the management receives too little information, most managers actually suffer from information overload. The challenge is to minimize the quantity of information while still providing the relevant information in time, and with reliability and quality that meets the demand. Certainly, this model can be considered complex. By breaking it down into two perspectives and several layers, while making sure to focus on the dependencies, this model will hopefully help you to lay the foundation for an effective strategy execution in your organization by aligning all organizational efforts.

What is the value of a model or a concept if it can't be applied? I do not want to leave my readers at this point. Now that I have explained the issues at hand, I intend to share how to apply it with the help of the following roadmap, called the **Strategic Alignment Process**™. The main activities of the Strategic Alignment Process™ are:

- Formulate your strategy.
- Identify stakeholder groups and their information needs.
- Establish meaningful key performance indicators, and understand cause and effect linkages or correlations between key performance indicators (e.g., leading indicators affecting lagging indicators, balancing, or reinforcing loops).
- Measure and collect performance relevant information. This typically includes extracting data from different source systems, transforming the data according to an established standard, e.g., measuring weight in kg or pound, and financial values in specific currencies. Information models should make the information available so it can be easily retrieved and communicated, e.g., aggregating frequently used performance indicators in data marts.
- Select the appropriate communication channels, e.g., alerts, dashboards, broadcasting agents, to fulfill the information needs of all stakeholders. This enables to analyze the performance of all stakeholders, to make appropriate decisions to improve performance, and to act, based on the decisions made.

In the following, the tasks involved shall be described in more detail, starting with the business perspective and followed by the information technology perspective.

2.1.1 Business Perspective

In their Harvard Business Review article *How Strategy shapes structure*, Kim and Mauborgne (2009) outline the three management tasks as attracting buyers with a convincing value proposition, motivating employees to help execute the organization's strategy, and to be profitable. They state that the key to sustainable success is to align these three tasks. Having a solid value proposition and profit orientation might create short term success, but, if there is no adequate people proposition, this may not be sustainable. On the other hand, motivating employees and having an attractive value proposition without a focus on profitability will also not be sustainable. What is needed is a holistic perspective and a management that understands balancing many different needs.

Using the model of the World of Strategic Business Intelligence™, a key task is to understand who the stakeholders involved in creating value are and how to fulfill their respective expectations, and deal with conflict of interest between these groups. One of the core questions the management should answer is what each of these stakeholders actually contributes to the success of the organization. Consequently, those stakeholders contributing the most need to be treated with extra care. While investors might have an interest in short term profitability by leveraging lower cost labor abroad, the employees might be interested in a stable employment opportunity rather than compromising short term profitability to secure their work.

The most critical stakeholders for most organizations are the customers, investors, regulators, employees, and suppliers (Neely, Adams, & Kennerley, 2002). Customers help to increase rofit. They also provide valuable feedback for product and service improvements. In return, they expect high quality products and services for the lowest price possible, and a convenient purchasing and service experience. Investors providing capital or credit expect a maximum return on capital. Regulators contribute a legal framework and infrastructure, while expecting compliance with the law, including financial contribution in the form of taxes. Employees contribute their knowledge and loyalty, and expect personal development, fair compensation, and loyalty from their organizations. Suppliers contribute their services and products on which an organization may depend, and expect revenue and profit in return. In all of these stakeholder relationships, trust is an important ingredient since both parties have expectations of their interests being fulfilled if they contribute to their part of the bargain. This network of relationships with their respective expectations, which need to be managed, contains a good amount of complexity.

Given the philosophy that you can only manage what can be measured, it is imperative that performance is measured related to what each individual stakeholder contributes and what the organization returns. Section 3.2 will describe key performance indicators related to different stakeholders.

To establish business performance goals related to each of the stakeholders allows to focus attention on the most critical activities. Measuring the performance also increases the visibility of positive or negative developments, and deviations from the planned performance. This increases the communication between different actors in a value chain, and can lead to team creativity and problem solving. When deviations from the target performance occurs, they can stimulate two different reflections. If the performance goals are not met, it might be debated as to which corrective actions should be taken to achieve the target. This feedback loop would help to improve the strategy execution. Alternatively, not meeting the objectives might lead to a reflection of whether the original target was realistic or if it should be adjusted. It might be even discussed if the key performance indicators used to define the business goals might be inappropriate and which other performance measures may be better suited. This could potentially lead to the establishment of new strategic objectives for the organization. The corporate dialog which happens in this process would be even more substantial since it questions the validity of the strategic objectives. It is an example of a feedback loop on the meta-level. I will refer to this later in Chap. 3 as part of the Preparation for Strategy Execution.

An example where a single performance measure might be inadequate is often found in sales, when sales representatives receive a bonus based on sales without considering the cost associated with the sales. In the end, a product or service sold may have a negative contribution to the organization if the cost is higher than sales. An example where this can be of significant importance are service contracts based on a fixed price. But why is revenue such a widely used measure for sales? It is much easier to measure at the end of an accounting period. In the case of the fixed price service contract mentioned above, if the services are performed over a period of 9 months, the bottom line contribution can only be measured after project completion. If the bonus is measured based on quarterly or annual performance, sales representatives might work hard to get the signatures under the contract, either in the current period or delay it until the beginning of the next period. Why: they play games with the numbers and try to optimize their bonus, because in non-linear bonus programs, e.g., incremental bonus programs, additional recognized revenue leads to different payouts. This kind of playing with numbers is not limited to sales representatives but can happen wherever performance is measured and where individuals benefit from manipulating numbers. These incentives for individual organizational members are not necessarily in line with organizational goals, they may actually be conflicting. Who does not know the example where spending is increased at year end in order to use the budget? In many organizations, not spending the budget in 1 year can lead to a reduced budget for the coming year. Since performance measurement in the above cases can lead to dysfunctional behavior, performance measures need to be designed with care.

In his book *Performance leadership*, Buytendijk (2009) outlines some of the most relevant, unintended, negative effects of performance measurement as:

- Tunnel vision: Focusing on what is easy to measure instead of what is important.
- Measure fixation: Trying to change definitions to make the numbers look better.
- Misrepresentation: Cheating the system.
- Ossification: Presenting outdated information.
- Gaming: Underachieving, once targets have been made.
- Misinterpretation: Incorrect or incomplete interpretation of the metrics.
- Suboptimization: Using corporate resources to optimize one's own targets, instead of corporate objectives.
- Myopia: Focusing on the short-term quick wins, instead of longer-term strategic objectives.

Buytendijk uses the example of a railway organization to explain the problem of measure fixation. After recognizing that a higher than planned percentage of trains either arrived late or left late compared to the planned time, they adjusted the margin. If deviating from the planned time by 1 min was previously recognized as "not on time," the margin was now adjusted to be 2 min. Consequently, the number of trains reported "late" could be significantly reduced despite the fact that nothing in the actual performance had changed. To avoid any misrepresentation and misinterpretation, it is critical to create a precise definition for each performance indicator, including the way it is calculated. Changes in this foundation for the reporting needs to be made transparent to all those working with these indicators. Where this is not secured, a manipulation is possible without it being recognized easily.

Why even care about establishing a measurement system if it is so complex and comes with these potential negative effects? Companies with established measurement systems are found to be more successful than those not utilizing performance measurement systems as comprehensively. One of the key benefits of performance measures certainly is their positive effect on coordination and alignment of the organizational efforts, enabling harmonization of different activities. The other benefit is fostering cooperation from all those that are responsible for the execution of the strategy, including all employees, investors, and business partners, even if they have divergent objectives.

One theory describing the problem of cooperation is the Principal Agent Theory (Grant, 2010), which deals with the problem that can arise when an agent fulfils a contract to act on behalf of a principal. The problem of the principal occurs if the agent does not act in the principal's interest, but in his own interest. The major cooperation problem within the organization is between the owners and the managers, and between managers and their subordinates throughout the hierarchy. Solutions to minimize the problem include establishing goals and monitoring performance or creating incentive systems to align the individual with the organizational objectives. Conflicts may still arise on this level or between organizational subunits with different goals. For example, sales may be trying to sell at the lowest price to be competitive, and marketing may be commencing a new expensive marketing campaign for a new product line intended to go on the market in the next quarter. At the same time, the finance department worries about discounts reducing the profitability and investments in marketing having a negative impact on the quarterly financial results for the current quarter. The list of potential conflicts of interest seems endless.

Have you experienced those or similar conflicts in your organization? This leads us to the next question: how to achieve an improved alignment of goals within an organization and, consequently, a better cooperation between the actors? Based on the differentiation of first-order control and second-order control introduced in Sect. 1.1, established mechanisms are:

- First-order controls
  - Direction and rules: Supervisors provide orders and directions to their subordinates.
  - Control: Supervision of the behavior and performance of subordinates in connection with reinforcement via performance incentives or sanctions.
- Second-order controls
  - Shared values and objectives: Ideally there is no conflict of interest between principal and agent and they share a common interest, purpose and values. Creating a shared organizational culture is the foundation for this to happen. Sharing and explaining the strategy to employees or involving them in the strategy creation process within their organizational unit allows them to identify with the organization. Once they understand their contribution to the whole, they can more effectively use their initiative and skills to contribute. Once this is reached, this mechanism is self regulating.
  - Routines: If tasks are performed repeatedly and frequently over time, the involved individuals develop routines to effectively coordinate their activities. This coordination is fostered by the actors being familiar with

their contribution in the overall value creation process. These routines provide direction without requiring much management attention.
– Performance incentives and sanctions: They link rewards to performance and, thereby, reduce the need for control from above.

The above mentioned first-order controls require direct involvement of the supervisor in the organizational structure, while the second-order controls are self-steering mechanisms. The first-order controls rely on the existence of a hierarchy of command and control to create vertical alignment. Since the cost for coordination is manifest in the number of managers needed to steer and control a system, significant efforts have been made in many organizations to remove layers of the hierarchy and to leverage partitioned subsystems with more autonomy. The **vertical alignment** can be created based on first-order controls but it is far more difficult to use those to create **horizontal alignment** along the value change. An efficient horizontal coordination can often not be directed from above as it requires an insight into the details of the process organization, which is mainly developed by those directly executing the tasks. Since processes cross the borders of organizational units, the respective supervisors might have departmental interests which are in conflict with each other. Direction from above might even lead to inefficiencies in process execution. This is where the second-order controls can help to solve business problems pragmatically by those responsible for the process execution. These individuals often have superior knowledge about the processes they execute and can make informed recommendations on how to improve them.

Increased information availability can facilitate improved decision-making by these individuals on the operational level as well as on the management level. Self-steering as well as horizontal and vertical alignment can be greatly enhanced by information technology. Let us focus on the IT perspective to understand exactly how information technology can contribute.

2.1.2 IT Perspective

Measurement-managed organizations are more successful, and more than half of the organizations don't have a consistently updated enterprise-wide analytical capability. Two-thirds believe that they need to improve their analytical capability.

Analytical capability is important to support managers with the right information at the time when they need it. It seems that more information is better for management. But is this really true? No; the quality of a decision depends not so much on how much data is supplied than on the relevant information being provided. Managers might actually suffer as much from information overload, including E-mails, as they lack access to critical information when needed. Having an effective strategy execution in mind, it is obvious that only the required facts should be provided to the information recipients, based on their articulated needs.

Data in itself carries no value. It is only when information, which is based on data, is requested and used that it creates benefits for the recipient. This should be the core philosophy and understanding. Basically, information technology is meant to add more benefits than create costs, thereby adding value. Maximizing this value creation is the task at hand. The IT perspective of the **World of Strategic Business Intelligence™** therefore covers a set of three layers which help to understand how value can be created based on data, always keeping the information recipients in mind, along with their specific information needs. The three layers are: data, information models, and communication. Together these three layers allow to design an infrastructure which enables the desired analytical capability and add value.

The core of an appropriate information technology solution consists of data. This data must be collected or acquired, and stored, and made available for analytical applications. Some of the data which is available might not be needed for reporting. Other data might be needed but stored in a format which does not allow to readily use it for reporting. Reasons can be manifold.

One example might be revenue data from different countries stored in the local currency while management in the headquarters wants to have it converted into a global reporting currency for some reports and utilizing the local currency for some country specific reporting. Questions arise: Which exchange rate should be used to convert the currencies? Should the date of the sales transaction be used, the rate at the end of the reporting period, or the rate at the time the report is generated?

Another example where data is stored but not readily usable for reporting is when the weight of products sold is available in pounds for the United States subsidiary, and in kg for the German subsidiary. In order to report the weight of global total sales, the data will need to be converted into one unit. Should standard reports use a corporate standard unit or should the user who creates the report have the choice to pick the unit used from pound, g, kg and many others?

Field lengths or the coding of information can also differ, based on the data source. Running a global headcount report by gender can be difficult in a global enterprise using a heterogeneous information technology infrastructure. In Mexico they might record a single digit number using 0 representing female and 1 representing male. Reports in Mexico work perfectly. Unfortunately, the subsidiary in Spain uses a single digit coding using 1 for female and 0 for male, exactly the opposite from Mexico. Running a global headcount report by gender will not work without prior transformation of the data to a unique standard worldwide. Other countries might even use a character field instead of a single digit field with ‘f’ for female and ‘m’ representing male and different characters will be used in the Chinese subsidiary system.

Clearly, something needs to be done before reporting across locations can be done properly. Access to the data alone will not be sufficient. What is needed to address the above mentioned questions and issues? The information needs of all stakeholders have to be understood. What information do they need, what is the format, the layout, the preferred communication channel, and how frequently should data be updated and distributed? These and more questions should be answered by performing a requirements analysis.

The relevant stakeholders who rely on analytics to make their business decisions should be contacted and asked what kind of information they need, and how they would like to access it, e.g., which communication channel they prefer. A simple approach to gather this relevant information might be the question: who needs what, when, where, and why. Primary communication channels, those where the individual has direct access to the facts, can be printed reports, access to a list of predesigned reports or to a dashboard, allowing the user to locate the relevant information via navigation operations. Another communication channel is broadcasting which allows users to subscribe or unsubscribe to recipient lists for specific information. This is specifically beneficial for periodic reports, which can automatically be delivered via E-mail as soon as they become available or are updated. Further communication channels are mobile devices or file access, e.g., to use established reporting tools like Excel. A comprehensive list of these primary communication channels is covered in Sect. 3.3. Obviously individuals who have direct access to facts via these primary communication channels, forward or communicate this information to additional information recipients via phone, in presentations, meetings, or conversations. These secondary communication channels are essential but they all critically depend on at least one person having access to the primary source. Ideally all decision makers can use a primary communication channel to avoid any delay. We have discussed the value of timely information in Sect. 1.2.

The final result of the requirements analysis is a list of information recipients and their detailed information needs. In an ideal world, all information needs can be fulfilled. Unfortunately, the fulfillment of the information needs typically requires preparation. First, one needs to find out if the needed information is available, where, and in which format. Once the information sources are located, the information models can be designed reflecting the appropriate granularity of data, aggregation or navigation needs. Granularity describes the level of detail in which data is available for reporting, e.g., answering the question as to whether it will be sufficient to provide monthly revenue numbers or if it needs to be accessible by week, day, or even hour or minute? Aggregation helps to improve the performance of the reporting by calculating frequently-used performance indicators once for all users accessing this information later. Navigation allows to slice, dice, drill-down, roll-up or sort data depending on the user needs. While theoretically any navigation is possible, performance needs to be optimized, which requires establishing indexes for fast access for those navigation options frequently used. Once the infrastructure to store this information is established, the data can be extracted from the source systems, transformed into the desired format and loaded in appropriate intervals into a so-called data warehouse or other destinations to fulfill the reporting needs. How exactly to design data models, a data warehouse and how to implement a business intelligence infrastructure will be covered in Sect. 3.3.

What are the typical information needs that should be fulfilled and supported by information technology? Managers typically want to know the current level of performance in comparison to a planned or past performance or benchmarks of similar business units within the organization, competitors or known best practices.

Performance levels might be displayed following a stoplight metaphor using color-coding with green, yellow and red, in table-format, as chart, map, dashboard or in any other format. One of the most important processes in measurement-managed organizations is establishing the performance targets during the annual budgeting and planning process. The purpose of the budgeting process is the optimal resource allocation for maximum value creation. The budgeting and planning processes typically rely on a solid understanding of past performance and benchmarks as well as trends, which display the performance over time. Trends can signal a declining, improving or constant level of performance. Comparisons as well as trends are based on data which stimulates a discussion about the potential causes for the performance, allowing an exchange of creative ideas on how to reduce or eliminate negative causes and reinforce positive ones. Based on an improved understanding of the current situation and potential initiatives that possibly help to improve performance, targets for the upcoming business periods can be determined. Information systems therefore should support at least the following two main tasks: target performance setting (Planning/Budgeting) and performance monitoring (Reporting). Both tasks are core elements of the strategy execution cycle: act, analyze, decide. Performance monitoring enables an analysis of the current situation. The analysis typically leads to decisions which can be either the setting or adjustment of performance targets or deciding which corrective action to take. The last step left in the strategy execution cycle is to act in accordance with the decisions, e.g., by actually taking the corrective action.

An issue related to information not discussed yet is, who should have the privilege to access the information, especially direct access to the primary information channels? Data needs to be protected for many understandable legal and business reasons. There is no point though in developing an information repository which may be costly and then limiting its potential by establishing access barriers, or lacking suitable communication channels to actually benefit from the available information.

A tragic example where an insufficient information supply led to many deaths was the Indian Ocean Tsunami, which occurred in December 2004. Tsunamis cannot be avoided, but the resulting damages they cause can be reduced significantly. As the UNESCO stated in their assessment in January 2005 about the consequences of a not-properly-working tsunami warning system: "Had such a system existed on 26 December, experts believe, scores of thousands of lives might have been saved from the giant waves that killed more than 200,000 people in a dozen Indian Ocean countries, since they would have been given up to several hours to flee to higher ground before the tsunami struck" (Adkins, 2006, p. 7). What had happened?

NOAA (2004), the National Oceanic and Atmospheric Administration, an agency of the United States Department of Commerce, reported about the Tsunami in their news online on December 29th 2004, just 3 days after the occurrence. The NOAA scientists at the Pacific Tsunami Warning Center in Hawaii received a seismic signal of the massive 9.0 undersea earthquake off the west coast of Northern Sumatra in Indonesia. This signal was sent by one of hundreds of tsunami buoys in the ocean detecting a centimeter's difference in ocean height. They issued a bulletin indicating that there would be no threat of a tsunami to Hawaii and the west coast of North America and coasts in the Pacific Basin. They then notified other countries of the possibility of a tsunami. There were no buoys placed in the Indian Ocean in 2004 and therefore the Pacific Basin tsunami warning system did not detect the tsunami, despite the fact that the tsunami already raced across the ocean at speeds up to 500 mph. Below is the timeline of events for December 25th and 26th reported by the NOAA Tsunami Warning Center (NOAA, 2004), Note: Items in brackets marked as waiting further verification at the time of publication on December 29th 2004:

- December **25, 2004, 2:59 p.m.**: The rupture of the great earthquake begins in the Indian Ocean off NW Sumatra, Indonesia.
- **3:07 p.m.**: Initial seismic signals from the earthquake trigger alarms at the NOAA Pacific Tsunami Warning Center (PTWC) in Hawaii.
- **3:10 p.m.**: PTWC issues a message to other observatories in the Pacific with preliminary earthquake parameters. Several geophysical observatories, including PTWC, initially underestimated the size as around a magnitude 8.0.
- **3:14 p.m.**: PTWC issues a Tsunami Information Bulletin providing information on the earthquake and stating there is no tsunami threat to Pacific coasts. It is a text message distributed by multiple means to participants of the Tsunami Warning System in the Pacific. PTWC also advises the following offices by telephone as part of its standard operating procedure: (1) Hawaii Civil Defense, (2) Pacific Command (PACOM) of U.S. Military Forces, (3) U.S. Navy-Hawaii Region, and (4) International Tsunami Information Center.
- **3:15 p.m.**: Tsunami waves begin striking the coasts of northern Sumatra and the Nicobar Islands.
- **4:04 p.m.**: PTWC issues a second Tsunami Information Bulletin to the Pacific revising the earthquake magnitude to 8.5, based on later seismic energy. The bulletin again indicates no tsunami threat to the Pacific, but language is added to advise about the possibility of a tsunami near the epicenter.
- **4:30 p.m.**: PTWC attempts to contact the Australian Bureau of Meteorology to verify they received the bulletin. As their main line was busy, they called Emergency Management Australia instead. EMA indicated Australia was aware of the earthquake.
- **4:45 p.m.**: Tsunami waves begin striking the coasts of Sri Lanka, India and Thailand.
- **6:21 p.m.**: A magnitude 7.1 aftershock occurs. PTWC staff evaluate the earthquake with some difficulty due to its signal being mixed with large seismic waves still active from the main event. No bulletin is issued for this event due to its much smaller size compared to the main shock.
- **6:30 p.m.**: Tsunami waves begin striking the Maldives Islands.
- **7:12 p.m.**: Reuters Internet wire service posts its first story indicating a tsunami has hit Sri Lanka, causing 150 casualties. It also reports 100 tsunami injuries in Thailand.

- **7:25 p.m.**: The first data from the Australian National Tidal Center gauge at Cocos Island gives a reading of 0.5 m crest-to-trough. This was the only sea level data in the Indian Ocean available to PTWC.
- **Also at 7:25 p.m.**: The Harvard University Seismology Department reports its preliminary Centroid Moment Tensor solution that indicates a magnitude of 8.9 (This was adjusted by Harvard the following day to 9.0).
- **7:32 p.m.**: PTWC issues a message to the Tsunami Bulletin Board that goes by E-mail to international tsunami scientists and organizations. The message reports that, based on the Reuters news wire article, a destructive tele-tsunami was generated by the Sumatra earthquake.
- **7:55 p.m.**: PTWC re-contacts the Australia Bureau of Meteorology and advises it of the increased earthquake magnitude and the 0.5 m reading at Cocos Island. They indicate that while they cannot make any kind of forecast, there is the possibility of destructive tsunami waves on Australia's western coasts.
- **8:00 p.m.**: PTWC re-contacts PACOM to advise of the increased earthquake magnitude and potential tsunami impacts in the western Indian Ocean.
- **8:15 p.m.**: The Australia Bureau of Meteorology calls PTWC to advise they have issued an alert to their western coasts.
- **9:00 p.m.**: PTWC receives a call from a Sri Lanka Navy Commander, inquiring about the potential for further tsunami waves from aftershocks.
- **9:15 p.m.**: The U.S. Ambassador in Sri Lanka calls PTWC to set up a notification point in case of aftershocks with tsunamigenic potential.
- **9:30 p.m.**: The NOAA National Weather Service Pacific Region director reports to PTWC that PACOM has informed him they did not observe a destructive tsunami at Diego Garcia.
- **10:00 p.m.**: The U.S. State Department Operations Center calls PTWC and is advised of the potential threat to the western Indian Ocean and eastern Africa. They agree to set up a conference call with U.S. embassies in the region.
- **10:15 p.m.**: The U.S. State Department Operations Center sets up a conference call with the U.S. embassies at Madagascar and Mauritius. PTWC advises that, based on the size of the earthquake and there being reports of tele-tsunami impacts in the Bay of Bengal, there is the potential threat of a damaging tsunami in the western Indian Ocean.
- **10:15 p.m.**: Tsunami waves have crossed Mauritius and are close to reaching Madagascar. They are also starting to impact the northernmost part of the east coast of Africa.
- **December 26, 2004, 5:36 a.m.**: PTWC issues a third tsunami information bulletin indicating that small sea level fluctuations from the Indian Ocean tsunami are being observed in the Pacific Ocean, probably from tsunami energy that passed south of Australia.

The NOAA also stated in its report that the need for a tsunami warning program outside the Pacific region had been raised since 1985 with little result. Now, after this tragedy happened, interest quickly rose again. As a consequence, the Indian Ocean Tsunami Warning System (Wikipedia, 2010b), with 25 seismographic stations relaying information to 26 national tsunami information centers bordering the Indian Ocean, became active in June 2006. The early warning system is now improved with additional key performance indicators being measured and monitored in the Indian Ocean too. The lack of information systems infrastructure clearly contributed to the disaster.

How does this apply to business? Clearly, early knowledge of significant events provides more time to take adequate action in business also. Political events like the current crisis in Egypt with President Mubarak having left office, the dramatic effects of terrorist attacks or natural disasters on businesses, the impact of the bankruptcy of major banks or the financial crisis of countries like Greece, or more traditional business news like a radical innovation, deregulation of industries creating new threats and opportunities, discount offers from competitors disturbing the markets, negative bottom line contribution of a product group because substitute products are significantly reducing demand – all these can be dealt with more effectively with more time on your hands. Having more time than the competition increases the chances to limit loss or improve profits.

But it is not only the measuring and availability of information that leads to success. In the case of the tsunami, those dying in Sri Lanka were hit much later than Indonesia, but still the information did not reach in time, leaving 35,000 dead in Sri Lanka. It is not only the information that is key to success, but the combination of information reaching the relevant recipients via suitable communication channels. Even with officials being informed about a tsunami, one of the problems was the issue of how to reach the individuals on the beach in time.

Research performed by the state of Washington in association with the U.S. National Tsunami Mitigation Program (UNESCO, 2005) uncovered that transmitting relevant information may not be sufficient, since a correct interpretation and preparedness to take action are also required. In a study to assess the usefulness of warning messages, they found that despite the dissemination of relevant information, the preparedness to act appropriately was still low-to-moderate because of some accommodating pre-existing beliefs and interpretation of information. They found that they needed to make sure that the provided information (1) was meaningful to the recipients, (2) motivated risk acceptance, (3) led to the adoption of risk reduction behavior, and (4) promotedearly risk mitigation. These and other findings led Mr. Gordon, Directorate General for Humanitarian Aid – ECHO, to state the following requirements for establishing sustainable and effective early warning systems (UNESCO, 2005, pp. 8–9):

- A major problem is the challenge of communication between a largely educated, literate project workforce and a little educated, often illiterate, beneficiary population.
- Message content must be as simple as possible for the end users.
- The mass media have a crucial role in assuring wide and effective warning dissemination and awareness raising.
- Education and training for the media is required.
- Message delivery systems must be cost effective.

- Regarding the issue of "false warning", credibility of the message is crucial for project acceptance.
- An early warning system is dependent upon the sustained investment of all stakeholders at multiple levels before, during, and after completion of the project cycle. An early warning system should not be attempted unless there is genuine grass roots demand for the system.
- An early warning system should have relevance from the perspective of the end-user: it may address pressing concerns of the community and individual households (rooted in risk to livelihoods rather than threat to life). This is particularly the case for communities vulnerable to low magnitude or low frequency hazards, and which require specific strategic dispensation.
- Perceived usefulness and effectiveness of a system is indispensable for project acceptance. Acceptance is essential for sustained end-user and system operator ownership.
- Low cost and technical assistance designs must be used that reflect the degree of sustained budgetary commitment that can realistically be expected from set budgets.

Several of these recommendations can be applied in a business context as well. Certainly, the first task is to define and measure what is important. Measurement requires an information technology infrastructure like the buoys in the ocean or IT systems in business, and then the relevant information needs to be communicated quickly. Reliability of the information is critical if the recipients shall be expected to consider the warnings seriously enough to take appropriate action. Obviously, the message content should be easy to understand. This means that information systems should be easy to use. Clearly, the implementation of a new system also requires a perception of usefulness and effectiveness. In a complex business environment, the management rarely finds time to monitor all relevant performance measures. Alerts established, based on individually-defined deviations from expected performance, can be triggered automatically and establish a 24×7 surveillance, freeing up scarce management time. This may be just one of the benefits of creating a measurement-managed organization.

How can the consequences of business tsunamis be mitigated effectively, and what are the new tools and philosophies available for managers in their organizations to improve the effectiveness of their strategy execution? This question shall be answered in the following section.

2.2 New Tools and Philosophies for Managers

We have discussed the challenges of increased speed, the complexity of business in dynamic environments, and the lack of information system support that can be alert to significant events. Managers need new tools and philosophies to be prepared for the challenges awaiting them. The concepts and technologies for Decision Support Systems have developed and matured. Information technology enabled better supply chain management and administrative tasks using Enterprise Resource Planning (ERP) applications since the 1990s and eBusiness has revolutionized many aspects of business since the start of the new millennium. Web 2.0, including social networking, has recently added new opportunities and created new business enterprises like Facebook, which is valued at $50 billion by Goldman Sachs after only 6 years of business operation (CNN, 2011).

One innovation based on new and mature information technology capabilities, which can be leveraged to deal with the increased speed and complexity of business, is **Business Intelligence**. More than 50 years ago, the term 'Business Intelligence' was first introduced by Luhn (1958). About the same time, the concept of Management by Objectives was established by Drucker (Drucker, 2006a) in 1954. The combination of these two landmark concepts is the foundation of a new management philosophy called **Management by Objectives** 2.0™ (*MBO 2.0*™). This philosophy can be applied easily by using a new management tool, the **Strategic Alignment Remote Control**™.

2.2.1 Business Intelligence

Information systems capabilities have developed significantly over time and can be leveraged to improve strategy execution. The term 'Decision Support System' was established in the late 1960s. Their purpose was to help decision makers in top management to gain access to relevant information using computer systems. This focus of decision support systems specifically for the top management is also reflected in the term 'Executive Information System', which was widely used in the 1980s. In the 1990s new terms like 'Data Warehousing' and 'Business Intelligence' were becoming more widely used.

It was in the year 1958 though that the term 'Business Intelligence' was used for the first time by Luhn (1958) in his article *A Business Intelligence System* published in the IBM Journal. He envisioned a flexible automated system identifying information needs and disseminating the information efficiently within the organization. His use of the word intelligence was defined in his article as "the ability to apprehend the interrelationships of presented facts in such a way as to guide action towards a desired goal" (Luhn, 1958, p. 314). Obviously, the technologies and mechanisms available at the time were far from where they are today, but the idea and concept remained. Despite his first mention of the term, Mr. Luhn is not widely credited with it (Information Week, 2008). The invention of the concept occurred 50 years ago, but the real innovation is happening only now.

Several factors drive the adoption and implementation of business intelligence in organizations. The Ness Technologies Market Pulse Study on Business Intelligence

(Ness Global Industries, 2010), conducted in 2009, identified the main factors driving business intelligence initiatives as:

- Better transparency into company data for business planning and decision making (54%).
- Desire for more insight into business to keep up with raid change (43%).
- Real-time analysis capabilities (43%).
- Increased demand from stakeholders for operational efficiency and performance management (42%).
- Data integration (37%).
- Early problem detection (29%).
- Higher standards of corporate governance (28%).
- Increasing revenue (27%).
- Reducing data management costs (26%).

The expected or already achieved benefits by establishing and utilizing a business intelligence solution were found to be, in order of significance:

- Improved operational efficiency (84%).
- Faster dissemination of information throughout the organization (83%).
- Faster, fact-based decision-making (81%).
- Enabled corporate performance management (78%).
- Increased business agility (78%).
- Early detection of problems (72%).
- Alignment of organization around consistent set of KPIs (72%).
- Improved compliance (68%).
- Identification of new revenue growth opportunities (67%).
- Improved identification of new business opportunities (63%).

The above list indicates that business intelligence is far from just another technology solution for IT fanatics. Instead, it is an innovative solution to help address key management issues.

Early decision support systems, developed only with the executives in mind, are now history and have been replaced by the concept of business intelligence, reflecting the information needs at all levels of the organization. Time wasted on searching for information, or the lack of access to relevant information, is an unnecessary waste of time not only for executives but at all levels of the organization. Based on improved data security, and with the availability of solutions to reach all decision makers, the benefit of decision support systems can now be multiplied.

The focus of decision support systems on top management would probably have been questioned by Drucker (2001) because his definition of the term 'executive' was based on the concept of the knowledge worker. Drucker asked the question "Who is an executive?" and provided the answer "Every knowledge worker in a modern organization is an "executive" if, by virtue of his position or knowledge, her or she is responsible for a contribution that materially affects the capacity of the organization to perform and to obtain results" (Drucker, 2001, p. 194). He emphasized the relevance of all organizational members' contribution to an effective strategy execution, and considered even individuals as executives in the above sense, if they did not manage anyone else but themselves. As Drucker phrased it: "The most subordinate, we now know, may do the same kind of work as the president of the company or the administrator of the government agency, that is, plan, organize, integrate, motivate, and measure. His compass may be quite limited, but within his sphere, he is an executive" (Drucker, 2001, p. 196).

To underline his argumentation, Drucker cited an interview of a young infantry captain in the Vietnam jungle being asked how he can retain command over his group in such a confused situation. The response of the captain was: "Around here, I am only the guy who is responsible. If these men don't know what to do when they run into an enemy in the jungle, I'm too far away to tell them. My job is to make sure they know. What they do depends on the situation which only they can judge. The responsibility is always mine, but the decision lies with whoever is on the spot" (Drucker, 2001, p. 195).

What does this mean for businesses which are experiencing turbulent times and for their managers? The captain understood that his level of direct control and influence was limited, given the complexities, a lack of detailed knowledge of situational aspects, as well as his limited time, which hindered his ability to be involved in all decisions. Managers have very similar constraints. Despite the fact that they are responsible, they rely on knowledge of workers to make independent decisions. While each of these individual decisions may not have the same magnitude as the decisions at higher levels, their accumulated relevance might be at least as high as those at the top, since the number of decisions below the top management are much higher and more frequent.

The increasing relevance of knowledge was also described by Drucker as a reason to review management practices. He mentions that very long ago people in higher positions knew what their subordinates were doing because they had been in the job of the subordinates themselves. This experience of the managers created authority and acceptance, since past challenges were similar to the present ones. Today, the present is increasingly different from the past and the future will be even more different in fast changing times. Therefore, past experience from managers might be not only irrelevant but even misleading, if the conditions have changed significantly. In this kind of environment, current knowledge becomes even more relevant and managers need to leverage the competencies of the knowledge workers.

The consequence is that decision support is needed on all levels of the organization to improve performance. Independent or interdependent decision-making to align the organizational efforts vertically or horizontally, as mentioned in Sect. 2.1.1, can be greatly enhanced with business intelligence and by applying Management by Objectives.

2.2.2 Management by Objectives 2.0

The late Drucker (2006a) has left a legacy of management knowledge. His book *The practice of management*, published in 1954, is an example of remarkable wisdom and foresight. In this legendary work, he introduced the concept of 'Management by Objectives' with the following words: "Business performance therefore requires that each job be directed toward the objectives of the whole business. And in particular each manager's job must be focused on the success of the whole. The performance that is expected of the manager must be derived from the performance goals of the business, his results must be measured by the contribution they make to the success of the enterprise" (Drucker, 2006a, p. 121).

This is a hymn on the value of corporate performance management and the need for alignment for effective strategy execution. The success of measurement-managed companies, as discussed in Sect. 1.3.3, show how this statement did not lose relevance over time.

On the contrary, Drucker even identified major barriers to an effective strategy execution. He stated: "Management by objectives requires major effort and special instruments. For in the business enterprise managers are not automatically directed toward a common goal. On the contrary, business, by its very nature, contains three powerful factors of misdirection: in the specialized work of most managers; in the hierarchical structure of management; and in the differences in vision and work and the resultant insulation of various levels of management" (Drucker, 2006a, p. 122). He further indicated that managers often develop their own empires and might be more concerned with their own or sub-unit's performance than with their contribution to the enterprise. Consequently, a major management challenge to create an effective organization is to create alignment between the individual and subunits goals and the strategic objectives of the enterprise.

When are managers effective? Drucker describes that individuals who are most relevant for a manager's effectiveness are those whom managers typically have no direct control over. He stated: "They are people in other areas, people who in terms of organization, are 'sideways'. Or they are his superiors. Unless the executive can reach those people, can make his contribution effective for them and in their work, he has no effectiveness at all" (Drucker, 2001, p. 198). This indicates the importance of alignment and cooperation with superiors, peers, and subordinate's objectives. What makes them effective is to have a shared overall goal and understanding. Having a well formulated strategy with clearly-defined objectives, including a breakdown with the measurable contribution of each subunit or individual, creates this kind of alignment with the corporate strategy. This is far more powerful than operating based on command and control.

Summarizing his philosophy for management, Peter Drucker stated: "What the business enterprise needs is a principle of management that will give full scope to individual strength and responsibility and at the same time give common direction of vision and effort, establish team work and harmonize the goals of the individual with the common weal. The only principle that can do this is management by objectives and self-control. It makes the common weal the aim of every manager. It substitutes for control from outside the stricter, more exacting and more effective control from the inside" (Drucker, 2006a, pp. 135–136). If this is applied to all organizational members, independent of the level in the organization, and to all organizational units, then organizational goals can be converted into individual or subunit goals. The concept of management by objectives needs to be applied side by side with the concept of self-control, which was already introduced in Sect. 1.1 as a solution which is a form of second-order control.

He described the benefits of self-control in the following words: "The greatest advantage of management by objectives is perhaps that it makes it possible for a manger to control his own performance. Self-control means stronger motivation: a desire to do the best rather than just enough to get by" (Drucker, 2006a, p. 130). The value adding capabilities of social systems including self-control are also described by Schwaninger (2009), p. 28, as:

- **Self-control:** A system's ability to control itself, which includes setting and adjusting its own goals, as well as autonomous adaptation.
- **Self-organization:** The autonomous, often spontaneous, formation of relationships, activities and structural patterns.
- **Self-reference:** A system's capability to reflect upon itself, and therewith on aspects such as its identity, values, purpose, goals and tasks or activities.
- **Self-transformation:** The ability of a system to reorganize and restructure itself.

This type of self-control, self-organization, self-reference, and self-transformation relies on knowledge workers on all levels. Organizations managed based on this philosophy should be well prepared to deal with the complexity and uncertainty which characterize these turbulent times. Authoritarian, first-order control oriented companies will be much less prepared. Or as Gary Hamel wrote in his landmark book *Leading the Revolution*: "It is universally apparent that we are living in a world so complex and so uncertain that authoritarian, control-oriented companies are bound to fail. Increasingly, intellectual capital is more valuable than physical capital, and it is employees who are becoming the true 'capitalists'" (Hamel, 2002, p. 27).

Empowering as well as holding accountable the knowledge workers on all levels also requires that they are provided with all relevant information they need to measure their own performance and contribution to the strategic objectives. This information should be provided via primary communication channels directly to the knowledge worker, not indirectly, and with delay via their superior managers. Information is power, and power should be given to all knowledge workers to manage their respective contribution to the enterprise. Obviously, the superior managers should also have access to primary communication channels; in essence, they are knowledge workers as well, and therefore the same rules apply, creating an information democracy where everyone receives the information needed to perform their job. The benefit of direct communication channels being available for knowledge workers is that managers no longer create unnecessary bottlenecks for the distribution and communication of critical information.

Drucker's concept of 'Management by Objectives' sounds fabulous, but as mentioned earlier, many companies have failed to make it work. What they lack is alignment of individual and subunit goals with the strategic objectives and the prerequisite to self-control. Self control relies on the availability of performance information for knowledge workers at all levels of the organization to create a measurement-managed organization.

The study from Harris Interactive (Covey, 2004) had found that two-thirds have no clear understanding what their organization's strategic goal is and how it is measured. About 80% have no clear "line of sight" between their tasks and their team's and organization's goals. About 90% have no clear, measurable, deadline driven work goals. Kaplan and Norton (2005) found that the strategies of 67% of subunit or departmental plans were not aligned with the corporate strategies and plans. Another study (Kaplan & Norton, 2001) had found that only 51% of senior managers in the United States and 31% in the United Kingdom had their personal goals linked to strategy. Ventana Research (Kugel, 2007) performed a study in 2007 which showed that a majority of organizations did not have enough ongoing feedback about how well they are performing to their objectives. This is alarming information and confirming that the concept of Management by Objectives is not practiced in many organizations.

Drucker had already stated that management needs special instruments to make 'Management by Objectives' work. With business intelligence, such an instrument is available now, and it can help to get the concepts of 'Management by Objectives' revitalized. More than 50 years after the concept was invented, it has now evolved to **Management by Objectives 2.0™ (MBO 2.0™)** by combining the concept of 'Management by Objectives' with an adequate instrument, business intelligence, to make it work in organizations.

Executives recognize that they can improve their operations by providing access to business intelligence not only to management. In 2006, the Economist Intelligence Unit surveyed 386 executives and found the following results: "BI will be shared among more employees. Business executives want to distribute analytical data to a wider range of employees. These include not just high-level decision-makers, most of whom already have access to BI data, but also middle management, operations employees and even front-line staff. The desire of our respondents to share BI with more people stems from a belief that workers can do their jobs better if they have the right information to improve operations" (The Economist Intelligence Unit, 2006, p. 2).

While making more information available is useful if the information is needed, business intelligence also includes mechanisms to help knowledge workers avoid drowning in too much data. And business intelligence can also be applied incorrectly. In some organizations, you find departmental data warehouses build on different platforms with different development tools, and not integrated with the enterprise data warehouse. As Adkins (2006) states: "Most companies are still unable to get the business intelligence they need; and the intelligence they do get is not delivered quickly enough to be actionable" (Adkins, 2006, p. 7). David Axson describes the difficulties in other words: "It becomes very difficult to improve decision making if management reporting is incomplete or contains incorrect information, the right people get the right information at the wrong time, the right information is in the hands of the wrong people, the right information is provided at the right time to the right people, but they do not know how to use it effectively" (Axson, 2010, p. 158).

Findings of a 2007 global survey of 162 chief information officers in North America and Europe conducted by the consulting firm Accenture (2008a) found that CIOs acknowledge that business intelligence is one of the cornerstones to achieving competitive differentiation. The survey found that 60% of the respondents admitted not using business intelligence for competitive differentiation, yet more than 57% of CIOs wanted to use business intelligence for that purpose. The drivers for this change were indicated by a group of 54% to be customer service/relations improvement, and for 50%, the capability to respond quickly to market situations. They also mentioned the need to move from basic or siloed analytics to enterprise-wide analytics. When compared for where they saw themselves at the time and where they wanted to be in their utilization of business intelligence, there was an increase of 233% for North America and a 267% increase in Europe.

With these intentions articulated in 2007, the interesting question is if organizations have been upgrading their infrastructures. A study published by IBM (LaValle, 2009) in 2009 confirmed that most organizations recognize the opportunity for analytics. It found that they are still very early in the adoption process. Only 14% of the respondents stated to take advantage of new analytics to leverage information to their advantage. The majority, 66% of respondents, stated to recognize the opportunity and getting started while 20% had not even thought about it. One in three respondents described their organization as frequently making major business decision with incomplete information or information they don't trust.

The above-mentioned problems or challenges might be stimulating you to ask yourself the following questions: Is something wrong with our strategy or how we execute it? Is there anything we can change to improve our strategy execution?

How complicated is doing business? I felt intrigued to conceptualize a tool that would help to manage the strategy execution process more effectively: The Strategic Alignment Remote Control™.

2.2.3 *Strategic Alignment Remote Control*

What is the value of concepts if they cannot be applied? Now that I have introduced the concept of Management by Objectives 2.0™, I do not want to leave you just with a new framework for effective strategy execution, but offer a new management tool which you can use right away.

In a complex world, all knowledge workers, including management, need to remain in control, and have visibility of all relevant performance indicators with zero latency. Is it not enjoyable to use the remote control for the TV? Whenever you make up your mind about what you like to view, you just click on a button and yes, you get what you want. I transferred this concept to management, which for obvious reasons is slightly more complex. But the idea should be the same. If an executive or manager has an information need, it should just be a click away. Now, is this realistic? How realistic has been the idea from President Kennedy, that Americans

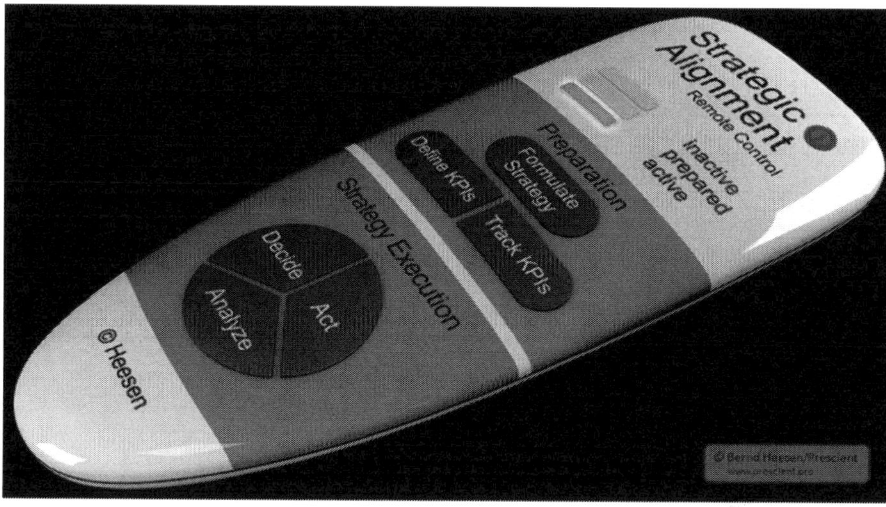

Fig. 2.3 Strategic alignment remote control™ (©Bernd Heesen/Prescient. Used with permission)

should put their feet on the moon? One has to have a vision to work towards in order to get there. With this in mind, the new tool I invented is the **Strategic Alignment Remote Control™** (see Fig. 2.3), which supports the preparation and execution of a strategy. It allows to access all relevant information at all levels of the organization across the globe, allowing the management team to focus their attention on the most relevant problems as well as opportunities. The final objective would be to create a measurement-managed organization. As indicated earlier, these organizations perform above average and are far better prepared to compete in dynamic environments.

A status indicator on the Strategic Alignment Remote Control™ indicates the maturity of an organization in regards to their strategic alignment. The level of strategic alignment is an indication for strategy execution effectiveness. The status of an organization can be inactive, prepared, or active.

Organizations which like to improve the effectiveness of their strategy execution can use the Strategic Alignment Remote Control™ to follow the **Strategic Alignment Process™**. It includes two major process steps with their subordinate tasks:

- Preparation for strategy execution:
  - Formulate strategy
  - Define key performance indicators to fulfill the information needs of all stakeholders
  - Track key performance indicators
- Strategy execution:
  - Analyze
  - Decide
  - Act

Organizations can advance step by step. The first step in the process is for the executives to understand the benefit of strategic alignment, and push the power button on the remote control. This switches the status light on with the status indicating "inactive" (red).

The second step is the preparation. It starts with the formulation of the strategy and the definition of measurable strategic goals. This can only be done based on a shared definition and understanding of the Key Performance Indicators (KPIs) suitable to measure progress. Following these two tasks, the KPIs need to be tracked with the help of a business intelligence infrastructure. The infrastructure should also enable the communication of relevant facts via different communication channels to the stakeholders, depending upon their information needs. Once these preparational tasks are completed successfully, the status indicator switches to "prepared" (yellow). There is no benefit and alignment yet. The benefit is only created once the information is utilized to improve the decision making at all levels. This happens during the execution of the strategy.

The final step is strategy execution. Now, knowledge workers at all levels of the organization can utilize the Strategic Alignment Remote Control™ to analyze their own or their organizational unit's performance, plan and act in a way that optimizes their contribution to reaching the strategic goals. They maintain the oversight over their business and can make more insightful decisions based on improved information access. An important element of the step call "decide" is establishing performance objectives for every individual or organizational unit, which lead to a maximum contribution towards reaching the strategic objectives of the enterprise. Strategic alignment is improved by this cascading of the performance objectives, which requires a dialog across the hierarchy as well as along the value chains, thereby improving the vertical and horizontal alignment within the organization. Given the magnitude of this communication and coordination effort, the business intelligence infrastructure needs to provide adequate communication support and information access for this planning and budgeting process. Continuous monitoring of performance and distribution of critical information to the knowledge workers supports the reflection of adequacy of business initiatives, and fosters continuous and accelerated learning. Once the strategy is executed in this fashion, the status indicator switches to alignment being "active" (green). Organizations with this status can consider themselves measurement-managed organizations and expect above-average success in reaching their strategic objectives.

The next chapters will guide you through this process. Chapters 3 and 4 will present how to perform the relevant tasks in more detail.

Chapter 3
Preparation for Strategy Execution

This chapter presents how management should prepare an effective strategy execution (see Fig. 3.1). The first task is to formulate the enterprise strategy and define associated measurable strategic objectives. A prerequisite to define measurable objectives is a shared definition and understanding of the performance indicators, which can be utilized to measure the current status of performance as well as the extent to which initiatives to reach the strategic objectives have been successful. But then there is one major task left to actually measure and track the performance over time. Tracking multiple performance indicators for different levels of the organization quickly becomes a complex task which can only be managed with the help of information technology.

How to formulate a strategy will be addressed in Sect. 3.1. The challenges of establishing meaningful performance measures will be introduced in Sect. 3.2, and

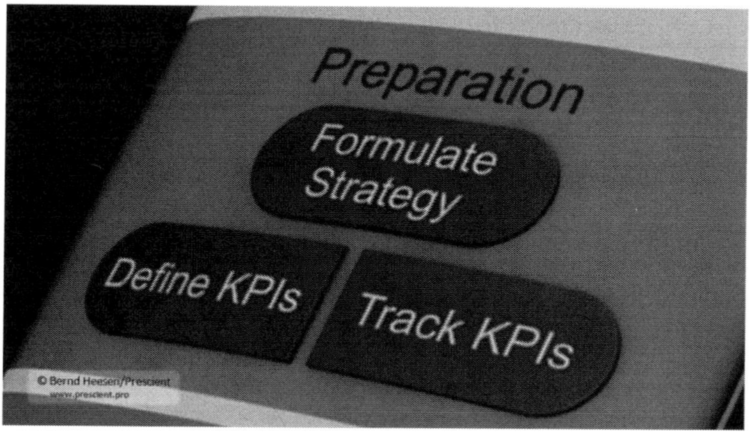

Fig. 3.1 Preparation for strategy execution (©Bernd Heesen/Prescient. Used with permission)

B. Heesen, *Effective Strategy Execution*, Management for Professionals,
DOI 10.1007/978-3-642-19205-0_3, © Springer-Verlag Berlin Heidelberg 2012

Sect. 3.3 will provide recommendations how to establish the needed **Strategic Business Intelligence Framework™**[1] to prepare an effective strategy execution.

3.1 Strategy Formulation

Strategy is a plan of action to achieve a particular goal. The strategic goals might be different for each organization but these goals can only be achieved if the organization continues to exist. Therefore the most basic goal is the survival of the organization. For companies this implies that in the long term they need to make sure their rate of return on its capital exceeds its cost of its capital since otherwise they go bankrupt.

The challenge to survive does not only apply to organizations but similarly applies to all species on our planet. Our species has gained a place in the top section of the food chain. This is not so much because of our size or strength as it is a result of the competitive advantage we gained based on our cognitive capabilities. We are not limited to simple learning but we possess the capability to learn how to learn more effectively. This core skill called metacognition (Wikipedia, 2010d) is defined as cognition about cognition and helps to develop knowledge about learning how to learn or deciding which strategies to use to solve problems. This capability of metacognition can also be applied to management. Managers need to plan, monitor, evaluate, decide and take action using their existing knowledge (cognition), and reflect on the effectiveness of the process (metacognition). If their management process is not effective, they need to search for ways to improve. Each individual knowledge worker also needs metacognitive skills to reflect on the effectiveness of the tasks they perform. The exercise of self-control depends on exactly these skills. The purpose of this book is to foster reflection. The free **Strategy Execution Effectiveness Survey™** is intended to help you to assess your organizational effectiveness in regards to strategy execution and thereby support self-reflection. In the first two chapters, I shared several examples and results from research-providing examples of ineffective strategy execution. For those organizations that, after reflecting on their process of strategy execution, conclude, that they might be able to improve, I will be providing ideas and recommendations for improvement of the organizational effectiveness on the coming pages. But let us return to the first task, which is strategy formulation.

Porter (2004a) talked about strategy formulation in his book *Competitive advantage: Creating and sustaining superior performance* (Porter, 2004a). He differentiated two types of strategy: (1) corporate strategy and (2) business unit strategy. Organizations typically divide their enterprise in business units or other forms of subordinate organizational units, departments, or groups. While the strategy of the enterprise usually determines in which industries and markets the

[1] Strategic Business Intelligence Framework™ is trademarked by Bernd Heesen/Prescient.

organization competes or operates and how it prepares for the future, the business unit managers develop a strategy for their sub-units which defines how they compete in the markets or how they perform their tasks leading to a maximum contribution to achieving the enterprise goals.

For companies the formulation of a strategy requires a solid understanding of the competitive environment (external) and the own capabilities, strengths and weaknesses, of the available resources (internal) and a conclusion of what should be done to improve the status quo of the organization. Basically, a competitive strategy requires (1) a selection of an attractive environment or market and (2) leveraging all available resources to create a maximum competitive advantage.

What is the process to select an attractive environment? Based on Michael Porter's landmark book *Competitive Strategy* (Porter, 2004b), the structural analysis of industries should be based on the Five Competitive Forces which indicate the profit potential of an industry: (1) Threat of new entrants, (2) Bargaining power of buyers, (3) Threat of substitute products or services, (4) Bargaining power of suppliers, and (5) Rivalry among existing firms. The threat of new entrants is influenced by the barriers to market entry (economies of scale, product differentiation, capital requirements, switching costs, access to distribution channels, cost disadvantages independent of scale), government policy, and expected retaliation from the existing competitors. The bargaining power of buyers is increased under the following circumstances: (1) if a buyer purchases large volumes relative to the seller's sales, products that represent a significant fraction of the buyer's costs or purchases, products which are standard or undifferentiated, (2) switching costs are low, (3) profits of the buyer are low, (4) buyers pose a credible threat of backward integration, (5) the product is unimportant to the quality of the buyer's products or services, or (6) the buyer has full information. The bargaining power of suppliers is affected by the level of concentration of buyers' and sellers' industries, lack of substitute products, importance as input to the buyer's business, switching costs, and a credible threat of forward integration. The rivalry among existing firms is influenced by the number of competitors, the rate of industry growth, high fixed costs, lack of differentiation or switching costs, capacity augmented in large increments, diverse competitors, high strategic stakes, and high exit barriers. Once an organization has assessed an industry's competitive forces and its own strengths and weaknesses, it can position itself in the market with its capabilities where the competitive forces are the weakest and its capabilities allow to establish a maximum competitive advantage. The industry and market should be selected based on the highest potential for success.

The potential of every industry and market is impacted by several actors including competitors, customers, suppliers, and regulators. It is also affected by factors like the replacement cycle for products, e.g., the average lifespan of a durable good like a car or a television, because it defines the market size when multiplied with the total number of actual and potential consumers and the product price. A first insight into the attractiveness of an industry may be gained by analyzing statistics about the average industry profitability (see Table 3.1) or taking a look at the most successful organizations (see Table 3.2).

Table 3.1 Top ten most profitable industries in America 2008

Company	Return on revenues		Return on shareholders' equity	
	2008 Profits as % of revenues		2008 Profits as % of equity	
	Rank	%	Rank	%
Network and communications equipment	1	20.4	12	19.5
Internet services and retailing	2	19.4	21	16.1
Pharmaceuticals	3	19.3	5	23.0
Medical products and equipment	4	16.3	9	21.2
Railroads	5	12.6	16	17.4
Financial data services	6	11.7	45	−2.0
Mining, crude-oil production	7	11.5	30	11.5
Securities	8	10.7	38	5.3
Oil and gas equipment, services	9	10.2	10	19.9
Scientific, photo, and control equipment	10	9.9	33	10.0

Fortune (2009)

Table 3.2 Top ten most profitable corporations in America 2009

Company	Profit		Return on revenues		Return on shareholders' equity	
	2009 Profit		2009 Profits as % of revenues		2009 Profits as % of equity	
	Rank	$ billion	Rank	%	Rank	%
Exxon Mobil	1	19.28	>50	6.8	>50	17.4
Microsoft	2	14.57	14	24.9	31	36.8
Wal-Mart Stores	3	14.34	>50	3.5	>50	20.3
Procter & Gamble	4	13.44	>50	16.9	>50	21.3
IBM	5	13.43	>50	14.0	18	59.3
Goldman Sachs Group	6	13.39	12	25.9	>50	18.9
Merck	7	12.90	3	47.0	>50	21.8
AT&T	8	12.56	>50	10.2	>50	12.3
Wells Fargo	9	12.28	>50	12.4	>50	11.0
Johnson & Johnson	10	12.27	23	19.8	>50	24.2

Fortune (2010)

Now, the above tables only provide a snapshot of the situation. To get a better understanding of the trends, an analysis of these performance indicators and rankings over many years might be useful. This still leaves a lot of uncertainty about how the potentials will be developing in future. Management should define a strategy which leads to outstanding performance over a long period of time. This implies that the best company value can be reached based on a strategy leading to a maximum net present value, the sum of the present values of cash flows over the lifetime of the company.

This requires a rough estimation of future cost such as investments in research, marketing, employee skill development, acquisitions, as well as the potential revenues. Even with this information being available, future cash flows remain difficult. The best management can do is to develop a solid understanding which factors might be the drivers for future profitability. The most relevant factors are often not the tangible resources which are reflected in the financial statements and key performance indicators such as revenue, profit, or return on shareholder equity because they are only reflecting past performance. The key drivers for future success are the intangible assets such as employees' knowledge and experience, customer satisfaction, or brand value (see Table 3.3) because they influence aspects such as product innovation leading to new products and the associated revenues or new customers or additional products sold based on customer satisfaction or brand value.

Table 3.3 Top ten most valuable global brands in 2010

Company	Brand value 2010		Brand value change 2010 vs. 2009
	Rank	$ billion	%
Google	1	114.26	14.0
IBM	2	86.38	30.0
Apple	3	83.15	32.0
Microsoft	4	76.34	0.0
Coca Cola	5	67.98	1.0
Mc Donald's	6	66.01	−1.0
Marlboro	7	57.05	15.0
China mobile	8	52.62	−14.0
General electric	9	45.05	−25.0
Vodafone	10	44.40	−17.0

Millward Brown Optimor (2010)

In times where consumers do not know whom to trust any longer, even feeling betrayed by major financial institutions, the reliability and quality associated with established brands, who are still perceived as delivering what they promise, has gained in significance. This is also manifested by an increase of 40% in value of the BrandZ Top 100 Global Brands (Millward Brown Optimor, 2010). Customers are willing to pay a premium for brand merchandise even if in recent years some of them might have had problems paying their mortgages. The BrandZ data found that only 7% of consumers made their purchase only based on price. Clearly, once the positive correlation of factors such as brand image on the product pricing is recognized, it is much easier to decide if an investment in a marketing campaign to strengthen the brand image should be included in the strategy formulation.

May be brand value is a key factor for your success. May be it is not if your major competitors have a great brand value as well and you do not gain a significant competitive advantage in your opinion. A lasting competitive advantage based on a competency, characteristic, or resource could be established if it has the following attributes(Collis & Montgomery, 1995):

- **Inimitability**: It must be hard to copy. Owning a resource which can be quickly copied by competitors is no lasting source of competitive advantage. An example would be Airbus's A380, which carried a development cost of about

$25 billion. Airbus will need to sell about 420 planes before reaching the break even (Flottau, 2010). This significant upfront investment in a limited size market creates market entry barriers for competitors who might never be able to reach sufficient economies of scale to recover their investment.
- **Durability**: Durability refers to the degree by which a resource depreciates in value.
- **Appropriability**: Who captures the value created by your unique resource? The value created by the unique resource is usually shared between groups such as shareholders, employees, distributors, and other groups.
- **Substitutability**: Can a unique resource be replaced by a different resource. An example is the substitution of typewriters by personal computers using word-processing software in the 1980s.
- **Competitive superiority**: Your special competence or resource truly should be superior to those of competitors, e.g., your most relevant rivals.

Understanding the industry and market combined with intuition is the key to decide which strategic actions to take and which competitive advantages to establish or increase. Once the management has selected the industry and market positioning, the strategy formulation also includes information about which strategic actions to perform in order to defend or improve the organization's position in this market. Competitive advantages can be manifold, e.g., unique and scarce knowledge, flexibility to adjust to changing market conditions, superior quality of products and services, competitive price, low production or procurement cost, unrivalled innovativeness or time to market, reliable and fast delivery to customers, exceptional recruitment, and personnel development. Everything could be a source of competitive advantage. The key is to know which ones are most relevant in your industry and market to establish a lasting competitive advantage. Strategy formation is not only about deciding what to focus on and what to do but at least as much about what not to do and not to make a priority.

3.1.1 Functions and Attributes of Strategy

We discussed earlier that a strategy means to develop a plan of action to achieve a particular goal. This sounds like a very positive statement. Is strategy formulation a task which has no downsides to it? Henry Mintzberg, Bruce Ahlstrand, and Joseph Lampel describe the positive and negative aspects which are associated with strategy (Mintzberg, Ahlstrand, & Lampel, 1998):

- **Strategy sets direction**:
  - Advantage: Charting the course of an organization which it can follow.
  - Disadvantage: Strategic direction can also limit the perspective and be blindfolding. Driving full steam ahead too quickly can limit the preparedness for threats surfacing and opportunities passing by.

- **Strategy focuses effort**:
  - Advantage: Strategy promotes coordination and avoids chaos. Organizational members pull in one direction.
  - Disadvantage: "Groupthink" can arise when everyone is so excited to work on reaching the shared goal that no one may be volunteering to articulate their concerns.
- **Strategy defines the organization**:
  - Advantage: Strategy provides an identity to the organization and allows to distinguish it from others. Strategy thereby provides meaning.
  - Disadvantage: A precise definition of an organization may take away the richness and versatility, sometimes to the point of stereotyping.
- **Strategy provides consistency**:
  - Advantage: Strategy is needed to reduce ambiguity and provide order. In this sense, a strategy is like a theory: a cognitive structure to simplify and explain the world and thereby facilitate action.
  - Disadvantage: Innovation and creativity thrives on inconsistency. It has to be realized that every strategy, like every theory, is a simplification that necessarily distorts reality. Because strategy is not an object of reality, misrepresentations and misunderstanding can have distorting effects.

Understanding these characteristics and effects of strategy, it is important to formulate a strategy with the following in mind: (1) Always keep monitoring the environment to remain flexible when needed, (2) appreciate the articulation of disruptive and innovative ideas which may lead to a change of direction in order to maintain an innovative climate, and (3) communicate the strategy and maintain constant dialog on how to best achieve the objectives by clarifying the contribution of individuals and each organizational unit.

There is one more major limitation to any strategy formulation, the lack of knowledge what will happen in future. This uncertainty leads to the dilemma that nobody can guarantee that a strategy is perfectly suited to reach the defined objectives. The available information will always be imperfect. A rational decision making of the management when formulating the strategy is impossible for many reasons, e.g., the lack of information about the past and certainly the lack of knowledge about the future and also an abundance of information which may not be utilized because of time and capacity restraints of management.

Since a perfect information supply cannot be guaranteed by any manager, also applying to the competitors, the challenge is not to be perfect but to have an information supply that is better than that of the competition. Using business intelligence can improve the timely access to information, presented in formats which are easy to interpret, including forecasts based on knowledge and extrapolation of past trends or correlations between different performance indicators.

Many organizations heavily rely on forecasts and predictions, such as airlines predicting the utilization of aircraft capacities, rental car agencies to predict the demand for vehicles based on type of car and location, consulting organizations to predict the demand for specific sets of skills to recruit and develop the right talent, or insurance companies to predict the likelihood of risks, just to name a few. Prediction is based on the law of large numbers and requires a sufficiently large body of data from the past which can be extrapolated to calculate the risks. As Colin White states “Successful strategic thinkers must have a view about the future. They should be able to read when human behavior is stable and can be relatively easily anticipated, including the special case when the law of large numbers allows easy interpretation of probabilities or when theory provides us with sequences of linked cause and effect, confirmed by empirical analysis” (White, 2004, pp. 130–131). Data mining, which is a function supported by an adequate business intelligence infrastructure, leverages statistical models to gain these kind of insights which help with predictive analytics.

An impressive example of an organization leveraging data mining is the case of Harrah’s (Pfeffer & Sutton, 2006). It started in the year 1998, when Gary Loveman was appointed COO of Harrah’s and took a leave from his position as associate professor at Harvard Business School. His experience in casino operations was limited at the time. Harrah’s wanted to predict what kind of promotion would be most effective to order to increase revenue and improve the bottom line. They tested control groups stimulation based on two different promotions: (1) the typical package including a free room worth more than $100, two dinners and $30 worth of free gambling versus (2) $60 worth of free gambling. What they found was that the $60 offer led to a higher gambling revenue than the offer of $130 plus the two dinners. They also found that their most profitable customers were locals, who played regularly and had little use for the hotel rooms. Predicting the future behavior of their customers based on this knowledge of past behavior Harrah’s decided to use less expensive direct mail campaigns instead of the traditional media advertisements and to offer the less expensive promotion to attract more of their most profitable clients and it worked.

But the commitment to use statistics to predict behavior and thereby to optimize the business has not halted since then. Harrah’s acquired Ceasars Entertainment in 2005 for $9.4 billion (Mihailovich, 2005). Both companies used loyalty programs. While Harrah’s operated a database with 25 million card members, Ceasars had 15 million loyalty card members in their data warehouse. Harrah’s was willing to invest $130 million to combine these sources in a single database of 40 million customers. At Harrah’s, about 80% of casino floor transactions were tracked compared with 30–40% at Ceasars at the time. Tracking individual transactions for gambling, meals, and entertainment and connecting this information with the identity provided via the loyalty card allowed to develop customer profiles and better understand customers’ preferences. Establishing different customer segments allowed them to tailor the promotional offers even further, having an understanding which segment prefers more gaming or entertainment promotions. Besides tracking the transactions, Harrah’s also uses surveys to 1 million customers annually with about 300,000 responding to collect additional information. Harrah's spent $863 million on casino promotional allowance, or comps, at its 28 U.S. properties in 2004. Leveraging their customer database and segmentation based on characteristics and predicting the effects on revenue and profit contribution, their marketing efforts are very effective. As Steven Mihailovich wrote in the Las Vegas Business Press, "Since 1997 the database has allowed Harrah's to ratchet up its share of gamblers' budgets from 36 percent to the current 45 percent. Harrah's Gary Loveman has said that every percentage point increase adds $1.10 to the stock price. Schibrowsky noted that Harrah's used to advertise in newspapers and on television to create a buzz in Southern California. Now a quick mailing or e-mailing to card players produces the same response at a fraction of the cost" (Mihailovich, 2005, p. 10).

3.1.2 Coordination and Alignment

Organizations have the need for a strategy to provide direction and purpose and to utilize the available resources most effectively. The process of planning how to implement the strategy provides an opportunity for the exchange of ideas and opinions within the organization. This dialog helps to establish a higher level of commitment and consensus for those that have been involved. The implementation process during which all actors work toward achieving their performance targets helps the strategy to be transformed from an abstract concept to a meaningful compass.

It is not the compass alone that stimulates and motivates the organizational members. The strategic goals (target) define where the organization wants to be, the goal setting establishes a vision and having a detailed strategy including the initiatives (means to reach the target) which need to be performed to get there provides the confidence (motivation) that these goals can be reached. Obviously, to create alignment, goals and initiatives need to be defined on all layers of the organization. In the end all individuals should be clear about how their goals contribute in reaching the enterprise objectives (see Fig. 3.2).

Goals should be SMART (Andler, 2008): specific, measurable, agreed upon, realistic, and time bound. If goals are not measurable then it will not be possible to find out if they are reached or if there was any improvement. In these cases, it might be necessary to search for a different specification of the goal which can be measured. All organizational members should be either involved directly or their interests and concerns should be adequately reflected by those deciding about the goals. Involvement creates ownership and adequate reflection of interests maximizes the chances for cooperation. In order for goals to be realistic the resources and time required to perform the planned initiatives should be provided to accomplish the goals. Since goals can be conflicting with each other, it is essential to assign each of the goals with a priority. This way the more important goals and related initiatives can be prioritized when resources or time is limited.

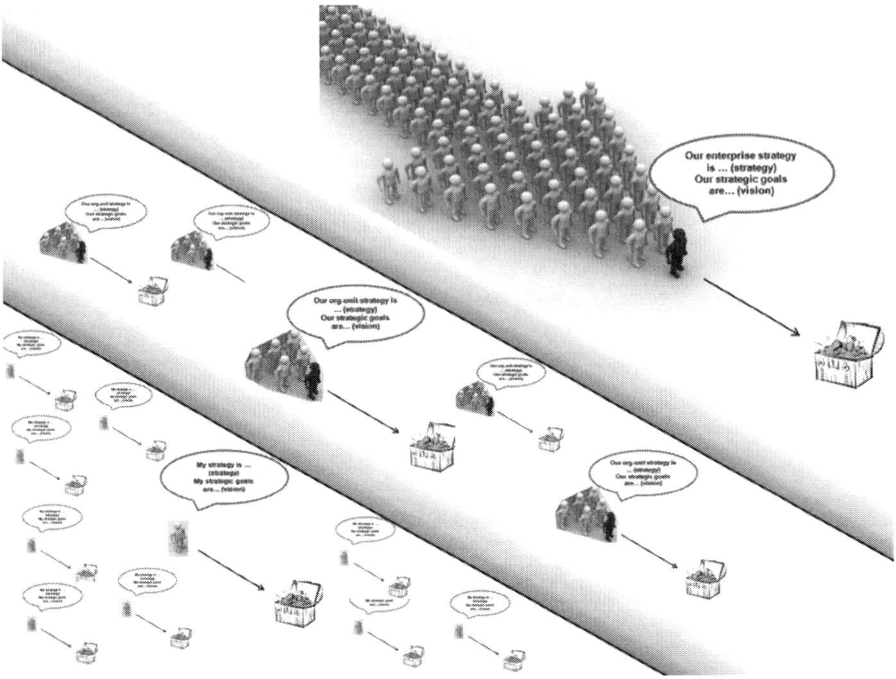

Fig. 3.2 Alignment toward organizational goals (©Bernd Heesen/Prescient. Used with permission.)

Not having clearly defined goal priorities can lead to an intense debate within the organization, leading to dissatisfaction and an inefficient use of resources.

Having a clearly defined goal establishes a vision to work toward. As Gary Hamel and C.K. Prahalad stated in their book *Competing for the Future*: "Competition for the future is competition to create and dominate emerging opportunities – to stake out new competitive space. Creating the future is more challenging than laying catch up, in that you have to create your own road map. The goal is not simply to benchmark a competitor's products and processes and imitate its methods, but to develop an independent point of view about tomorrow's opportunities and how to exploit them. Pathbreaking is a lot more rewarding than benchmarking" (Hamel & Phahalad, 1994, p. 24).

3.1.3 Emergent Strategies

Great visions have led to great discoveries and advances. Think of Christopher Columbus (Wikipedia, 2011a), who's strategy was to find a sea route to India. At the time kingdoms were seeking wealth from the establishment of trade routes and colonies. His lacking knowledge of facts led him to believe that the sea route from

Spain to India would be shorter than the land route, gaining a potential competitive advantage of Spain over the Italians and Arabs, who were dominating the lucrative spice trade. His strategic goal was to reach India. The stakeholders involved to make this happen were, besides himself, Queen Isabella and many sailors joining him for the journey. Isabelle had rejected his plan for years before she finally agreed to fund his expedition in 1492. Columbus himself had the strategic objective to be an Admiral and to gain governship of the new lands for himself and his descendents as well as 10% of all profits. Queen Isabella and he agreed on these terms. Many of the sailors might have had the vision for a better life in the new world. Interestingly, we know, despite failing to reach the intended target India, Columbus gained the Admiral's rank, governship, and shares of the profit. This is a valid example that a strategy motivates individuals to risk their life and for investors to fund projects often based on wrong assumptions, e.g., incorrect expectations of the world. Nevertheless, with the new knowledge of the new territories the Queen and Columbus adjusted their strategy. Instead of trying to find India on their next trips, Columbus repeated his trips to the Americas three more times. This is proof for strategy to be evolving based on new insights from an intended, deliberate strategy to a realized, emergent strategy. Strategy formulation therefore is not a once a year task but a permanent activity.

In the business world, new insights are gained continuously. The actions of rivals or changing customer demand can undermine the own strategy. As George Day, David Reibstein, and Robert Gunther correctly state: "The strength of a given strategy is determined not by the initial move, but rather by how well it anticipates and addresses the moves and countermoves of competitors and shifts in customer demands over time" (Day, Reibstein, & Gunther, 1997, p. 2). The renewal or modification of a strategy certainly requires new alignment. In turbulent times, the reflection of the adequacy of the strategy, its adaptation and the capability to align the organizational members with the emerged strategy is a core element of an effective strategy execution. During turbulent times, it is no longer adequate to develop 5-year strategic plans and execute them without adjustment.

A continuous reflection and adaptation of the strategy should not be confused with chaos. A strategy is needed to set direction, to establish strategic objectives which motivate the organizational members. In turbulent times, it is even more essential to have a clear direction to create alignment within the organization.

How does one realize that the strategy and the initiatives should be adjusted? Gathering new information about the external world and about the performance of the own organization helps with this process. It is necessary to evaluate the effectiveness to see if the objectives are reached, and to evaluate the efficiency to make sure that the resources are used to maximize the positive outcomes. The foundation needed to perform such evaluations is the definition of Key Performance Indicators (KPIs) and the establishment of a monitoring system. These two topics, promoting learning, will be addressed in the remainder of this Chap. 1.

3.2 Definition of KPIs

Organizations typically describe how they envision their future or how they want to be perceived in vision and mission statements. These kind of statements are often communicated on the websites or in annual reports. What these statements often lack is specificity. If these visionary statements are supposed to become the foundation for a strategy, they should be converted into measurable objectives because only what can be measured can be managed.

We know, based on our own experience, what is measured is important. Something that is measured might be noticed and may be used for evaluations and decisions. It can have an effect for those that are measured. Something that is not measured is likely to be ignored and therefore of lesser relevance. Naturally, we have to spend our time wisely, where we believe it has the most impact. Now, if something is measured and potentially being used for decision making, it makes sense to focus our efforts on that matter. Consequently, the use of measurements has an impact on behavior, specifically if the performance is made public and leads to positive or negative recognition by colleagues or is used as a basis for incentive compensation or promotion.

Performance indicators are used nearly everywhere. Given their obvious importance, it is critical to understand that KPIs have to be used with care. Their correct interpretation requires a precise definition as well as a detailed understanding of the measuring process.

We are all familiar with a KPI called weight. We might use a scale at our home to find out how much we have gained over the holidays. Depending on the comparison of the planned or expected value with the current reading we might decide to take action, e.g., doing more sports or starting a diet. The measuring process provides us with the relevant information which influences our decision making. We trust the scale because we have used this KPI and the same measurement instrument in our home many times. We know that we cannot easily compare our weight measured at home with our weight measured on a scale in the fitness studio since they might not be calibrated identically. Even if the scale at home is not calibrated properly, if the measure is always taken from there it can be used to compare one's own weight over time. Unfortunately, under these circumstances, the own weight measured at home cannot be compared to the weight of other individuals who use a different measurement instrument. For organizations, this indicates the relevance of applying consistency in the measuring process for KPIs internally and in order to benchmark with other organizations to follow an accepted standard.

Let us take another KPI which is widely used, the gross domestic product (GDP), which measures the market value of all final goods and services from a nation in a given year. You would expect that using such a KPI is suited and reliable for reporting as well as benchmarking? Far from true. Take a look at the table below (Fig. 3.3). The values for the GDP and the derived ranking reported by the International Monetary Fund and the World Bank are NOT identical. This example

2009 List by the International Monetary Fund[1]

Rank	Country	GDP (millions of USD)
—	*World*	57,843,376[4]
—	*European Union*	16,414,697[4]
1	United States	14,119,050
2	Japan	5,068,894
3	People's Republic of China	4,984,731[2]
4	Germany	3,338,675
5	France	2,656,378
6	United Kingdom	2,178,856
7	Italy	2,118,264
8	Brazil	1,574,039
9	Spain	1,467,889
10	Canada	1,336,427
11	India	1,235,975
12	Russia	1,231,892

2009 List by the World Bank[2]

Rank	Country	GDP (millions of USD)
—	*World*	58,133,309
1	United States	14,256,300
—	*Eurozone*	12,455,979[3]
2	Japan	5,067,526
3	People's Republic of China	4,984,731[2]
4	Germany	3,346,702
5	France	2,649,390[4]
6	United Kingdom	2,174,530
7	Italy	2,112,780
8	Brazil	1,571,979
9	Spain	1,460,250
10	Canada	1,336,067
11	India	1,310,171
12	Russia	1,230,726

2009 List by the CIA World Factbook[3]

Rank	Country	GDP (millions of USD)
—	*World*	58,150,000
—	*European Union*	16,240,000
1	United States	14,260,000
2	Japan	5,068,000
3	People's Republic of China	4,909,000[2]
4	Germany	3,353,000
5	France	2,676,000
6	United Kingdom	2,184,000
7	Italy	2,118,000
8	Brazil	1,574,000
9	Spain	1,464,000
10	Canada	1,336,000
11	Russia	1,255,000
12	India	1,236,000

Fig. 3.3 List of countries by GDP (nominal) in 2009 (Wikipedia, 2010c)

is not used to criticize either of these organizations but just as an indication how important it is to know the basis of the calculation of each KPI in order to be able to interpret them correctly. In internationally operating organizations, the application of currency exchange rates, e.g., the transfer from original currency in reporting currency using an exchange rate, is one potential cause for the distortion of monetary values.

One of the KPIs which is utilized in most organizations is revenue. Your organization probably reports revenue numbers per period? If your organization reports revenue numbers, please take a break right now to write down your answer to the following question, before proceeding further with your reading!

- What is recognized as revenue in the reports stating revenue and how is this revenue calculated?
  It is ok for you to look up the definition and calculation formula for the KPI revenue, if it is readily available to you.

Take your time to answer the above question now! If you are not able to provide the answer, then you probably belong to those individuals who either (1) have no direct or indirect responsibility for revenue and therefore do not work with the KPI revenue for planning nor execution, or (2) you are used to work with numbers that you do not understand. Working with numbers you do not understand would be dangerous as it would imply that decisions you make depend on information which you do not understand, which can be worse than having no information. Frank Buytendijk, Vice President at Oracle, has done a great job to describe 12 different variations of what can be recognized as revenue, which may be appropriately used depending on the context (Buytendijk, 2009): (1) gross revenue: total sales before discounts and incentives for partners, (2) net revenue: total sales after discounts and incentives for partners, (3) net own revenue: net revenue minus royalties to third parties, (4) recognized revenue: accepted booking in the finance system, (5) revenue U.S. GAAP: revenue according to U.S: accounting rules, (6) revenue local GAAP: revenue according to country-specific accounting rules, (7) management revenue: total revenue for a region including revenue coming from other regions or countries for local customers, and excluding local revenue for customers belonging to other regions or countries, (8) commission revenue: total revenue matched against a salesperson's targets, (9) invoiced amount: the amount that is invoiced in the current period. Not all of this revenue may be revenue for the current period, e.g., in cases where payment for work is provided upfront or in scheduled installments, (10) statutory revenue: revenue as reported to the outside world, (11) fiscal revenue: revenue as reported to the tax office, and (12) cash inflow: technically not revenue, but the last metric in the process. All of these calculations of revenue are reasonable. The key is that all individuals receiving a report which includes revenue should know, not guess nor have no clue, what the reported number means and which effects could potentially distort the perception. If management revenue shall reflect regional association then a reclassification of a customer order from one region to another might impact the numbers reported for the affected regions. If a fixed price project lasting 18 months is paid in two installments, 50% after 9 months and the remaining 50% at completion after the customer signed off on the deliverables, the revenue recognition may occur when work is performed or when the invoices are sent out. Depending on the size of the project this could significantly impact the reported monthly performance as you can imagine.

Now compare your answer to the question on the previous page to see if you do understand how the revenue is calculated in your reports. In case you do not know, you may want to find out, specifically if it impacts the way your work is evaluated or your bonus is calculated of if you use revenue as an indicator to evaluate the performance of other individuals or organizational units.

Revenue, profit, and other financial measures such as GDP are used to measure the performance of many organizations or countries. The problem with these KPIs is that they only measure what happened in the past and they have little predictive value.

The fact that financial measures are insufficient to manage organizations was already recognized by Robert Kaplan and David Norton in their Harvard Business Review article *The Balanced Scorecard: Measures that drive performance* in 1992. They used the example of pilots navigating their plane and their need to have a multitude of indicators and instruments. As they stated: "Reliance on one instrument can be fatal. Similarly, the complexity of managing an organization today requires that managers be able to view performance in several areas simultaneously" (Kaplan & Norton, 1992, p. 72). They recommended the balanced use of external measures, e.g., related to customers or shareholders, and internal measures, e.g., measuring process efficiency or innovativeness. They also recommended to balance outcome performance measures such as revenue and profit with measures impacting future performance like customer satisfaction or brand value (Kaplan & Norton, 1996). Their balanced scorecard was separated in four dimensions, separated to cluster KPIs: Financial, customer, internal business process and learning, and growth.

Since the task of management is to make sure the performance in future periods will be in accordance with the strategic objectives, they need a comprehensive set of KPIs to manage future performance. They need to measure what impacts their organizational performance in future periods and they need to maximize the value creation process. How this can be accomplished will be presented in the following section.

3.2.1 The Value Scorecard

Each organization needs a legitimation for their existence which typically describes the overall purpose or vision and gives the organization a unique identity. The organization should have an idea how to leverage existing value potentials based on their core competencies to supply solutions to existing problems thereby fulfilling a demand from the constituency they serve. For-profit companies may focus on customer needs while public service organizations focus on the needs of their citizens or the overall population. Let us use the World Health Organization (WHO, 2011) as an example. They define their purpose as directing and coordinating efforts to improve the health within the United Nations system. In their 2011 World Health Report Margaret Chan, Director General of the World Health Organization states: "At a time when money is tight, my advice to countries is this: before looking for places to cut spending on health care, look first for opportunities to improve efficiency. All health systems, everywhere, could make better use of resources, whether through better procurement practices, broader use of generic products, better incentives for providers, or streamlined financing and administrative procedures. This report estimates that from 20 to 40% of all health spending is currently wasted through inefficiency" (WHO, 2010, p. 4). An effective strategy execution is exactly what organizations try to achieve, both for-profit and not-for-profit organizations. They intend to do the right things and at the same time focus on utilizing the available, always limited, resources to maximize, what they consider to be of value. The ultimate value can be defined in terms of value of shareholders, e.g., measured in return on capital, value for citizens, e.g., measured in public health status, unemployment rate (see case study in Sect. 6.5), or social satisfaction index (see case study in Sect. 6.3). One of the key questions for management is how to maximize the value created and captured by the organization.

Adam Brandenburger and Harborne Stuart published an article *Value-based business strategy* (Brandenburger & Stuart, 1996) in 1996, which provides a valuable framework describing a generic model of the entire value chain and the associated value creation, which can be applied to any organization (see Fig. 3.4).

The value chain includes suppliers, the organization, and the buyers. The organizational value can be optimized by maximizing the difference between the price the buyer is willing to pay and the cost for all suppliers including employees

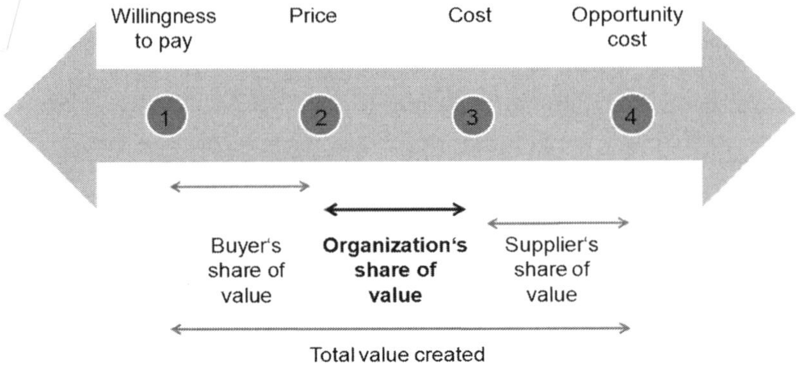

Fig. 3.4 Distribution of value created (©Bernd Heesen/Prescient. Used with permission)

who provide their work at a defined cost. The suppliers gain extra value if the cost at which they sell their goods or services is higher than their related transaction cost, costs occurred to sell their goods and services, plus their opportunity cost, the cost at which they could have sold their goods and services to other organizations. The buyers capture extra value if they can buy the goods or services at a price which is lower than what they would have been willing to pay as their maximum price. Consequently the overall value created is split between all actors and it is not only important for organizations to add a maximum value but to secure a maximum share of this value for the organization by reducing the cost paid to suppliers and by increasing the price for buyers. The bargaining between the players will determine how the value will be divided. A maximum value appropriation for the own organization therefore requires good negotiation skills as well as knowledge of the willingness to pay and opportunity cost, since these two present upper bounds in the negotiation process.

This price for buyers must be low enough so that they are still interested to perform the transaction. This only happens if the situation after the buying is considered as better than the original status quo prior to the transaction. Complete information transparency is required to have an exact knowledge of the price the buyer is willing to pay or the price a supplier is willing to accept based on their individual opportunity cost. It is unrealistic to ever have such a transparency. But business intelligence can contribute to gain insights which help to predict these important variables, e.g., finding a price close to the willingness to pay. I will provide examples of these applications in the coming chapter.

Good negotiation skills are always contributing to a higher share of value for the organization. Other strategies to improve the capturing of value for the organization can be differentiation, so that buyer's needs are uniquely met and therefore the willingness to pay is increasing. Another option is to effectively manage the supplier relationship and thereby lowering the opportunity cost for the suppliers. An example for an effective management of the value chain is Dell.

In their book *Execution: The discipline of getting things done*, Bossidy and Charan (2002) describe that Dell turns its inventory over 80 times a year, compared with its rivals with 10–20 times. Their efficient supply chain even generates cash, contributing to a negative working capital. Dell gained a cash flow of $1 billion from operations in the fourth quarter of 2002 based on a revenue of $8.1 billion realizing an operating margin of 7.4%. This led to a return on invested capital of 355% in 2001. The quick inventory turnover also had the consequence that Dell did not develop an inventory of outdated products which still need to be placed in the quickly evolving technology market. Their customers gained the benefit of being offered up-to-date products while Dell was able to quickly benefit from lowered component prices while the competition still sold products which included more expensive components. This allowed Dell to either reduce prices or increase their share of the value created. An effective strategy execution of the complete value chain provided the framework for this success.

The question at hand is, how can management effectively execute their strategy to generate a maximum value for the organization? It certainly requires to manage the negotiation process with different business partners, suppliers, and buyers. A tool to help monitor and manage these relationships is the **Value Scorecard™** which is based on the concept of value creation and the understanding that the management has the task to secure a maximum value appropriation for the own organization (see Fig. 3.4). The naming of the relevant dimensions follows the logic of the model. There exists a *supplier* dimension. It is essential to note that this dimension includes equipment suppliers as well as capital suppliers (investors, banks...) and workforce suppliers (employees, contractors...). The *internal* dimension includes KPIs related to manage the effective execution of processes such as supply chain management, customer relationship management, human capital management, business support via information technology, and the order to cash cycle. Brandenburger and Stuart had used the term buyer and in the balanced scorecard one dimension is called customer. Reflecting the fact that recipients of services and products may not be paying for these directly or at all, e.g., citizens being served by their government or disaster victims receiving aid at no cost, and because even buyers might not maintain a direct relationship with the organization and still need to be managed, e.g., customers buying products or services of the organization via retailers or wholesalers, this dimension is called more generically the *demander* dimension. In addition to the three dimensions, demander, internal, and supplier, which reflect the value creation process, one dimension still missing is needed to measure the value actually captured by the organization, the *value* dimension. Many organizations focus their effort to maximize return on capital and monitor other KPIs. In the balanced scorecard, these indicators would belong to the so-called financial dimension. Not all organizations primarily focus on financial objectives, e.g., organizations such as the World Health Organization, Greenpeace, NOAA Tsunami Warning Center, governments or religious organizations have far different objectives and measures for value. To use an example, the success of the NOAA Tsunami Warning Center might be measurable in a minimal time from the occurrence of a tsunami to its communication to those responsible to initiate rescue efforts and finally in a KPI measuring the death toll of tsunamis, which should be minimized. To reflect whatever is considered to be most valuable the dimension to capture the most important KPIs, and not limited to the financial KPIs, is called the *value* dimension.

This new creation of the **Value Scorecard™** (see Fig. 3.5) is reflecting the value creation process as well as the appropriation of value. In its design it is equally suited for for-profit as for non-profit organizations.

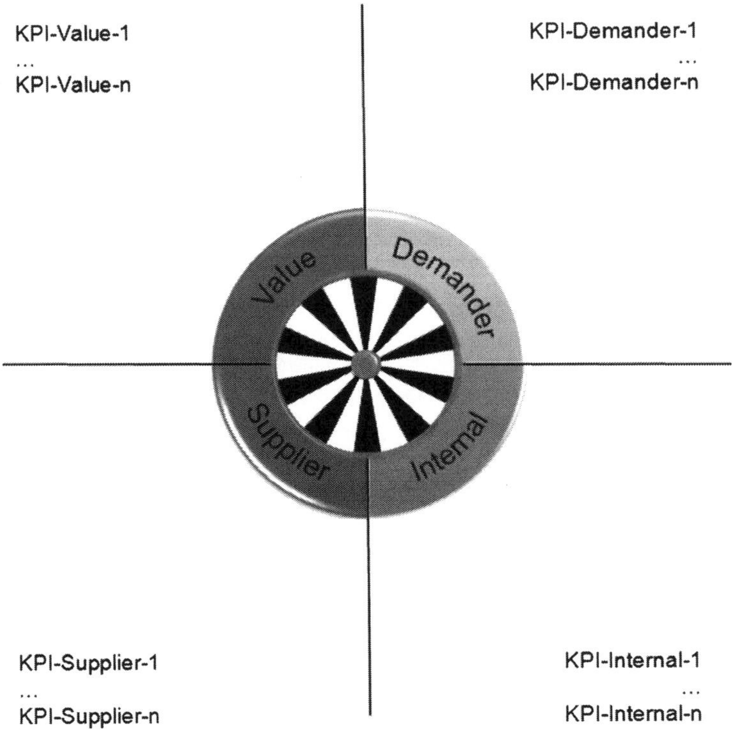

Fig. 3.5 Value Scorecard™ (©Bernd Heesen/Prescient. Used with permission)

Every organization needs to determine which KPIs are important for their business. There are a couple of performance indicators, which are frequently used. I want to share a couple of those KPIs with you for each of the four dimensions of the Value Scorecard™.

For-profit organizations will typically focus on financial KPIs to measure profitability, debt, or shareholder return in the value dimension. KPIs suitable for this purpose might be gross profit margin, net profit margin, revenue per employee, revenue from new products, rate of growth, cash flow, credit rating, return on total assets, debt to equity, times interest earned, return on capital employed (ROCE), return on equity (ROE), earnings per share, or share price. Non-profit organizations will likely add KPIs which reflect their main purpose, e.g., the social satisfaction index for the city Aix les Bain (see case study in Sect. 6.3) or the #job vacancies filled, duration of unemployment, and #benefit recipients for the Federal Employment Agency of Germany (see case study in Sect. 6.5).

In the demander dimension KPIs such as market share, price relative to competition, sales channel distribution of revenue, cost per sale, customer visits per sale, revenue from new customers, revenue from new products/services, revenue growth from existing customers, account share, customer profitability, customer acquisition cost, marketing cost relative to sales, marketing campaign effectiveness, brand recognition, customer complaints, time to solve customer complaints, customer satisfaction, or customer loyalty by customer segment. Non-profit organizations might use similar KPIs replacing the term customer by citizen or the corresponding term for their respective constituency. Starbucks is an example of an organization that was able to create a new customer segment with a high customer loyalty rating, leading them to grow coffee sales with an annual growth rate of 55% compared with a 1.3% overall growth for coffee consumption in the market (Zook & Allen, 2010). One of many organizations that leveraged the internet to create a new sales channel is Charles Schwab who developed from a follower to a leader with a high market share in online trading, a distribution channel for which the profit margin is estimated at 70% compared to 12% for traditional trading.

KPIs used in the internal dimension include time to market, first to market, research and development expense, #patents, internal rate of return on new products, lead time from placing an order to its arrival at the customer site, average stock-outs, on-time delivery, cash-to-cash cycle time, average collection period, capacity utilization for infrastructure, equipment and labor, inventory turnover, part-per-million defect rate, product returns, warranty claims, waste, disposal costs as percent of total manufacturing costs, environmental emissions, safety and health incidents, average waiting time in customer service, and information coverage ratio measuring perceived accessibility of relevant information. Dell was given as an example where a negative cash-to-cash cycle time was leveraged to improve the business. Given their efficient supply chain management, Dell was able to receive payments from customers prior to the company paying their suppliers. Instead of paying interest, they were able to earn interest by doing business.

The following are examples of KPIs used in the supplier dimension: average cost of capital provided, employee satisfaction, recruitment cost, employee retention, employee productivity, employee competency fitness, personnel development cost, employee absenteeism, part-per-million defect rate, on-time delivery. The purchase price paid for products, services, or funds from suppliers is only reflecting a portion of the total cost for the organization. There is cost associated with the procurement and management of the relationship, which is significantly impacted by aspects such as quality, reliability, and ease of communication.

3.2.2 Use of KPIs for Strategy Execution

Since you can only manage what is measured, an effective strategy execution requires the formulation of a strategy including measurable strategic objectives. Establishing these strategic objectives for the enterprise and for each individual or organizational subunit requires to know the current performance and define the expected target performance and strategic initiatives to help improve the performance from the current level to the intended level of performance. KPIs, targets, and initiatives therefore need to be cascaded within the organizational hierarchy to document the contribution each unit is expected to make toward the achievement of the overall goals (see Fig. 3.6).

Because of the interdependence of organizational units on each other it is not only important to document the own contribution but also the expected contribution of other organizational units. This can include the approval of a budget and resources from above (vertical) or support from organizational units along the value chain (horizontal) as well as from subordinate organizational units (vertical). This way, management by objectives is enabled in combination with self-control and coordinated teamwork.

One of the tasks when establishing goals is to operationalize strategic, long-term objectives into short-term objectives, whose outcomes are achievable in the next month, quarter, or year. To reach a 10% increase of customer satisfaction within the next 3 years, this may be broken down to a 2% increase this year, 5% increase next year, and the remainder in the third year. Appropriate action plans including detailed initiatives with assigned timeframes and responsibilities can be developed for the respective timeframes to lead to the intended improvements. This concludes the preparation for strategy execution. Evaluating the effectiveness of the

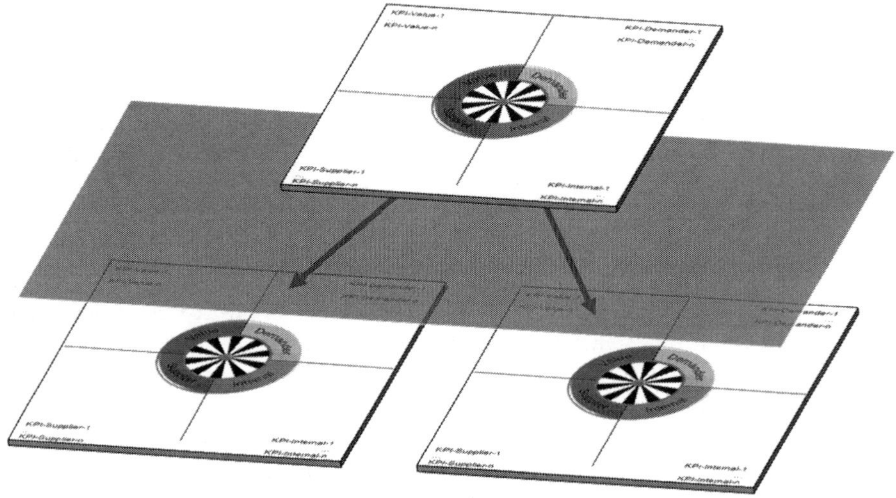

Fig. 3.6 Cascading the Value Scorecard™ (©Bernd Heesen/Prescient. Used with permission)

individual initiatives as well as the overall plans should be performed by management to decide if corrective actions are required and need to be implemented. Short-term objectives have the benefit of allowing early feedback on the effectiveness of the business execution. Applying this procedure ensures that decision making on all levels is consistent with the strategy of the organization while also allowing considerable latitude.

If KPIs are so important, how can they be used to make strategy execution more effective? Let us take a look at AVIS Europe.

Rental car companies have one KPI which allows them to diagnose their level of performance: The number of days cars are rented divided by the number of days the company owned the cars. Avis Europe serves more than 8 million customers at more than 3,800 locations (Fair Isaac Corporation, 2009c). In 2007, Avis was Europe's No. 2 car-rental agency, controlling 17.7% of the €8.81 billion market, which included the operation of 1.2 million vehicles. Avis had no sophisticated forecasting system but instead relied on the experience of fleet and station managers to predict future demand. They also followed established routines, e.g., to bring one transporter load of cars from London Heathrow to Mayfair every Friday at 7 a.m. because of the increased demand for cars in downtown on weekends. This had been a routine for many years but Avis management did not know if there was any extra room for the improvement of their fleet utilization. They searched for, invested in, and implemented a software to support a precise recommendation for fleet distribution and utilization. It may tell that only four cars need to be transported from Heathrow to Mayfair this week. The program also has built-in business intelligence. It automatically suggests sales restriction based on rental duration and locations for pick-up and car return, thereby contributing to a higher percentage of cars to be available for the most profitable customer segment. Jens Utech, Avis Europe's director of backoffice and station systems, estimated that the program has accounted for a two-point increase in the company's fleet utilization, which correlates to a $19 million increase in incremental benefits. Besides this benefit for the organization, the customers also benefit because the likelihood that Avis is able to meet customer demand in any location has increased.

The example of Avis also demonstrates the concept of leading and lagging indicators, which shall be addressed in the next section. In Avis's case, the investment in information technology created additional cost in the year prior to the system being used. The leading indicator of investment in process improvement caused a negative short-term effect on profitability. With a delay, until the system could be used to improve the fleet utilization, the lagging indicator of fleet utilization was improved. At the same time, a positive long-term effect was recognizable on profitability. In consequence, the financial indicators can be misleading. If management would have tried to optimize profitability without compromise, they would not have funded the innovative information technology solution. The reflection of the estimated net present value of the investment, including upfront cost and long-term benefits, allowed management to make a wise decision.

3.2.2.1 Leading and Lagging KPIs

The majority of financial KPIs are lagging indicators, measuring the results or performance of the past. This can be compared with driving a car just by looking in the rearview mirror. How safe would you feel driving a car this way and without having any vision to see what is in front of you? How many companies are driven by short-term financial results? A focus on short-term profitability alone can be very risky because there is limited vision to observe obstacles on the way.

On the other hand, leading performance indicators are early indicators for future success or failure. An example is customer satisfaction. A reduction in the number of customer service representatives working in the call-center will improve the financial KPI profitability in the short term. But with longer waiting times on the phone, customers may not receive the quality service they expect, and their satisfaction may decrease. At the time of their next purchasing decision they will evaluate many aspects including product features, product quality, price, and service. A lowered customer satisfaction of x% may lead to a loss of y% customers, who choose to buy the competitor's product. This way, in the long-term, the lowered customer satisfaction will potentially lead to reduced revenues and profits. Consequently, the monitoring of KPIs related to customer retention or customer satisfaction are early indicators of future problems. On the opposite, rising customer satisfaction may be an indicator for future success. To understand more precisely to what extent any leading indicator impacts a lagging indicator, statistical evaluation is required – one of the main features of business intelligence solutions.

You may ask yourself if it is really necessary to understand the correlations of leading and lagging KPIs in detail or if it suffices to understand that a good customer satisfaction should always be secured? Not knowing the details would potentially mean not to be able to benchmark against competition or to know if a further investment to improve a KPI is worthwhile. This can lead to an ineffective strategy execution and waste of resources.

There always are conflicting objectives in an organization. How would you know if an annual investment in additional customer service with an associated cost of $300,000 is worthwhile if you have no realistic expectation about the effect of this investment on customer satisfaction and therefore indirectly on future revenue and profit? From a business standpoint, the investment should be approved if the net present value is positive, reflecting all current and future costs and benefits. This might be influenced by additional factors, e.g., how does the own service compare to that of the competition and what is the strategic position the own organization intends to maintain or to reach? The decision may depend on the strategy of the organization. If it follows a strategy of a cost-leader, providing a standard product to the lowest possible price, the current service may be sufficient. If it follows a customer-focused strategy offering exceptional services and products for a premium price it could be a necessary investment. To make a smart decision, more knowledge of the situation is beneficial since outstanding customer satisfaction is only beneficial if it impacts future revenue and profit sufficiently as the following example illustrates.

Ittner and Larcker (2003) studied a company in the telecommunications industry where customers' switching costs were minimal. The company management decided to target a 100% customer satisfaction rating in order not to lose customers. What the company did not know was the correlation between customer satisfaction and revenue or profit generation. Ittner and Larcker found a very weak positive correlation to exist but customers who were 80% satisfied spent nothing less than those who were 100% satisfied. Basically, in this case, the investment in improved customer satisfaction did not lead to additional revenue or profit; it was an investment without payback.

Wrong management decisions cannot be avoided completely for many reasons but more knowledge about facts can contribute to improve management decision making in many instances. A key consequence from the above example should be that better performance on a single KPI does not necessarily mean a better performance of the overall organization. This is like it is in team sports, e.g., soccer. Having a good offense does not make you win all games if you lack quality in the defense. The overall result counts. In the case above, the money invested in the increase of customer satisfaction might have been more effectively invested in a marketing campaign to increase revenue and profit or saved.

Further examples of leading and lagging indicators might be:

- Absenteeism by employees as leading indicator for low employee satisfaction and increased workforce turnover as lagging indicator.
- Customer loyalty as leading indicator for sales growth as lagging indicator.
- Lower price than competition as a leading indicator for revenue as lagging indicator.
- Investment in research and development as a leading indicator for revenue from new products as lagging indicator.
- Investment in a customer satisfaction survey as a leading indicator for improved customer retention as lagging indicator.
- Customer problems solved in first call to customer hotline as leading indicator for improved customer satisfaction as lagging indicator.

A solid understanding of leading and lagging indicators means to have knowledge about the correlation of different KPIs. Since statistics just evaluate the correlation it not possible to conclude cause and effect without doubt. Nevertheless, in the previous example, the knowledge that an increase in customer satisfaction does not lead to higher revenues is valuable as it helps to answer the question: If we invest additional $300,000 annually in customer service, does it improve our profit? The answer is: No. Consequently, the investment may not be made. Similarly, it can help to answer questions like: If we reduce our price by 5%, does it lead to an increase in products sold of at least 15%? An understanding of the price elasticity of demand is required to answer this question.

For some products a change in price has a significant impact on demand while for others it does not. The dramatic increase in gasoline price in the past years has only caused a modest change in consumption. Why? People still have to get to work and if they own a car they typically have to accept a significant transaction cost for selling it and buying another one. Obviously there are many more reasons including the preference to drive a specific brand or type of vehicle. Cooper (2003) found that oil demand was highly price-inelastic in the short run in 21 of 23 analyzed countries. Demand was only decreasing significantly in China and Portugal when prices were rising. Price elasticity of demand is much higher for those products with many substitutes. A recent publication summarizing the findings of 160 studies on the price elasticity of demand for major food categories found that the price elasticity varied between 0.27 and 0.81 (Andreyeva, Long, & Brownell, 2010). The highest values in the range between 0.7 and 0.8 were found for food away from home, soft drinks, juice, and meats. To use an example, a 10% increase in beef price should reduce its consumption by about 7%. Consumers might be switching to chicken if its price did not increase. Finding out how price-sensitive customers are could be done by evaluating the purchasing behavior via direct experimentation, e.g., in online shops by changing prices or via surveys. The determination of the price elasticity of demand is one of the many valuable applications of business intelligence. See, how Marriott is leveraging price optimization based not only on price elasticity but a more complex model, helping to improve the effectiveness of strategy execution.

Marriott International, managing more than 3,400 properties with over 600,000 rooms in 70 countries with 18 brands generated $11 billion in sales in 2009 (Hormby, Morrison, Meyers, Dave, & Tenca, 2010). The application of data analytics, based on a database with 2 years of data with transaction and lead information, with a solution called the *Group Pricing Optimizer* leveraged information about the available inventory, displacement cost, probability of winning at a recommended rate to propose a negotiating range for the price based on customer segment, season, booking window, hotel, group size, and other descriptive variables. Understanding the customer buying behavior allowed to use different price curves for each segment and optimized the profit based on existing reservations, premium rate, regular rate and discount rate bookings for each hotel. A simulation allows to view the profit without the candidate group booking and with the candidate group including the reflection of displacement costs. As Carl Wilson, Executive Vice President & Chief Information Officer at Marriott, mentioned: "Our ability to pair the science and technology that dynamically provides Marriott's sales force and Marriott.com with group rates based on daily market conditions sets us apart from the competition" (Hormby, Morrison, Meyers, Dave, & Tenca, 2010). The introduction of the Group Pricing Optimizer improved revenue by $200 million. Bill Marriott, Chairman, stated "Two things that make our company successful are taking care of our customers and innovation. The Group Pricing Optimizer shows our sales managers just the right amount of information they need to book a group profitably while meeting the needs of many of our many group customers. I am proud of our Revenue Management team for developing an industry-first pricing system that has already booked over 1 billion dollars in revenue for our North American hotels" (Hormby, Morrison, Meyers,

Dave, & Tenca, 2010). Marriott International's Group Pricing Optimizer was recognized as the winner of the 2010 Practice Award at the 10th Annual INFORMS Revenue Management and Pricing Section Conference for their industry leadership in the application of management science, managing both group and individual travel demand to maximize total profitability and improve customer service by using innovative analytics (INFORMS Revenue Management and Pricing Section, 2010).

Another example where the use of KPIs and analytics helped to improve strategy execution is described in Sect. 6.4 in the case study. Würth was able to improve the leading KPI "Number of customer visits" as well as knowledge about the correlation of products sold together. Using this information during the customer visits, made available on mobile devices during the visit, facilitated improved cross-selling. Sales as a lagging indicator could be increased.

Just as a note for all those familiar with statistics. Using statistics or data mining to uncover exact correlations between KPIs you can never be 100% confident. You can determine the confidence level of the correlations you receive. They are often determined as sufficient when the confidence interval is set at 95 or 99%.

An important consequence of understanding the difference between leading and lagging indicators is that one needs to first impact leading KPIs in order to experience a positive change on the lagging KPIs. The lagging KPIs are most essential measures of the success of the organization. Organizations trying to create a competitive advantage need to do this by positively changing leading indicators first before realizing the benefits. As Markus Schwaninger states: "One basic fact is that building value potentials requires a substantial, long-term effort. It creates future benefit and therefore demands sacrifices in the present. Value potentials must be controlled separately from value, on the basis of independent criteria. Research on strategic management has clarified the nature of these criteria and shown, for instance, how to apprehend the critical success factors (such as market share, relative market share, experience, quality and customer benefit, speed, flexibility, etc.) in a given business system" (Schwaninger, 2009, p. 54). This confirms that short-term success is not easy to realize without potentially accepting sacrifices in the longer term.

There is a chance that a focus on short-term profitability might lead to decisions like reducing the investment in research and development, processes improvements, personnel development, or other activities which only provide their return on investment with delay. Reducing the spending in the above-mentioned areas or by reducing the headcount reduces cost and improves profitability in the short term, making the financial numbers look good. These decisions can reduce the value-creation potentials for the organization in the longer run and thereby harm an effective strategy execution.

It is key to understand that the leading indicators, typically the non-financial ones, are the foundation for competitive advantage. They are also the ones to keep an eye on to identify positive or negative developments in business performance early on. How to leverage KPIs to receive early alerts of critical developments is covered on the following pages.

3.2.2.2 Diagnostic KPIs

Not all KPIs have the same relevance. As introduced in the last section there is a difference between leading and lagging KPIs. Another differentiation introduced by Kaplan and Norton (1996) are diagnostic measures. They use the example of a body where a couple of KPIs need to be within specific intervals for the body to work properly. This applies to the KPI body temperature or blood pressure. When we are getting close to the border or outside of the defined interval, then the existence might be in danger and all energies should be utilized to get back into normal operations. As long as they stay within the defined limits, we do not need to focus on them more than on any other KPIs. This is why they are called diagnostic KPIs. Management by exception best describes how to deal with them. Normally we treat them the same way as any other KPI, but in exceptions, when the KPI leaves a defined bandwidth, then we need to focus on them immediately. This is similar to a car where you do not need to monitor oil temperature or the fuel gauge permanently but you rely on a warning light or another signal to indicate if the PKI leaves a predefined bandwidth. Some cars even monitor tire pressure. This allows us to focus on traffic and steer the car to our destination. This is exactly what we want to do as managers: steering our business to reach our strategic objectives.

What is the benefit of applying this concept of diagnostic measures to business? Management time is always scarce and to continuously monitor all KPIs for which a manager has responsibility is often impossible. Managers typically focus their attention on the most pressing issues and this is exactly what diagnostic KPIs support. They only alert managers when a problem needs to be escalated or requires the attention on this level.

Like most tools, they should be used adequately. The purpose of alerts is lost if there are too many of them, leading to the manager ignoring them. In a flood of information, critical alerts could be lost. This may already happen today every once in a while to important notifications we receive via a tool called E-mail. Has this ever happened to you? It certainly happens more frequently if there are too many messages to adequately deal with them in the limited time available. As a consequence, the information recipients of the alerts should be able to define their own bandwidth for each KPI, one that, based on their management experience, is sufficiently early to notify them of the deviation in performance.

Which KPIs might be suited as diagnostic measures? There is really no ultimate list because they need to be tailored to the needs of each information recipient for them to be relevant. While there is no ultimate list there are applications, specifically for risk avoidance, which can be found in many organizations. One of the risks for organizations is to go bankrupt. Therefore it makes sense for at least one person in the organization to establish an alert if the cash-flow forecast indicates a shortage of funds. If such an alert is received early on, there may be enough time to cut expenses, make an extra effort to collect accounts receivable, or get an extension of the credit line. Other useful diagnostic measures might indicate unexpected radical negative developments, e.g., in KPIs such as customer retention, employee

turnover, on-time delivery, defaulting accounts receivable, cap
inventory turnover, part-per-million defect rate, and product retur

Why would organizations potentially miss to recognize risks?
could be not to recognize a risk at all or to recognize it but not con
enough to initiate change and commit adequate resources. This happened in the Indian Tsunami case, where previous statements about missing infrastructure to recognize such events was ignored. The second problem might be to have no adequate business intelligence infrastructure which automatically alerts the individuals in charge. In this case, the use of KPIs would not be effective.

3.2.3 *Effective Use of KPIs*

First of all, there is no purpose in defining KPIs, whether they are leading, lagging or diagnostic ones, if they are not utilized. Utilization requires that the performance information is tracked, stored, and available for analysis. Analysis of the data should include data mining to detect correlations between KPIs in order to effectively monitor early indicators of performance. An automatic monitoring system should be utilized to relieve managers from the tedious and time-consuming task of looking up performance measures just for the sake of validating that diagnostic KPIs are within their expected bandwidth. It should be possible for managers to establish their individual alert levels for any of the KPIs they work with. In order to perform these tasks it is necessary to establish a business intelligence infrastructure. This will be covered in Sect. 3.3.

Sadly enough many companies do not fulfill the above prerequisites for an effective use of KPIs. Many companies do not even realize the significance of the non-financial KPIs as early warning indicators and predictors for future performance (Ittner & Larcker, 2003). Other companies do have inappropriate performance measurement systems where the meaning and calculation of KPIs is not clearly defined, documented, and readily available for everyone working with the KPIs. Another problem may be not to perform benchmarking of the own current performance with the own past performance, the expected performance and the performance of your competitors. What counts is not only absolute performance but also relative performance. As Michael Vitale and Sarah Mavrinac correctly state: "Quality and satisfaction levels that improve by 5% each quarter might seem impressive until one discovers that competitors are bounding forward with quarterly performance improvements of 10%" (Vitale & Mavrinac, 1995).

In addition to what was already mentioned, what are the characteristics of effective KPIs? Wayne Eckerson developed a list with 12 important attributes, which can be considered essential for effective KPIs" (Eckerson, 2006, p. 201):

1. Aligned: KPIs are always aligned with corporate strategy and objectives.
2. Owned: Every KPI is "owned" by an individual or group on the business side who is accountable for this outcome.

3. Predictive: KPIs measure drivers of business value. Thus, they are "leading" indicators of performance desired by the organization.
4. Actionable: KPIs are populated with timely, actionable data so users can intervene to improve performance before it is too late.
5. Few in number: KPIs should focus users on a few high-value tasks, not scatter their attention and energy on too many things.
6. Easy to understand: KPIs should be straightforward and easy to understand, not based on complex indexes that users do not know how to influence directly.
7. Balanced and linked: KPIs should balance and reinforce each other, not undermine each other and suboptimize processes.
8. Trigger changes: The act of measuring a KPI should trigger a chain reaction of positive changes in the organization, especially when it is monitored by the CEO.
9. Standardized: KPIs are based on standard definitions, rules, and calculations so they can be integrated across dashboards throughout the organization.
10. Context driven: KPIs put performance in context by applying targets and thresholds to performance so users can gauge their progress over time.
11. Reinforced with incentives: Organizations can magnify the impact of KPIs by attaching compensation or incentives to them. However, they should do this cautiously, applying incentives only to well-understood and stable KPIs.
12. Relevant: KPIs gradually lose their impact over time, so they must be periodically reviewed and refreshed.

This list of characteristics provides a good checklist for organizations to start evaluating their preparedness to leverage KPIs.

One obstacle that frequently surfaces is the lack of available data to actually measure one or many of the KPIs that business managers would like to use to track performance. If this occurs it is a signal that this specific performance must have been ignored in the past. By closing this gap, management can potentially uncover new opportunities or detect problematic performance earlier. On the other hand, it is equally essential to limit your wishlist of KPIs and to always consider the additional cost the tracking, storing, and reporting related to the additional KPI might be causing. Looking at it from a holistic enterprise perspective, the accumulated benefits should outweigh the related costs. The justification of any investment in information technology via a business case is in the best interest of everyone involved.

Effective KPIs also help to surface otherwise often undiscovered or hidden conflicts of interest. Transparency by providing access to KPIs helps to uncover potential conflicts between organizational units. An example could be a conflict between the marketing and sales and the manufacturing department. While the marketing and sales department has an interest in frequent production runs to have the most current products available and be able to deliver make-to-order products quickly to the customers, the manufacturing department might be interested to have as few as possible manufacturing runs in order to minimize their manufacturing cost per product. Similarly sales and marketing might have a preference for warehouses in the field, close to the customers, while manufacturing might prefer warehouses in the manufacturing plant to minimize delivery times and the finance department might have an interest in a minimal number of warehouses in total as to reduce capital cost. These are just a few examples where the definition of targets for KPIs can lead to a valuable exchange and understanding of positions. This shared understanding across the value creation process provides the foundation for an effective strategy execution.

Despite the obvious advantages of measuring different KPIs and understanding relevant correlations between them, Ittner and Larcker (2003) found that only 30% of the surveyed companies analyzed correlations between KPIs. Ittner and Larcker had conducted field research in more than 60 manufacturing and service companies and supplemented it with survey responses from 297 senior executives. The companies that analyzed these correlations had superior business success. They had a 5.14 higher return on equity (ROE) than the companies that did not. This, in addition to the other successful examples of organizations should motivate organizations to establish the necessary infrastructure to create an effective measure-managed organization.

3.3 Tracking KPIs and the Need for Business Intelligence

There is not much value in knowing what needs to be measured, the KPIs, without actually collecting the required information. And it is not only the capturing of the information that is important, but also the communication to all those interested in the KPIs for performance measurement or diagnostic purposes. This is the foundation for measurement and learning from feedback as well as the ability to align employees with the organizational objectives by linking their performance to strategic objectives. How should these tasks be accomplished without information systems?

Implementations of scorecards frequently fail because of a lack of IT-infrastructure to provide correct calculation and timely availability of the performance indicators. Data might not be available or the quality of the data is insufficient or they are not integrated or centrally available for reporting. A solid IT infrastructure is needed to support the collection, calculation, and distribution of critical information. Unfortunately, many companies lack this kind of infrastructure. A 2008 survey of 254 executives conducted by the consulting firm Accenture (2008b) found that more than half of the organizations do not have a consistently updated enterprise-wide analytical capability and two-thirds believe that they need to improve their analytical capability. One of the specifically mentioned challenges was their limited IT capabilities, as indicated by 39% of the executives. Another survey of 600 executives conducted by Accenture (2010) in 2009 confirmed that data silos and outdated information technology limited the organizations from gaining relevant insights based on the data they have and lead to suboptimal business decisions. Isolated data was reported as a problem by 45% of the respondents and 40%

described their IT infrastructure not to be at the point to support enterprise-wide analytics. Opportunities were specifically seen in improving the quality of the data in regards to its consistency, accuracy, and completeness. The key is to exploit the maximum value of information.

3.3.1 Value of Information

Information is an asset with unique characteristics. In contrast to many types of assets, the asset “Information” is not losing value when used. It can be exploited without depreciating the value (see Fig. 3.7).

The total value of the asset information even increases when it is used by many individuals. This implies that once information is available it should be communicated to as many individuals as possible if they are expected to benefit from it. Since there are costs to gather and store information, it is essential to recover the cost by sharing the information with those who have a respective information demand. Consequently, this also implies that only that kind of information should be gathered and stored which contributes enough value to recover its cost (see Fig. 3.8). This also applies to key performance indicators. Organizations should limit themselves to those KPIs which are valuable. A business case should be used to justify the investments in information technology.

Maximizing the value of information also requires to control the amount of information since this does not automatically lead to more value. Information overload can actually be a burden for mangers. With information sharing being so easy via communication channels like E-mail and internet/intranet, one of the

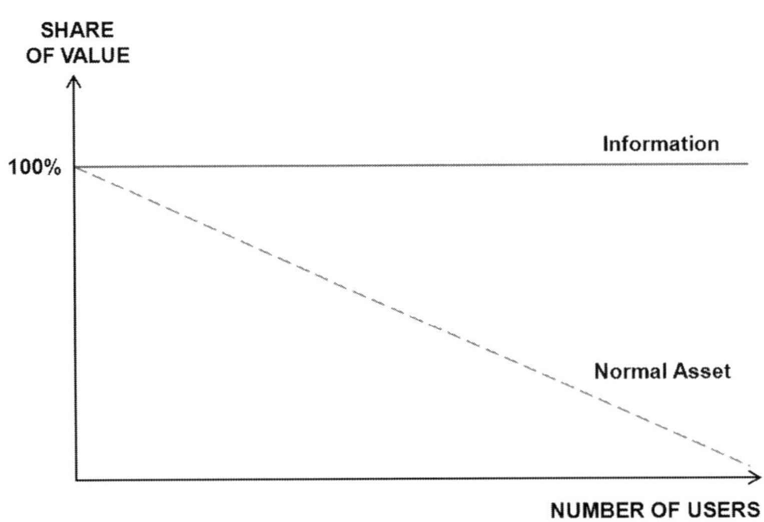

Fig. 3.7 Depreciation of assets (Reproduced based on Moody and Walsh 1999, p. 500)

challenges is to find the right balance between not providing enough information and supplying too much (see Fig. 3.9). Sharing more does not automatically lead to higher value, even when the information is of relevance. Each individual has limited capacities and time for information processing.

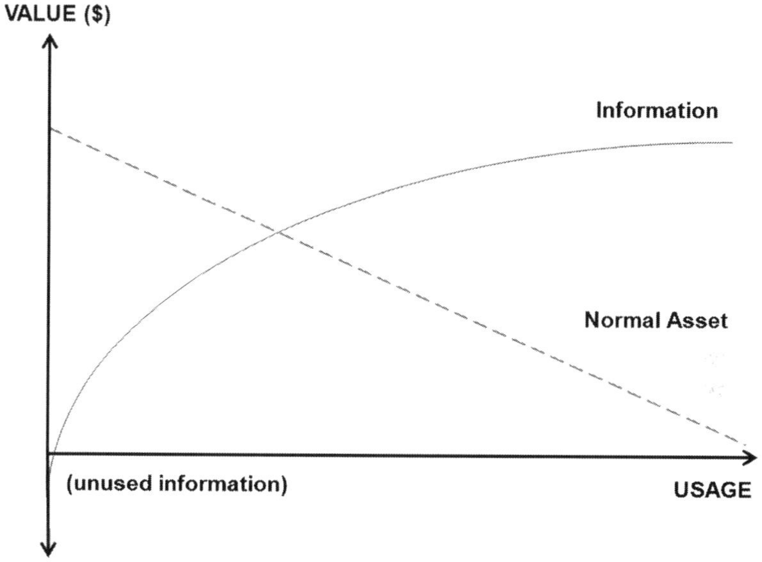

Fig. 3.8 Value increase with usage (Reproduced based on Moody and Walsh 1999, p. 501)

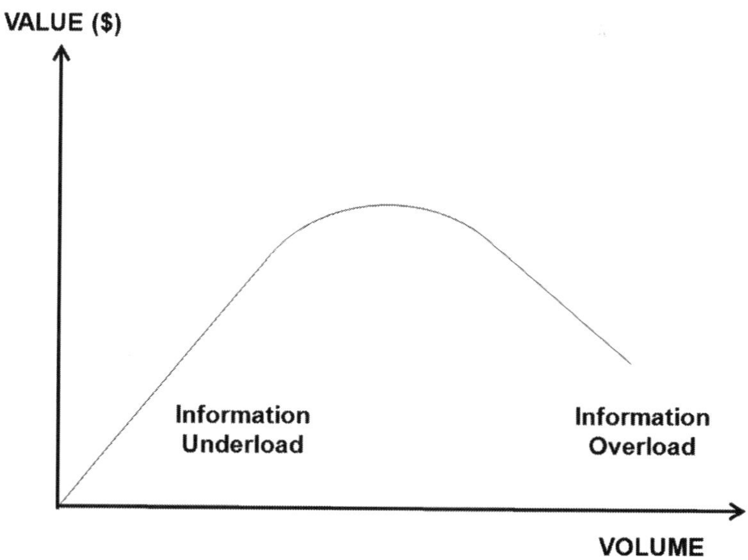

Fig. 3.9 Volume versus value of information (Reproduced based on Moody and Walsh 1999, p. 504)

Information systems can help with finding this balance. Business intelligence infrastructures can provide access to standard reports, offer ad-hoc analysis tools to analyze performance KPIs, and automate the monitoring of diagnostic KPIs via exception reporting and alerting. A flexible and proactive way for each individual to balance their own information access is information broadcasting. Information producers publish information in defined communication channels to which each individual can subscribe or unsubscribe any time based on their preferences and information needs. Once they have subscribed, the information from this communication channel is automatically broadcasted to them, e.g., via periodic newsletters. Ideally the subscribers can even select the periodicity in which they want to receive the information. Some information requires immediate attention and should trigger an immediate alert while other information might be sufficient in form of a weekly, monthly, or annual summary. The right and appropriate timing largely depends on the role and responsibilities of an individual.

The key to maximize the value of information is not only having more information but to understand which information is needed by whom, increasing the overlap between information demand and information supply, to improve decision making (see Fig. 3.10).

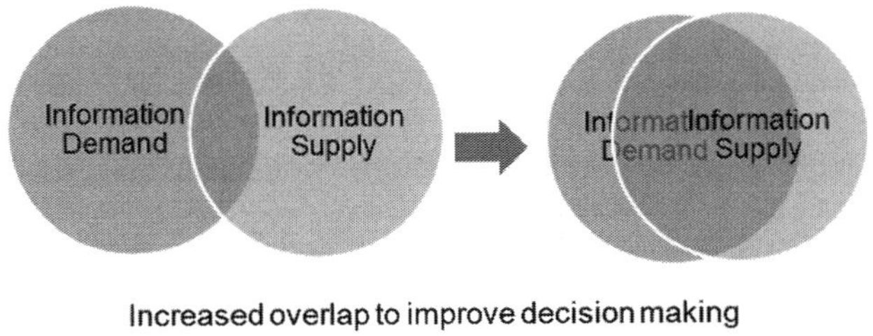

Fig. 3.10 Maximizing information availability (©Bernd Heesen/Prescient. Used with permission)

Another relevant factor influencing the value of information is accuracy and correctness. Decisions based on incorrect information can lead to a negative value. Incorrect information about the price customers are willing to pay for a product can lead to pricing below the optimal price or incorrect information about the risks associated with lacking information technology, and communication infrastructure may lead to an incapability to appropriately deal with a tsunami or a comparable event in business. Accurate information, on the other hand, can hold significant added value as demonstrated in the many examples given in this book.

To define an exact value of information is difficult. A couple of established valuation models can be applied:

1. Historical cost: What has been paid to acquire information.
2. Market value: What is the value at which the information can be sold.
3. Utility value: What are the expected economic benefits from the possession of the information.

A maximization of the value of information typically depends on the cost in comparison with the utility value. But the value contribution of information is not limited to the internal benefits and efficiency gains. The customers, suppliers, investors, and other stakeholder groups may similarly benefit from improved information access.

Customers benefit from easily available product and service information as the following example from FedEx demonstrates. Federal Express Corporation (Lendio, 2011), a company incorporated in 1971 has evolved to a company with more than 10 billion in revenue with their courier service. Their articulated aim is to continually apply new information technologies, strategic management initiatives, and aggressive marketing strategies to better connect with customers, reduce operating costs, and improve profitability. In the late 1990s, they introduced an innovative new service, the tracking of packages at any point in time. In a very competitive market, this added value via information helped to gain competitive advantage. It was not the service of package delivery itself but additional information which enabled this progress. Already in 1978, Fred Smith was famously quoted as saying, "The information about the package is just as important as the package itself" (Federal Express Corporation, 2011). Today, FedEx provides customers access to near real-time information that has enabled new supply chain models and efficiencies. This unprecedented access to information is connecting customers around the world to economic markets and communities.

Another example where information adds value is in vehicle maintenance. Think of your car breaking down on the road in nowhereland. Would you not like to call the customer service and get an immediate analysis of the problem? Now, if the car does not start or provides an alert that the vehicle should not be operated to avoid larger consequences, the only remaining option often is to have the car towed to the next repair shop. Depending on the seriousness of the issue they may spend a good amount of time analyzing the problem. Would there be a benefit to you as a customer if your customer service representative would have remote access to a communication device on your vehicle which stores all malfunctions? This would allow them to quickly identify the cause of the problem. This could enable them to provide you with directions how to solve the problem without any further assistance or to send a service vehicle with the required spare parts to fix the problem without the vehicle to be towed to the service shop. This would reduce the cost and the time for the customer. I can recall my own experience with my Mercedes-Benz car last year. It was Friday afternoon and I happened to be in Grenoble/France. I had just finished my lecture and was ready to head back to Germany, a several hours trip. The engine started but made an unusual sound and a red warning light indicated problems with the engine. Reviewing the warning details in the operating manual I found a note telling me that the engine had a serious malfunction and I should immediately drive to the next service station. The motor was throttled automatically to limit further damages and I was only able to drive with a speed of about 30 km/h. The motor did not operate smoothly at all. I located the closest Mercedes service station, checked if they were still open at this time on Friday and drove there very carefully. When I arrived I was certainly relieved to find them open and immediately drove my car into the garage. With about 10 h left to drive home, it was my sincere interest for them to solve the problem quickly and get back on the road. With the weekend approaching, I was also concerned that they may not be able to repair the car in the remaining time. But I was lucky because my car had a built-in computer recording all major vehicle operations and problems and they used a special networking cable to hook up their analysis station to my car's recording unit. I had not even known that my car had this feature. The data transfer to their computer took about 2 min. I was looking over the shoulders of the service technician as he was analyzing my car's performance. It showed several malfunctions together with the associated times they happened. The main problem seemed to be an underperformance of my third combustion chamber, which was leading to a rattling and reduced performance of the engine. The information allowed the technician to quickly identify the issues and by accessing their world-wide support database with prescribed solutions for recognized types of problems, he was able to solve the problem within less than an hour and I was on the road again. The information gathered by my car, stored in the recording unit, and the business intelligence of Daimler significantly contributed to a positive service experience. In this kind of scenario, the information availability adds value for the customer right away and for the manufacturer it helps to increase customer loyalty. Additional details on the KPIs used by Daimler to optimize their service are described in the case study in Sect. 6.2.

Unfortunately the information is not always as readily available as in the above example. The Economist Intelligence Unit (2006) reported, based on a survey of more than 300 executives, that almost 72% of the survey respondents perceived the information available within their organizations not to be consistent across departments because of unreliable methods for data gathering and missing corporate standards. Another mentioned source of problems were heterogeneous IT landscapes, e.g., caused by the acquisition of organizations with different IT systems and data formats. It takes time to integrate the systems of acquired companies and until this is accomplished, corporate-wide analyses are limited. The integration of systems is a major task for IT departments.

But data are not only managed by the IT department. Actually, most managers utilize tools such as Microsoft Excel to manage data they do not appropriately receive, either in format or detail, from the IT department. Maintaining data locally is detrimental in two ways: (1) the locally maintained information is not accessible by other organizational members and consequently the same data may be maintained redundantly by different groups in the organization, which can lead to inconsistencies and (2) these tools often incorporate incorrect formulas or allow data to be captured without validation, which leads to errors and miscalculations. Based on Panko's (2008) analysis, an audit of 113 spreadsheets in seven studies reported that 88% of the spreadsheets contained errors. In his report, he stated that many companies utilize spreadsheets as part of their financial reporting, which may not be well controlled. Panko referred to the following sources, confirming the urgency of the issue:

- Financial intelligence firm CODA reported 95% of U.S. firms using spreadsheets for financial reporting.
- International Data Corporation (IDC) interviewed 118 business leaders and found that 85% were using spreadsheets in reporting, budgeting, and forecasting.

- The Hacket Group surveyed mid-sized companies and found that 47% of companies used stand-alone spreadsheets for planning and budgeting.
- CFO.com interviewed 168 finance executives, all of whom confirmed to use spreadsheets.
- A.R.C. Morgan interviewed 376 individuals responsible for overseeing Sarbanes-Oxley compliance in multinational organizations. More than 80% of the respondents stated that their firms used spreadsheets for financial reporting.

Many of the errors in spreadsheet calculations were caused by a lack of understanding on the developer's side (Panko & Aurigemma, 2010). This leads to the question who is actually modifying these spreadsheets; are these professional software developers? Obviously this is not the case, and typical software testing to validate the proper functioning is also not performed. Documentation of the spreadsheet functionality is typically not developed and therefore the functionality of the spreadsheet often relies on the competence and availability of individuals. When they leave an organization or are unavailable this can have a negative impact on the availability or quality of reports. This kind of dependency should not exist for any mission-critical reporting since the value of information increases with its immediate availability when needed.

The difficulty with spreadsheets is not only limited to the unquestionable high probability of errors, but also the different validation and calculation rules across the organization. Even though spreadsheets may contain their own validation and calculation rules, it is likely that they differ across the organization. These local spreadsheets can lead to confusion in meetings where executives debate about which information is correct, the local data from the spreadsheet or from another source, while they should focus on the decision making instead of debating IT issues. The reason why spreadsheets are frequently used is their flexibility. The more restrictive and limiting the enterprise IT solutions are for local management, the more they seek their own avenues to fulfill their local information needs, partly with the help of spreadsheets. The maintenance of these spreadsheets can become a full-time job for many individuals in the organization. The effectiveness of local data maintenance and manipulation can be questioned from an enterprise perspective since these data cannot be aggregated or used for corporate reporting or benchmarking across organizational units.

What is needed is a centralized enterprise business intelligence infrastructure, providing a single version of the truth, supporting the comparison of key performance indicators across the enterprise. No doubt, this infrastructure needs to fulfill not only corporate, but also local information needs. If the local information demand is met, there is no need for the local managers to establish their independent data marts and spreadsheets. Also, the appreciation of spreadsheets by end users for their ease of use and flexibility needs to be recognized. Enterprise business intelligence infrastructures need to provide easy-to-use applications and flexible access to information via tools which are widely accepted. The business intelligence software has evolved in the recent past and is now able to meet these expectations, e.g., via the use of portals, dashboards, and mobile devices. The use of spreadsheets can still be supported but should be used with care, avoiding the above-mentioned disadvantages.

It is important though to maximize the value of information by establishing an enterprise data warehouse based on a shared metadata. This kind of a business intelligence infrastructure can fulfill the local as well as corporate information needs. The following examples from Marriott and Barnes & Noble demonstrate some of the benefits of replacing disparate systems with an enterprise business intelligence infrastructure.

Marriott was able to streamline their procurement process and customer management via the consolidation of IT systems (Radcliff, 2000). Originally each of their hotel groups purchased supplies such as shampoo, soap, towels etc. from their preferred vendor. Because of their disparate systems, Marriott was not able to benefit from consolidated procurement for the Marriott group with the according volume discounts. They also lacked a consolidated view on their customers across the group, e.g., to track and improve revenue per customer. Realizing these deficiencies, Marriott established a consolidated system tying their procurement as well customer management systems together to enable a consolidated procurement as well as customer management. Carl Wilson, Marriott's executive vice president and CIO, confirmed the relevance of appropriate IT solutions for business execution by stating: "IT at Marriott is a key component of the products and services that we provide to our customers and guests at our properties" (Radcliff, 2000).

Barnes and Noble used to have nine different data warehouses, one for point-of-sale data from 730 retail stores, another one for 630 college bookstores, and another one for their website and so on. Similar to Marriott with its different systems, this infrastructure did not enable the analysis of sales across the different sales channels. Barnes & Noble recently implemented a consolidated enterprise data warehouse project. Marc Parrish, VP of retention and loyalty marketing, stated that Barnes & Noble is now doing a better job of cross-channel analysis, which was next to impossible with the previously existing data silos: "Before, when somebody visited us online, we only knew about their online purchases. Now that all our data is in one place, we can understand their interactions across our entire ecosystem" (Henschen, 2010, p. 26).

With executives understanding the relevance and value of timely and correct information for their business operations the question is: How confident are executives about having timely and reliable information at their disposal when they need to make strategic decisions? Wm Schiemann & Associates Inc. conducted a national survey of a cross section of 203 executives in the United States (Lingle & Schiemann, 1996). They found that only 60% of the executives placed confidence in the data they had available. The uncertainty was attributed to a lack of clarity in the measurements as well as the limited frequency of capturing key performance indicators such as information about customers, employees, or external stakeholders. A significant gap existed between the executives' value for information and their confidence in the quality of the available information. These gaps regarding the following key performance indicators surfaced:

- Customer satisfaction (value: 85%, confidence: 29%, gap: 56%)
- Employee performance (value: 67%, confidence: 16%, gap: 51%)
- Operating efficiency (value: 79%, confidence: 41%, gap: 38%)
- Financial performance (value: 82%, confidence: 61%, gap: 21%)

Executives who realize a gap between their demand and the reality of their information supply for decision making should improve their business intelligence infrastructure to improve quality and timeliness. Clearly they might not want to continue to operate without valuable information when they make decisions, following an effective information processing framework as displayed in Fig. 3.11.

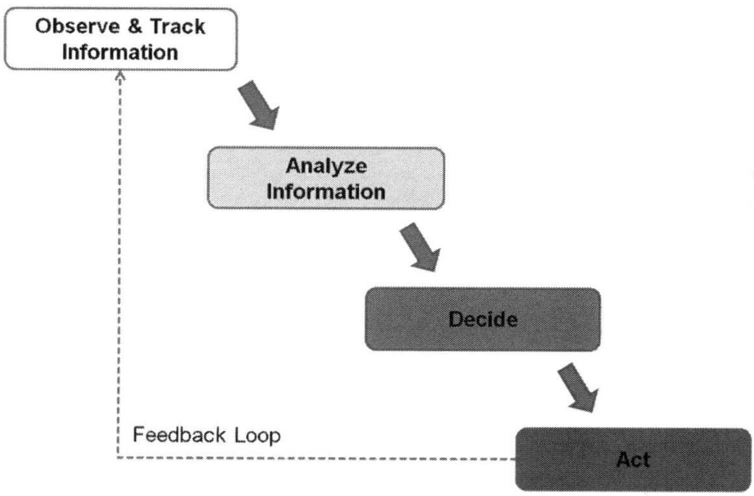

Fig. 3.11 Information processing framework (Heesen, 2010, p. 142)

The value of information and the competitive advantage of its availability is decreasing over time. Therefore executives should shorten the process of collecting data, analyzing the information, deciding, and finally business execution (see Fig. 3.12). An organization which is acting quicker than their competition can gain competitive advantage.

The effectiveness of the information processing and limiting the loss of value of information can be reached by shortening the action distance. From an information processing standpoint, this can be done by reducing the data latency and the analysis latency by utilizing business intelligence. From an execution standpoint, a quicker business execution is possible by reducing the decision latency in combination with the execution latency. Since the effectiveness depends on the sum of all four latencies, the key is to create a performance culture which equally addresses all phases in a holistic approach. The following chapters in this book will demonstrate how business intelligence helps to reduce:

- Data latency: Sect. 3.3
- Analysis latency: Sect. 4.1
- Decision latency: Sect. 4.2
- Execution latency: Sect. 4.3

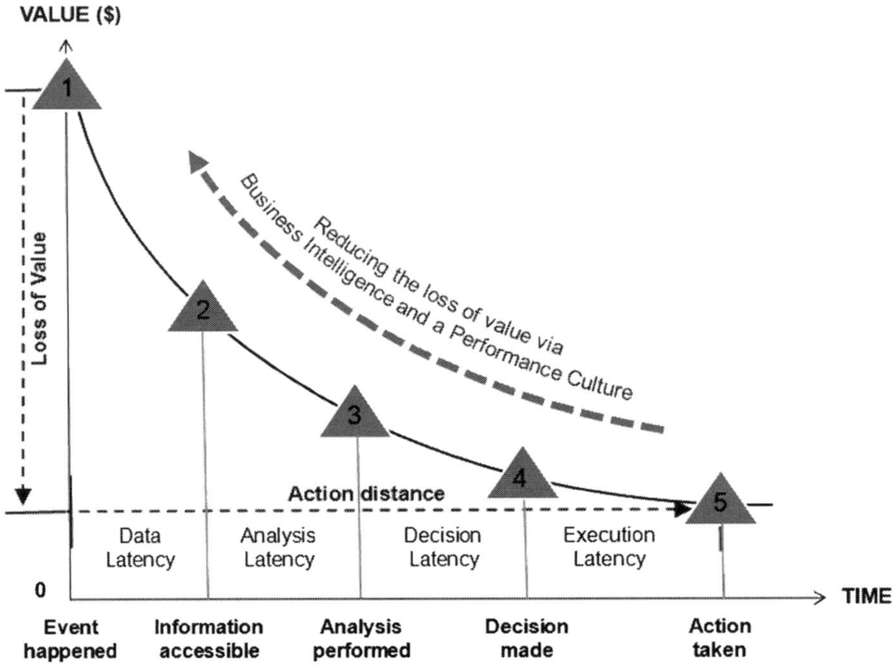

Fig. 3.12 Time as a critical success factor for effective strategy execution (©Bernd Heesen/ Prescient. Used with permission)

Obviously the timeliness of information needs to be complemented by adequate quality. While some information used for legal reporting has to be provided in compliance with the law and 100% correct, information for decision making does not have to the same accuracy in all cases. Sometimes a decision maker might prefer to have close to perfect information right away over precise information two weeks later. In any case, the decision maker needs to trust the reliability of the information and the degree of exactness needs to fit the requirements of the decision maker. If they can have access to better information before their competition, they probably gain a relevant competitive advantage, if their competition has access before them, they probably have a competitive disadvantage.

3.3.2 Business Intelligence

Information technology can help companies in several ways to complement or substitute information processing performed by humans, especially leveraging the advanced capabilities to store and retrieve information or perform calculations and analytical tasks quickly and finally present and communicate the information.

Information technology is (a) supporting an efficient and effective way to perform business transactions in online transactional processing (OLTP) systems, e.g., Enterprise Resource Planning (ERP), Customer Relationship Management (CRM), Supply Chain Management (SCM) or similar systems, and (b) access to and distribution of information for improved decision making. The access to information includes reporting and analytics on demand, e.g., access to standard reports or reporting tools, delivering information via broadcasting for subscribed users, as well as automating the monitoring and alerting in case key performance indicators significantly deviate from expected performance or reach defined thresholds. Information technology is also facilitating the communication process via synchronous as well as asynchronous electronic communication channels independent of time and place.

As mentioned, OLTP systems are used to perform business transactions, e.g., ATMs are performing millions of banking transactions effectively or retail cashier systems are collecting million of sales transactions effectively. These OLTP systems are designed for an optimal support and performance of these types of transactions but they are not optimized for the analyses of the data. While there are standard reports and options to develop ad-hoc queries in many of the OLTP systems, the reporting options may not be sufficient and the complex calculations required for the reporting can have a negative impact on the performance and response times of the system. If reporting is used extensively on these systems, it can interfere with their main purpose, a quick execution of business transactions. You would not want to have your customers at the ATMs or at the retail cashier systems wait extra long on the receipt just because someone at the administration is running a couple of reports. Clearly, the OLTP systems have an important task to fulfill to perform business processes and at the same time collect important information for later analyses. One further disadvantage of OLTP systems is that they can only analyze the data captured within a single system. Typically organizations utilize several OLTP systems with disparate databases and much additional value can be gained by integrating the data from these multiple OLTP systems in a single data warehouse for complex analyses and advanced reporting, called Online Analytical Processing (OLAP).

One of the first publications using the term OLAP was from Codd, Codd, and Salley (1993). They defined twelve requirements for OLAP systems: 1. Multidimensional conceptual view enabling users to slice, dice, drill-down, zoom out, 2. Transparency, 3. Accessibility, 4. Consistent reporting performance, 5. Client/server architecture, 6. Generic dimensionality, 7. Dynamic sparse matrix handling, 8. Multiuser support, 9. Unrestricted cross-dimensional operations, 10. Intuitive data manipulation, 11. Flexible reporting, and 12. Unlimited dimensions and aggregation levels. OLAP requires the availability of an OLAP server, a data warehouse, storing the data from the OLTP systems in a multidimensional format rather than a relational format used in OLTP systems. While reports in OLTP systems or spreadsheets are typically restricted to display data only from one OLTP system and in two dimensions, OLAP reports allow users to slice and dice information from multiple systems and across multiple dimensions and hierarchies in the OLAP cubes. Each cube can hold multiple key performance indicators, multiple dimensions, and multiple hierarchies as displayed in Fig. 3.13.

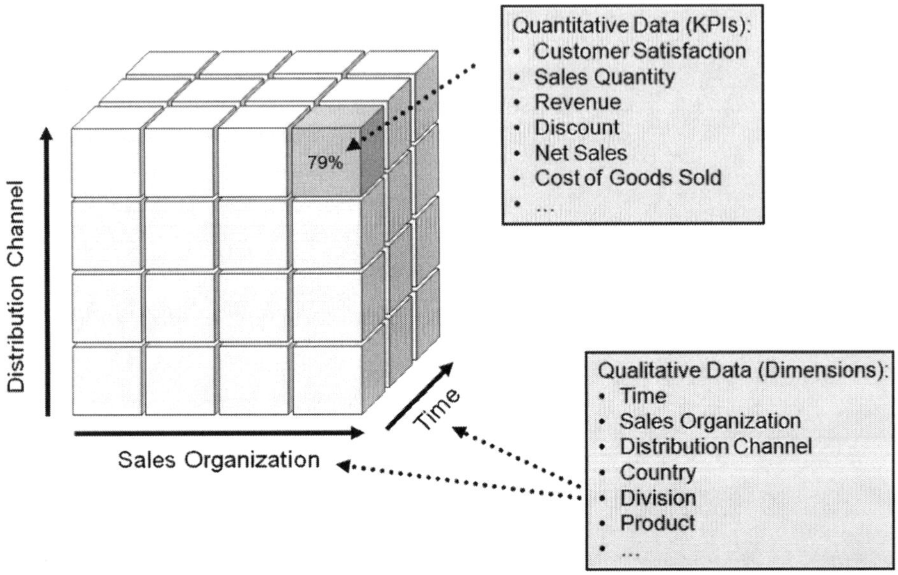

Fig. 3.13 OLAP cube (©Bernd Heesen/Prescient. Used with permission)

The OLAP cube in the above figure contains several KPIs and supports navigation and selection based on several dimensions. Each of these dimensions can contain hierarchies, e.g., products being organized in product group hierarchies or time allowing a drill-down from year to quarter, month, week, day, hour, and minute. These hierarchies enable the end users to display the KPIs in a granularity which fits their information needs. While the above OLAP cube only displays three dimensions, distribution channel, sales organization, and time, this is a simplification because we are used to visualize objects in a three-dimensional space. In reality, this example of an OLAP cube offers navigation in six dimensions and data warehouses can easily store data in OLAP cubes with more than twenty dimensions. These complex models are so powerful because the end users can restrict their perspective on those dimensions they really need to locate their desired information. In the above example, an end-user might just be interested in the distribution channel "Retail" (not "Wholesale", "Internet", or "Catalog"), in the sales organization "East" (not "West", "South", or "North"), in the performance of the "Current year" (not "Last year", "Year before last year"), and exclusively in the KPI "Customer satisfaction" (not "Sales Quantity", "Revenue", or any other one). The information displayed would be 79% customer satisfaction based on the given selection criteria. This is just one example of how to locate information. Additional navigation operations on OLAP cubes are slicing, dicing, drill-down, roll-up, and drill-across as displayed in Fig. 3.14.

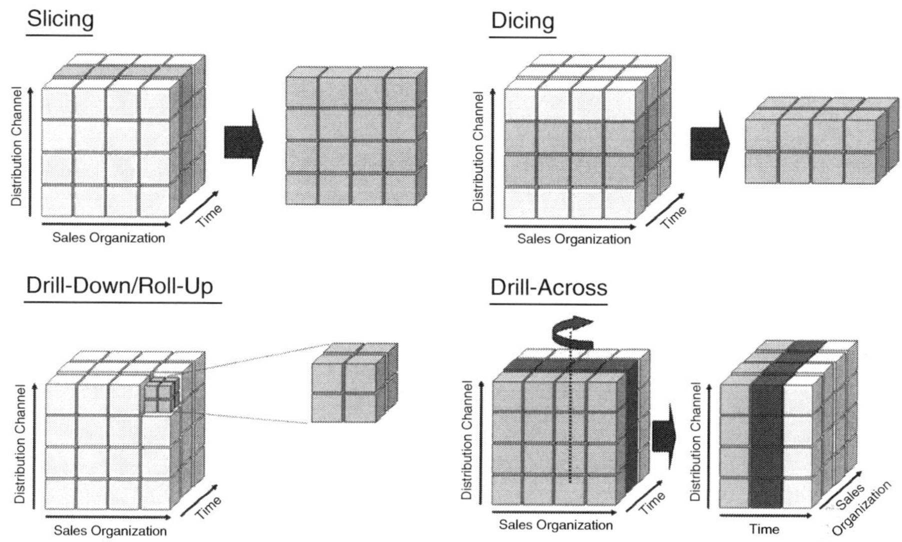

Fig. 3.14 OLAP navigation (©Bernd Heesen/Prescient. Used with permission)

Slicing could be used to display the customer satisfaction for all distribution channels and all sales organizations just for the previous year. Dicing could be used to display the customer satisfaction for two of the four distribution channels across all sales organizations for the current and the previous year. A drill-down might be used to display the customer satisfaction for the distribution channel "Retail", the sales organization "East" for the current year. A drill-down might also be used to view the data based on different products and for each of the twelve months of the selected year. To reduce the amount of detail, a roll-up can be used at any time to remove the monthly detail perspective and just show the annual performance. A drill-across can be applied to change the perspectives and allows to switch the sequence of the dimensions and decide if we want to view the dimension horizontally or vertically in table view. The benefit of OLAP cubes is the simple and easy navigation for end users and the improved performance without compromising the execution of transactions in the OLTP systems. To accomplish this task effectively, OLAP systems store their data in specific ways.

Vitt, Luckevich, and Misner (2002), p. 46 describe the different storage paradigms typically used by OLAP systems to support a multidimensional analysis, as follows:

- DOLAP: Desktop Online Analytical Processing using desktop files. Because data is stored on individual desktop machines, you will tend to find DOLAP existing by itself in smaller-scale applications where there is minimal need for multiple users to have access to a single data source on a central server. You will also find DOLAP as a part of many OLAP vendors' overall offering to facilitate analysis when users are away from their company network, such as when they are on an airplane.

- ROLAP: Relational Online Analytical Processing using relational database servers. You will find lots of ROLAP environments in various size implementations. Storing data in a relational database allows you to take advantage of one of its greatest benefits – being able to store lots of data. What tends to happen, however, is that the data retrieval performance for ROLAP will often not be as fast as other storage options, such as multidimensional servers. Some OLAP vendors store data only in relational databases regardless of the data volume. Other vendors provide ROLAP as one of several options.
- MOLAP: Multidimensional Online Analytical Processing using multidimensional databases serves. In MOLAP storage, data are placed into special structures that are stored on a central server. MOLAP tends to offer the greatest data retrieval performance – generally outperforming all other storage modes. However, there are some arguments that MOLAP cannot handle as much data as ROLAP. The performance and storage really depends on the particular OLAP product and the type of analysis that you are trying to accomplish.
- HOLAP: Hybrid Online Analytical Processing using a mixture of ROLAP and MOLAP. HOLAP is the ability to spread data across both relational and multidimensional databases in order to get the best of both worlds. Whether this is true or not depends on the particular vendor.

The OLAP paradigms for information storage are relevant for ease of use and performance, but from an end-user perspective all of them support an improved multidimensional analysis via interactive reports. But where arethe data coming from and how is the permanent data supply managed to feed the OLAP databases? The data are managed by a data warehouse. The advantages of using a data warehouse as a foundation for corporate reporting compared to reporting based on OLTP systems are:

- Improved online transactional processing performance: By using a data warehouse for the majority of the reporting, the OLTP systems can support the OLTP users with improved performance during peak times of operation. OLTP operation is not negatively impacted by intensive reporting.
- Improved reporting performance: OLAP cubes are optimized for reporting based on a specific multidimensional database design and preaggregated data. A predetermined number of aggregations, those most frequently used, are typically calculated in batch operations overnight and stored in the OLAP cubes. In consequence, these preaggregations allow reporting users to read the aggregated figures without any calculation at runtime of the report. This reduces the runtime significantly, wherever large volumes of data are processed. The more users access these preaggregated figures, the more CPU time is saved, and in any case the IT infrastructure is freed of these calculations during peak reporting times during the day.
- Easy access to data: Data marts are created to fulfill the specific reporting needs of user groups. There might be an OLAP cube with marketing data for users

from marketing and another OLAP cube with employee data for users from human resources, etc. The benefit of these data marts is that they offer the relevant information to fulfill the end-user expectations from the decision makers gathered in the analysis phase, prior to the implementation of the data warehouse. Each of these data marts is an extract or subset of all data available in the data warehouse. This design of each data mart limits the complexity to what the users really need. In addition to OLAP cubes, the data warehouse is also able to store detailed transactional data in operational data stores (ODS). Transactional data from OLTP systems are transformed and loaded in an integrated format into the operational data stores. ODS data can be used for reporting but also to load the integrated data into OLAP cubes.

- Integrated and consistent data from multiple sources: Data are first extracted from the OLTP systems. In a second step, these data are transformed into an enterprise standard format, which is defined using a metadata repository. The transformation is accomplished by using a shared format, shared units, e.g., kg, lb or tons for weights, and shared codes for master data. Shared codes for master data mean that the same code is used to specify the gender of an employee as male or female. In some OLTP systems, this may be coded as m for male and f for female or 0 for male and 1 for female. While this does not impact the reporting for any of these isolated OLTP systems, a consolidated enterprise reporting requires for all employees to be coded based on a shared standard, e.g., m for male and f for female. The same applies to codes for products. While product numbers in a single OLTP system are unique, the same product-ID may be used for two different products in different OLTP systems. In order to show proper enterprise revenues per product, the associated product-IDs need to be transformed based on a unique enterprise-wide product-ID. These enterprise-wide IDs are maintained in so-called master data tables in the data management layer of the data warehouse. The same applies to other master data such as the IDs and corresponding texts for product groups, customers, industries, distribution channels, and many more. Based on this concept of enterprise-wide coding using shared master data, the data warehouse is able to transform data from multiple sources for enterprise reporting, which cannot be done in any of the many stand-alone OLTP systems. If all data are transformed using a defined standard, all reports are based on the same facts, thereby creating what is referred to as “one single version of the truth.”

The use of multiple data warehouses operating independently from each other can actually eliminate one of the main benefits of data warehousing, the access to integrated, and consistent data from multiple sources, the single version of the truths. In the absence of an enterprise data warehouse concept, many organizations develop their own decision support systems and local data warehouses serving different user groups. One of the major risks, besides the inefficiency of maintaining redundant data, is the potential loss of integrity and consistency of the data if no shared meta data and enterprise master data is used. Reports from these different systems meant to help decision makers easily lead to confusion if they provide inconsistent information about key performance indicators. The solution to this problem is to use an enterprise data warehouse with enterprise meta data and master data as displayed in Fig. 3.15, the Strategic Business Intelligence Framework™.

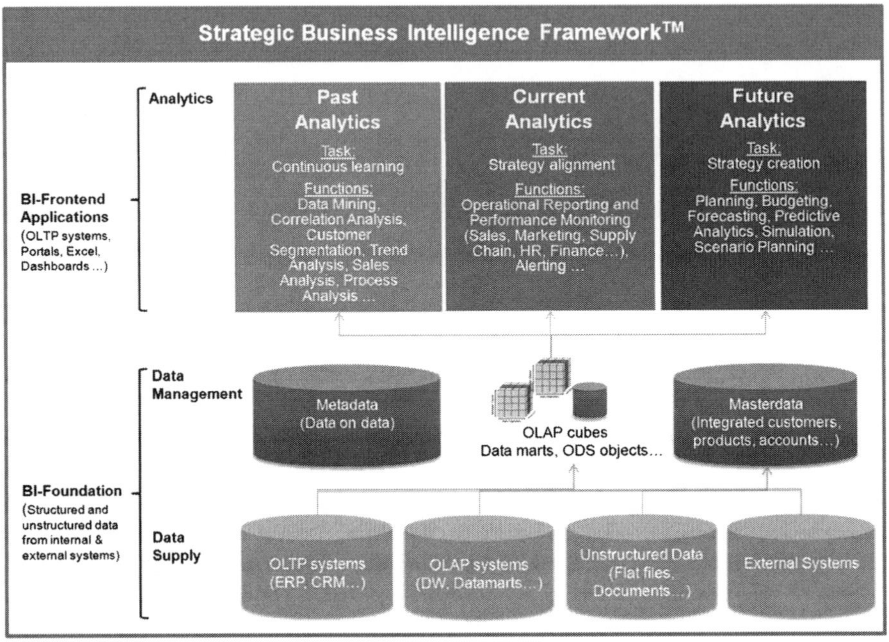

Fig. 3.15 Strategic Business Intelligence Framework™ (©Bernd Heesen/Prescient. Used with permission. Strategic Business Intelligence Framework™ is trademarked by Bernd Heesen/Prescient)

The term business intelligence was first used by Luhn (1958). He envisioned a flexible automated system identifying information needs and disseminating the information efficiently within the organization. He was ahead of his time with this innovative idea. The information systems still lacked the capabilities and sophistication he envisioned. The concept was a great one but it would take several decades until his idea of business intelligence would become a reality. It was in the year 1992 that the Research Fellow at Gartner Group, Howard Dresner (Dresner Advisory Services, 2011), reintroduced the term business intelligence. He described business intelligence as a set of concepts and methods to improve business decision making by using fact-based support systems. Even in 1992, the sophistication of the concepts and the tools still needed improvement. But now, as I write this book in the year 2011, business intelligence seems to be at the point where the concepts and the tools have evolved to a point where organizations can easily utilize the systems. Organizations may even be forced to leverage this innovation to remain competitive. Not to leverage the new opportunities offered by the use of business intelligence to improve strategy execution can create significant disadvantages.

The term Business Intelligence is often used as a synonym for data warehousing or decision support systems, as an IT-solution or an OLAP infrastructure. This is only partly correct and does not adequately reflect the benefit business intelligence adds to an organization and an effective strategy execution, if applied properly.

Therefore I created a new definition of what I consider to be **Strategic Business Intelligence™**[2]: "Strategic Business Intelligence™ is a set of concepts and tools to improve decision making on all levels of the organization and enable an effective strategy execution. Strategic Business Intelligence applies the concept of the Value Scorecard™ and leverages information technologies in a Strategic Business Intelligence Framework™ to enable past, current, and future analytics to support continuous learning, strategy alignment as well as strategy creation."

The **Strategic Business Intelligence Framework™**[3] (see Fig. 3.15) consists of a BI-Foundation, including a Data Supply layer, a Data Management layer, and BI-Frontend-Applications to support past, current and future analytics.

The Data Supply layer represents all structured and unstructured data from internal and external source systems, including OLTP systems and local OLAP systems. This data needs to by integrated and harmonized using an extraction, transformation, and load process (ETL-process) to make this information available in the Data Management layer in an integrated format, a single format for all data of one object type, e.g., customers, products. These enterprise data definitions are called metadata. Metadata defines the enterprise data definition for master data tables, e.g., customers, products, . . ., as well as OLAP cubes and other information objects used within the data warehouse. The ETL-process uses this metadata as the target format for data which are transformed from source systems and loaded into master data tables, OLAP cubes, or operational data stores and other information objects. Master data tables are used for validation during the loading of data in OLAP cubes or ODS to make sure that, e.g., only sales transaction data with valid product identification numbers (IDs), customer IDs, and sales organization IDs are loaded and made available for reporting. This procedure contributes to an increased data quality. Once all data are loaded into the data management layer, BI-Frontend applications are used to access, distribute, and present the information. While only a small number of individuals, namely IT experts, us the tools on the BI-foundation, the majority of users leverage BI-Frontend applications for analysis. All decision makers or knowledge workers will likely be utilizing analytical applications either using OLTP systems, portals, dashboards, or DOLAP tools such as spreadsheet applications. Data warehousing solutions have reached a level of maturity in the past years and created a solid BI-foundation infrastructure. Most of the current innovation regarding BI is happening on the BI-Frontend layer. Many organizations

[2] Strategic Business Intelligence™ is trademarked by Bernd Heesen/Prescient.

[3] Strategic Business Intelligence Framework™ is trademarked by Bernd Heesen/Prescient.

are just now starting to develop dashboards and management cockpits for their decision makers and understanding the value and potentials of analytics.

In many books about business intelligence, the OLTP systems were only considered as a source system for the data warehouse but often ignored as a relevant infrastructure on the analytics and reporting side. From the perspective of the decision maker, it does not matter where the data reside, if in an OLTP system or a data warehouse. For the decision maker, all that counts is that the information should be available just in time and in the appropriate quality to support the decision making. Therefore it is important to consider all IT systems including the OLTP systems as components of the BI-Frontend applications. OLTP systems provide many essential reports for decision makers and can be easily integrated into management cockpits or dashboards together with OLAP reports.

The Strategic Business Intelligence Framework™ also distinguishes different types of analytical applications and their main purpose: (a) Past analytics such as data mining, correlation analysis, and trend analysis should help to gain insights about what happened in the past and digging deep to find short- and long-term correlations between key performance indicators. This may lead, e.g., to an understanding which marketing campaigns for which customer segments were most effective for improving the company image, customer satisfaction, or sales. Via this kind of analysis, the organization understands and learns more about their own operations and how to potentially improve the effectiveness. (b) Current analytics include operational reporting and performance monitoring as well as automated alerts. The purpose of these analytics is to align all activities of the organization with its strategy. (c) Future analytics support business planning, budgeting, forecasting, simulating alternative business scenarios based on predictive analytics and are part of strategy creation. The strategy is defined based on the forecasts and simulations of business scenarios and the strategic objectives are defined during the planning process. Budgets are allocated to enable the organizational units to accomplish these strategic goals. Obviously past analytics and current analytics are supporting this important decision making process as well. The decisions made during the planning and budgeting process define the strategic contribution of each organizational entity and thereby establish strategies on all levels, which align toward the shared objectives.

The invention of the concept of business intelligence may have occurred 50 years ago but it is only now that the concepts are more widely recognized and the tools have matured to a point where the diffusion of the innovation can happen. Managers and decision makers at all levels of the organization should have access to this information, e.g., using management cockpits or dashboards summarizing the key facts (see Figs. 3.16–3.18), similar to the cockpit of an airplane, which displays the key performance indicators in a transparent, consistent, and timely manner. Management cockpits help managers to "drive" their business. They use graphics similar to regular dashboards including dials, gauges, and traffic lights and complement these with charts, maps, and text. A live ticker may be used to display alerts.

This management cockpit has been developed with the dashboarding tool SAP Crystal Solutions (SAP, 2011), formerly known as SAP Business Objects Xcelsius.

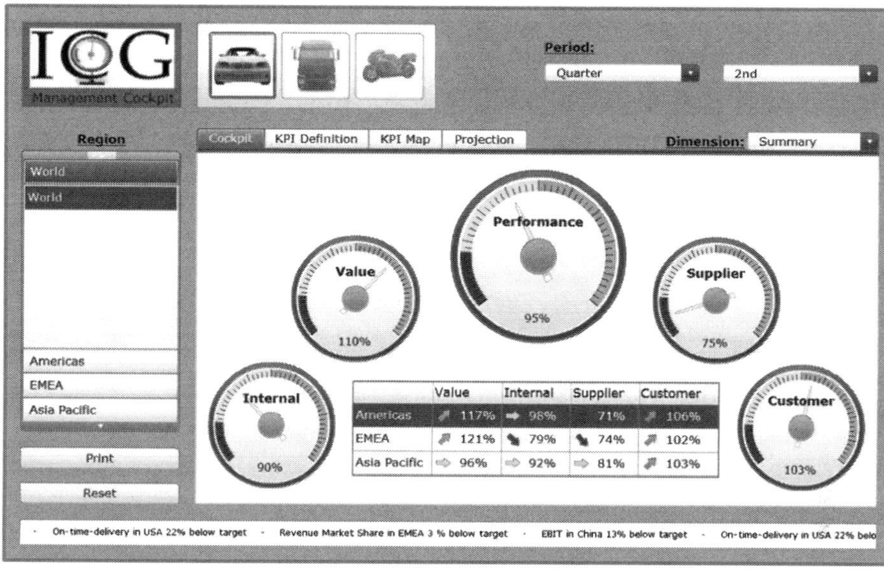

Fig. 3.16 Management Cockpit (©Bernd Heesen/Prescient. Used with permission)

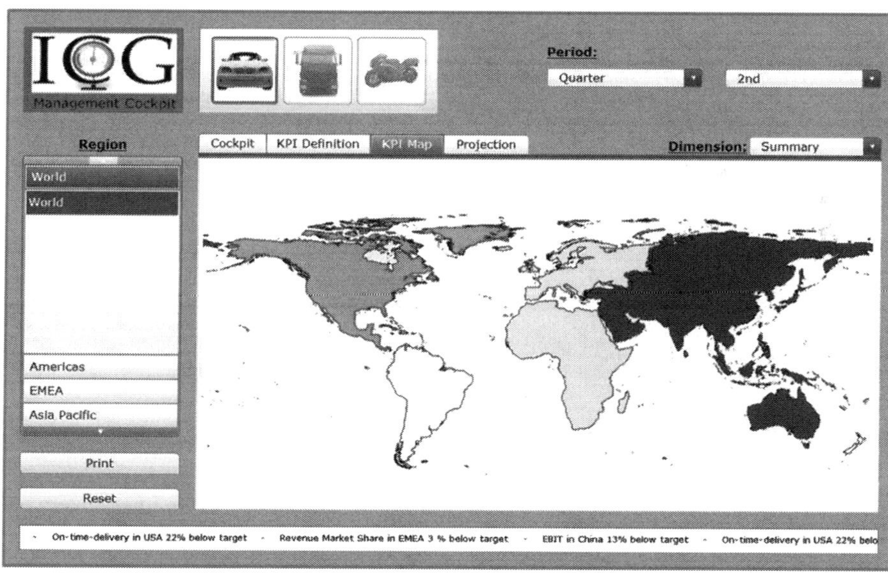

Fig. 3.17 KPI Map (©Bernd Heesen/Prescient. Used with permission)

It displays the aggregated performance in the four key dimensions of the Value Scorecord™: Value, demander, supplier, internal. The dashboard allows an easy navigation on the left side to select the geographic region and on the top to select the division: Cars, trucks, motorcycles. Another key selection criterion is the

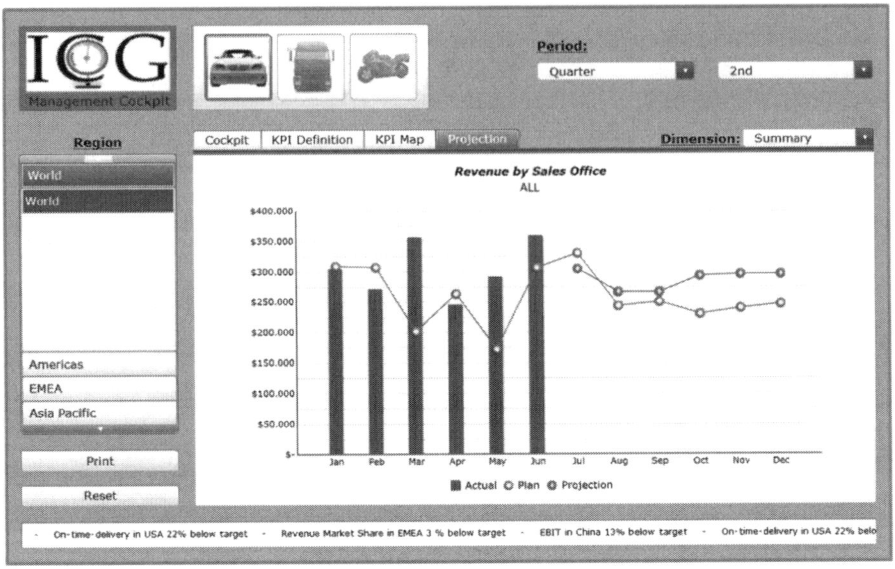

Fig. 3.18 Revenue projection (©Bernd Heesen/Prescient. Used with permission)

dimension: Summary, value, demander, supplier, internal. The selection of the period type allows to select from year, quarter, and month, and an additional drop-down menu is used to specify the period. For each of these combinations, it is possible to display the Cockpit (see Fig. 3.16), the KPI definition, the KPI map (see Fig. 3.17), or a projection of sales (see Fig. 3.18).

The KPI map uses color coding to display the performance of the selected metrics in green (current performance better than planned), yellow (performance as expected), or red (performance below plan). In this case, the maps reflect the overall performance of the cars division for the second quarter of the current year with a perspective on the regions Americas, EMEA and Asia Pacific.

The projection displays the actual sales based on the year to date information in a bar chart. The planned values and the projection for the remaining months are displayed in form of a line chart. In this case, the projection is better than the planned performance.

This kind of information access on demand, using dashboards, portals, or access to OLTP or OLAP systems works well if the decision makers have a specific information need and take the initiative to locate the relevant information. Business intelligence utilizes these pull applications as one information distribution channel.

Additionally, business intelligence leverages a second channel to push information via periodic reporting, broadcasting, and alerts to a defined group of individuals (see Fig. 3.19). Alerts are specifically useful to reduce the demand on management time to monitor performance for diagnostic KPIs (see Sect. 3.2.2.2) to recognize exceptions. The example cockpit displayed in Fig. 3.18 also uses a live ticker to

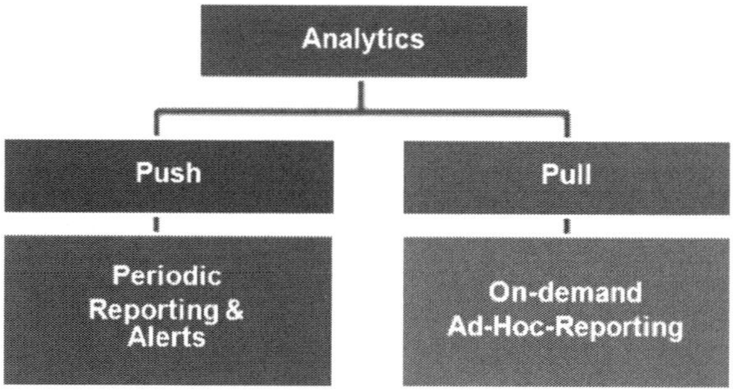

Fig. 3.19 Information distribution channels (©Bernd Heesen/Prescient. Used with permission)

display alerts. In addition to displaying them in the dashboard, alerts can also trigger SMS or E-mails to a defined recipient list.

The information recipients and users of decision support applications have changed over time. The fact that business intelligence solutions have a far broader audience than what executive information systems (EIS) were designed for also requires the use of a more versatile set of communication channels and formats. Business performance management applications have a more balanced mix of users consisting of executives, midlevel managers, business analysts, and operations personnel according to research from TDWI (Eckerson, 2006). A TDWI Best Practices Report (Eckerson, 2009) published in 2009 found that about 20% of business intelligence users are so-called power users (IT developers, super users, business analysts, analytical modelers) while the majority of 80% are casual users (executives, managers, staff, business analysts, customers, suppliers). Clearly the tools provided for casual users must be easy to use and superior to what they currently utilize if they shall be accepting the new solutions. One of the key problems with the implementation of new IT solutions has been a lack of user acceptance. It has been found that the casual users most widely use static reports and dashboards (76%) and export data to spreadsheets for local modeling (35%). Therefore, these need to be supported specifically well and should be adaptable based on individual roles and responsibilities. Additionally, users should be able to personalize their reporting solutions and dashboards. With so much information being available, one of the key considerations when designing a dashboard should be its ease of use, simple navigation, switching of dimensions and formats as well as providing adequate documentation of the KPIs and dashboard functions. Now, these dashboards should be available via different communication channels, e.g., online on desktops and wireless devices, offline in formats such as PDF. It may be even useful to attach commentary to the dashboard. These comments can be helpful to document interpretations, decisions or recommended courses of action.

With all these opportunities to benefit from utilizing business intelligence, the question remains to what extent companies actually use it. The following two stories of CompUSA and Volkswagen allow to see how businesses leverage business intelligence. Further examples are given throughout the book.

The company CompUSA, Inc. (2011) is one of the largest computer and computer-product retailers in North America, with more than 200 computer superstores and an online shop with inventory of 50,000 in-stock products. What was the situation prior to the implementation of a data warehouse at CompUSA? Every morning the store, regional, divisional as well as corporate management were reviewing sales analysis reports from the previous day. While sales and profitability between stores and regions could be compared, the legacy system did not provide all relevant details such as discretionary discounting at individual stores that affect a store's performance. Managers needed more details to interpret the other KPIs correctly and take corrective actions where needed. One of the obstacles to capture this information centrally were the many disparate point-of-sale systems in place within each store, which could not provide all data and were not able to provide consolidated information during the day, e.g., prohibiting to interpret data by hour during the same day. To have this information in a timely fashion was especially important when promotions were running to evaluate their effectiveness. A data warehouse, using a Microsoft SQL Server, was implemented to solve these problems, to consolidate data from multiple sources during the day and to update OLAP cubes for reporting. The benefits were measurable in performance improvements and data quality improvements. Productivity gains could be realized because now managers were able to focus on analyzing information and acting based on it. They do not need to spend much time searching for this information or ask support personnel to consolidate data from multiple sources into a usable format. Cathy Witt, Vice President and Chief Information officer at CompUSA stated "The data warehouse has simplified data access for general managers, individuals who run retail operations and work very long hours. They work seven days a week. They do not have a lot of time to go in and dump data to an Excel spreadsheet. So the real goal is to make the data simple and concise, summarize it, and show them the exceptions so they can go fix it" (Vitt, Luckevich, & Misner, 2002).

Today the use of business intelligence is also a core element of the IT strategy at Volkswagen Group (Volkswagen Group, 2011), one of the largest automobile manufacturers of the world with a world market share of 11.4% of the world passenger car market representing well-established brands like Volkswagen, Audi, Bentley, Bugatti, Lamborghini, Skoda, and Scania. In 2005, CIO Klaus Hardy Mühleck initiated the development of a BI strategy (Alexander, 2008). During the gathering of the current use of information systems they found that more than 120 decision support systems were used as isolated solutions in different departments and processes. Mühlbeck decided to build a team to establish a consolidated landscape based on a shared framework documented in the "Book of Standards." Business intelligence is now viewed as the long-term solution for process controlling, reporting, and analytics including data mining and corporate planning for all business units.

This problem of disparate systems which was solved in the case of CompUSA as well as Volkswagen is one of the frequently cited problems in a study conducted by The Economist Intelligence Unit (The Economist Intelligence Unit, 2006). Other frequent problems included the use of too many different business intelligence tools within one organization. Sixty-three percent of the respondents indicated their interest to consolidate their information on fewer BI platforms, also because some of these platforms are incompatible with each other, not sharing a single set of metadata. The survey identified additional challenges with using business intelligence to improve performance because of the following reasons (numbers in brackets indicate the percentage of respondents stating to be dealing with this challenge):

- Improper association of metrics with business processes (34%).
- Inability to generate metrics (27%).
- Lack of monitoring of KPIs (26%).
- Inability to determine KPIs in the first place (25%).
- Inability to disseminate data in a timely manner (17%).

This list confirms that an effective strategy execution requires preparation including the definition of useful KPIs as well as establishing the business intelligence infrastructure to capture the data in a consolidated format and in a timely manner. Once this preparation is completed, the strategy can be executed effectively.

Chapter 4
Strategy Execution

This chapter presents how management can improve strategic alignment by utilizing the management section of the Strategic Alignment Remote Control™ (see Fig. 4.1).

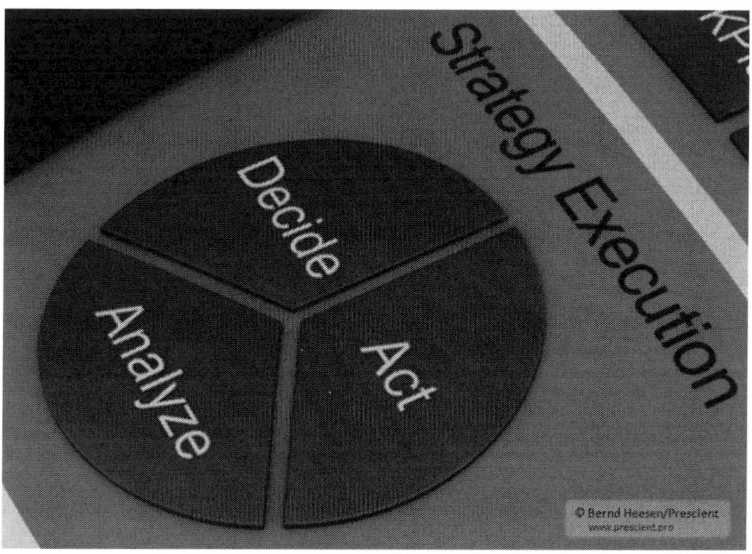

Fig. 4.1 Management control loop for strategy execution (©Bernd Heesen/Prescient. Used with permission)

An effective strategy execution typically starts with an analysis and understanding of the current situation, which will be addressed in Sect. 4.1 in more detail. An analysis not only includes past and current analytics of the performance, but also future analytics. Insights gained from the analysis can be used as an input in the decision making process, e.g., establishing performance targets and a plan of action consisting of a list of strategic initiatives which shall help to reach the set targets.

B. Heesen, *Effective Strategy Execution*, Management for Professionals,
DOI 10.1007/978-3-642-19205-0_4, © Springer-Verlag Berlin Heidelberg 2012

The decision making should include appropriate budgeting to fund the necessary initiatives and operations. The decision making process is covered in Sect. 4.2. Decision making in itself does not help with strategy execution unless the decisions lead to their consequent implementation. Section 4.3 provides examples of organizations taking action. Following the management process for strategy execution helps decision makers to align their actions with the organizational objectives, and the timely availability of information for analysis and decision making helps to reduce the action distance, thereby improving the effectiveness of the strategy execution.

4.1 Analyze

Analysis is defined by Craig Fleisher and Babette Bensoussan as: "The skilled application of scientific and non-scientific methods and processes by which individuals interpret data or information to produce insightful intelligence findings and actionable recommendations for decision makers" (Fleisher & Bensoussan, 2009, p. 4). This definition defines an implicit sequence: Analysis is the first step, decision and actions follow from it. This definition fits the model of the management control loop for strategy execution, as presented in Fig. 4.1.

An effective strategy depends on a systematic and continuous monitoring, evaluation, and control process to ensure that business interventions are effective and help to achieve the set goals. Trend extrapolations and the scanning of the business environment are of utmost importance in dynamic environments to complement the analysis of past and current performance. The key question the management teams on all levels of the organization might ask themselves is: Are we reaching our goals and are we executing our strategy effectively? This kind of strategy execution effectiveness evaluation should be a continuous process, triggered whenever new opportunities arise or when such problems arise which might require a swift decision and action. Past success is no longer a guarantee for future success.

One example that demonstrates how analytics are not only useful to avoid threats to organizational survival, but also have the potential to create a significant competitive advantage, or can be the foundation of new business models is Google (2010). Google was founded in 1998 and their value add was to provide information about websites, such as a search function using key words and an associated page rank for each site. The name Google was picked to express their intent to organize the masses of information available in the internet as a slight modification of the mathematical term "Googol," which represents the number 1 followed by 100 zeros. In 2000, they launched Google Adwords, offering advertisements to be displayed for specific keywords. They use analytics to show recommend prices for advertisements depending on the keywords used. They also offer advanced analytics for their customers, allowing them to improve the effectiveness of their marketing investments. In 2001, their index grew to 3 billion database entries.

A more current initiative is Google Instant, which predicts what you're interested in and shows search results to you as you type, so you can more quickly get to the information you are looking for. Analytics is the core of their business model and they continually fine-tune their offerings. In 13 years, they have reached a market capitalization of more than 190 billion US dollars based on analytics.

The success of Google is impressive, but each organization has to find their own way how to do business most effectively and how to leverage analytics. The three main benefits of analyticsare their support in organizational learning, strategic alignment with the organizational goals, and in the strategy creation process (see Fig. 4.2).

The following three chapters will address these areas in more detail.

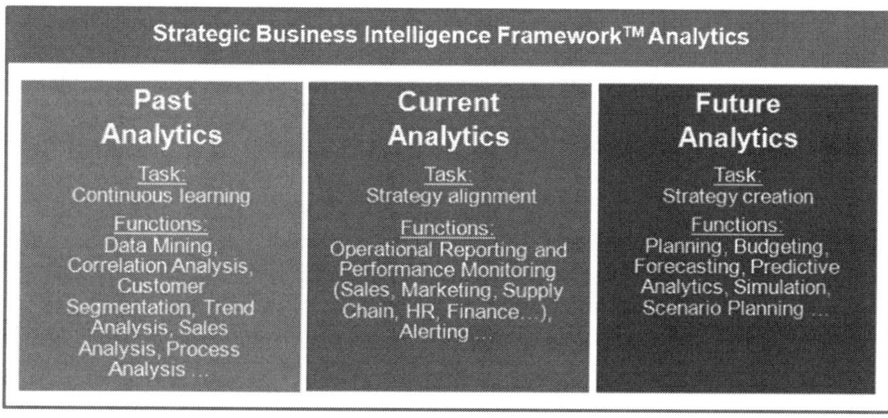

Fig. 4.2 Strategic business intelligence framework™ analytics (©Bernd Heesen/Prescient. Used with permission)

4.1.1 *Past Analytics for Continuous Learning*

Continuous learning happens whenever we receive feedback on something we did or missed to do. Taking a detailed look might even be possible to uncover opportunities for improvement when the expectations were met. Total quality management is a philosophy where continuous learning plays a vital role. Learning from problems to avoid them in the future and uncovering opportunities for improvement can be equally useful. Often, more management attention is given to the recognized problems. They often require immediate attention and a detailed analysis. The chance for improvement is automatically triggered by the problem. Ideally both, a recipe to deal with the problem when it occurs and a way to reduce the likelihood of the problem's occurrence in future, are identified and applied. This kind of continuous learning is specifically useful if these solutions are documented and accessible to all those who might benefit from them within the organization.

The key to a real improvement of the effectiveness of an organization is to avoid experiencing the same problems over and over again. Experiencing the same problem again often is an indication that the cause of the problem has not been found and only the symptoms were dealt with. The Toyota (Liker & Meier, 2006) management system is an example of a philosophy which tries to fix problems right away and also put countermeasures into play to avoid the reoccurrence of the problem in future. To determine effective solutions, Toyota applies a problem-resolution cycle containing the following steps: 1. Recognize, 2. Elevate, 3. Evaluate, 4. Control, 5. Contain, and 6. Prevent. Another key element of Toyota's management system is to develop exceptional people, individuals who share this culture and value high quality. Toyota is no longer the only organization using Kanban and Andon or other methods and tools. In their opinion, the key advantage does not lie in the tools themselves but in the individuals using the tools and how they use them. The same probably applies to business intelligence and analytics and how it is used for continuous evaluation and learning. It is not the tools but how they are used which decide about the added value.

Liker and Meier (2006) also share in their book *The Toyota way fieldbook* that many Japanese are intentionally slow in decision making. They seek to invest the necessary time to find the root cause and involve everyone who is affected in gathering ideas and developing a consensus for a solution, called Nemawashi. Once this time-consuming process leads to a decision, they can quickly execute it.

Below you find a grouped catalog of common analytical applications:

- Customer: Customer satisfaction analysis, customer segmentation, customer loyalty, customer churn analysis, customer profitability analysis, customer lifetime value analysis.
- Product: Sales by product, product profitability, cross-selling analysis, product warranty case analysis.
- Finance process: Profit and loss analysis, pricing analysis, fraud detection, credit scoring.
- Marketing and sales process: Marketing campaign analysis, promotion analysis, lead management analysis, pipeline analysis, sales channel analysis, call center analysis, business partner analysis, website analysis.
- Manufacturing process: Productivity analysis, quality analysis.
- Supply chain management: Supply chain analysis, inventory analysis, procurement analysis, yield management.

Analytics help to utilize resources more efficiently and to improve the effectiveness of process execution. One example where this applies is matching demand to supply. Analytics can be used to forecast market demand more accurately, e.g., by developing a more detailed understanding of demand patterns per customer segment. This allows us to manufacture more effectively in time with a lower inventory level and to optimize capacity utilization of assets, while still being able to avoid stock-outs.

Another frequent application is customer segmentation. The purpose is to better understand each customer segment's financial value and loyalty characteristics.

Segments can be established based on geographic region, demographic variables (e.g., age, gender, family status, education, income), or psychographic variables (e.g., attitudes, values, interests, lifestyle). A better understanding of loyalty helps to determine an appropriate amount of funding for actions related to retain customers. More loyal customer segments require less spending than those with lower loyalty. Similarly, the customer value in a customer segment in proportion to the respective acquisition cost for new customers helps to evaluate the effectiveness of actions like discounts, incentives or marketing campaigns and their related spending. In the end, the allocation of funds should be based on an evaluation where one extra Euro or Dollar spent creates the highest return on investment. But how do you find out which customers are of high value and what their loyalty is or how can you predict the likelihood of them reacting to a marketing campaign?

To answer these types of questions, you can use data mining. You analyze the results of past marketing campaigns to identify the characteristics of customers who responded or did not respond to the campaigns. Via statistical regression, you can use past results to predict future results. If timing, e.g., the season, plays a vital role it may also be useful to apply time series analysis to predict variances over time. These models, which are used for predictions, can be developed using the following steps (Eckerson, 2007, p. 11):

1. **Project Definition**: Define the business objectives and desired outcomes for the project and translate them into predictive analytic objectives and tasks.
2. **Exploration**: Analyze source data to determine the most appropriate data and model building approach, and scope the effort.
3. **Data Preparation**: Select, extract, and transform data upon which to create models.
4. **Model Building**: Create, test, and validate models, and evaluate whether they will meet project metrics and goals.
5. **Deployment**: Apply model results to business decisions or processes. This ranges from sharing insights with business users to embedding models into applications to automate decisions and business processes.
6. **Model Management**: Manage models to improve performance (i.e., accuracy), control access, promote reuse, standardize toolsets, and minimize redundant activities.

The value of these models does not lie in their complexity or their predicting correctness alone. The extent to which the decisions based on the models produce extra value for the organization is important. Consequently, the cost to develop these kinds of models should be lower than the extra value generated.

With data on product sales being available, standardized statistical evaluations like a conjoint analysis or multiple regression analysis can be used to identify the key factors impacting a customer purchasing decision. These factors can include variables like price, service quality, and location.

Not surprisingly, price optimization is a topic of relevance to many organizations. Based on the *Value-based business strategy* (see Fig. 3.4), the organizational value can be optimized by maximizing the difference between the price the buyer is willing to pay and the cost for all suppliers. Understanding the price elasticity of demand, the effect of price changes on buying behavior, helps to maximize the value gained by the organization.

One way to determine the price elasticity of demand is to perform market experiments, e.g., offering the same product at different prices in different markets, evaluating the effect of discounts and promotions. These kind of experiments can be easily performed via internet offerings, where prices can be changed each minute and the reaction of web site visitors can be quickly monitored. The same kind of experiments can be applied to test other variables and product attributes.

Web-based advertisements via banners, pop-ups, or other instruments work similarly well as experiments since they allow to evaluate the effectiveness of ads right away via the number of visitor clicks. Google AdWords provides this analytical knowledge about the effectiveness of ads to each advertiser. The availability of these metrics help their customers to be more effective and, consequently, motivate them to spend more with Google AdWords.

Another example of an organization leveraging experiments and developing models to predict customer behavior is Capital One. They perform several thousand experiments each month, which allows them to predict which products and programs might be successful before they make them available to a broader audience. In their book *Competing on analytics: The new science of winning*, Davenport and Harris state: "In its savings business, for example, Capital One found that its experiments in terms of CD interest rates, rollover incentives, minimum balances, and so forth had very predictable effects on retention rates and new money coming into the bank. Through such analyses, the savings business increased retention by 87 percent and lowered the cost of acquiring a new account by 83 percent" (Davenport & Harris, 2007, p. 42).

A new avenue to leverage data on the internet is text analytics analyzing unstructured information to gain insights on reports, comments, and chat sessions, which can be used to evaluate brand image and other details. Given the amount of the available information and the unstructured format, appropriate and effective procedures of evaluation are still evolving.

4.1.2 Current Analytics for Strategy Alignment

Managers and knowledge workers at all levels of the organization have limited time and need to focus their energy on the most essential tasks in their daily business. Continuous learning obviously helps them to not only solve current problems but more importantly to avoid their recurrence. The reality of the business is that they will still use some of their time to fire fight problems and use past analytics in combination with operational reporting to better understand issues and solve problems.

Besides managing their business and solving problems, they also need to make sure to utilize their resources to achieve the strategic objectives, which they established during the corporate planning process for all organizational units when they were cascading the Value Scorecard™ objectives (see Sect. 3.2.2). Managers need to make sure that they do not deviate too much from their goals, at least not negatively. Obviously it would be inefficient if managers continually spent time in front of their computers to run reports and monitor all their KPIs. Given the lack of time managers have, much of this monitoring does not happen, unless it is automated, increasing the risk of ignoring important developments.

Fortunately, with the help of business intelligence, much of this monitoring task can be automated via alerts. Obviously, managers should be able to define thresholds for KPIs, defining when they would like to be notified via an alert. This can be applied to all types of KPIs, but is specifically useful for diagnostic KPIs (see Sect. 3.2.2.2). Supporting this flexibility of the altering mechanism for all managers individually supports their specific information needs. In consequence, managers are relieved from the burden of monitoring and can therefore focus their time on those management tasks which cannot be automated. This way of operating is similar to a thermostat. Once, in the beginning of a period, the desired temperature is configured and allows the system to operate without further management attention. Obviously, if exceptions occur in these control systems, either the system needs to automatically take action (automated decision making) or for those tasks where an automated response is not possible or adequate, an alert (alerting) needs to be triggered to generate the needed management attention. Automation, also called embedded business intelligence, is more effective and should be preferred where it is considered suitable.

Decisions can typically be automated if prescribed, standardized routines can be applied based on the existence of certain conditions being fulfilled. The automation is valuable if the standardized routines can be applied many times or occasionally. Besides efficiency gains, the benefits of an automated versus manual process execution lie in the improvement of speed and consistency. One example for automated decisions are automatic reordering of stock for replenishment, automatic calculation of credit scores, or the automatic yield management and price calculation described in the case of Marriott (see Sect. 3.2.2.1). But even in the Marriott case, the system-generated proposed price can be overridden by the management. So overrides may be justified if experts know more than the system has been programmed to reflect and use for its decisions. Basically, the overrides are justified if they lead to better decisions. In consequence, the reasons for overrides should be captured and subsequently considered as input to further improve the automated model. Even if an exception does not happen often enough to justify its automation, capturing the reasoning may still be useful for similar decisions to come.

Legal or ethical issues may also limit a complete automation of the decision making. For example, a pre-selection of candidates proposed by a system based on comparison of capabilities of the candidates and the requirements of a position may be utilized as a starting point for the recruitment process, but leaves the final decision to the management after they have had a chance to interview the candidates. This would be an example of a partly-automated process execution.

Where automation is not possible, useful alerting might still be an option to improve the efficiency of operations. Another partly automated process is Jidoka (Liker & Meier, 2006), the self-monitoring and self-stopping machines, one of Toyota's philosophies. It is important to understand that in their philosophy, the machines are expected to relieve humans from a burden, e.g., constantly supervising a machine. Because only people can think and solve problems, the self-stopping machines allow the employees to focus their talents on more value-adding tasks and only in case the machine stops, an audible and visible alert helps to direct the attention to the defective machine.

Monitoring can be applied to machines as we have seen. Another application is the monitoring of KPIs which are calculated in data warehouses. KPIs with associated threshold values to trigger alerts could include variables like the interest rate, share value, exchange rates (for companies with significant revenues or cost in foreign currency markets), raw material price or demand, credit risks (major bad debt losses), environmental incidents, or competitor's discounts. The importance of a quick response to important events has been discussed already in the case of the Indian Ocean Tsunami (see Sect. 2.1.2) or General Motors (see Chap. 1). You can test your own alerting readiness by asking a question like this one: "How long does it take me to receive an alert if one of my main KPIs in the value perspective is more than 10% below the threshold I defined?" In case you did not even define a threshold for your main KPIs, your alerting readiness can obviously be improved.

But alerts can be equally valuable to leverage opportunities as the following example from Wal-Mart demonstrates: "On September 12, 2001, Wal-Mart's systems alerted the business to the increased demand for U.S. flags and automatically triggered increased orders from the company's suppliers, ensuring that the retailer was able to meet demand. Many of its competitors found the supply of flags exhausted because of Wal-Mart's superior execution" (Axson, 2010, pp. 136–137).

4.1.3 Future Analytics for Strategy Creation

Strategy creation is a complex process. Sometimes the strategy is put together too quickly and without sufficient prior analysis and understanding of the market. In this case, the strategy document might not have much meaning nor impact on how the business is executed. Another problem might be that the strategy creation process is too focused on short-term objectives at the expense of long-term objectives. A third potential problem during strategy creation can be the time it consumes, with too many meetings and procedures to be followed properly. During such a formalized process, if overdone, the creativity that should be part of the process can easily get lost on the way. Another concern with strategy creation is how to shield it from your competitors gaining insight into your strategic moves too early. From a strategy perspective Sun Tzu argues that "all warfare is based on deception" (McNeilly, 2006). Following this logic would imply that some strategic decisions need to be kept secret. The case study in Sect. 6.7 is an example of a hidden strategy creation process.

The benefit of having an open strategy creation process is that managers and knowledge workers at all levels of the organization can contribute to the process, thereby understanding how they can support it and develop commitment. They also feel more valued by being allowed to participate in the process. External partners, like investors and suppliers, can better decide if and how to support the strategy. Keeping the strategy hidden to a good extent helps to maintain a competitive advantage over rival firms who, otherwise, may act in a way to limit and undermine the success of the planned activities. Since many organizational members are not involved in such a strategy creation process, they are limited in their criticism which may be in the interest of an autocratic management team. But independent from the approach taken, the analytical tools used are the same. The difference is about how many individuals need to be involved in the process and working with the tools: Forecasting, predictive analytics, simulations and scenario planning, planning, and budgeting.

One example of utilizing predictive analytics and forecasting is the bus fleet operator Metro St. Louis (Accenture, 2008a). They partnered with Accenture to develop a system to forecast bus equipment failures before they occur. They used sensors for monitoring in all buses and statistical analysis to identify deviations and operating anomalies in the engines and transmissions. The predictive analytics application helped them to reduce vehicle failures and maintenance expenses. In addition, they were able to extend the vehicle life by customizing the maintenance intervals for each individual vehicle based on the collected information.

Wendy's (May, 2009) also used forecasting to predict food and labor demand using predictive analytics. Wendy's offering was based on a custom hamburger production in many combinations, a built-to-order manufacturing process. Originally, they used the past 6 weeks of data to forecast the demand without details related to the specific product mix. This estimate was not exactly precise. So, in 2001 they started introducing a data warehouse and used 2 years of data as the foundation for their forecasting in their 1,300 stores. The new system enabled them to forecast the demand by product mix for every half an hour with a 95% accuracy, avoiding waste and improving resource utilization.

Other applications of predictive analytics and forecasting are part of customer relationship management, e.g., the predictive evaluation of a marketing campaign effectiveness based on behavior modeling and past experience. Simulating the effectiveness may also rely on data mining including clustering, association analysis, regressions, and scoring. A research conducted by TDWI (Eckerson, 2007) in 2006 surveyed 833 individuals and produced the following results: Predictive analytics can yield a substantial ROI and helped a Canadian bank to increase their campaign response rates by 600%, and to reduce customer acquisition cost by 50%, while an airline used it to improve their estimation of no-show passengers, thereby reducing the number of overbooked flights as well as empty seats leading to increased revenue and customer satisfaction. Despite these and other successful examples, the research survey showed that 61% of participants are either still "exploring" or have "no plans" to use predictive analytics. Those respondents who have implemented predictive analytics, used it for cross-selling/up-selling, campaign management, customer acquisition, budgeting, and forecasting, attrition/churn/retention management, fraud detection, promotions, pricing, demand planning, customer service, quality improvement, and many other areas.

Another application is scenario planning, e.g., simulating different customer adoption rates for newly introduced products based on the schedule of their market entry or the effects of an increased sales force or a modified pricing. These factors and additional ones can be used to simulate the potential effects on the business from sales via different distribution channels to manufacturing and procurement up to delivery.

Two of the most critical processes during strategy creation are the strategic planning process and the budgeting process. Both of these processes need to be supported heavily by analytics as well as communication support for an effective dialog within the organization. Sharing new ideas, evaluating different scenarios, reflecting the effectiveness of past actions, new trends and forecasts, basically all available knowledge should be used in the process of defining the strategic plan, objectives, and initiatives. Using business intelligence applications to align these plans, objectives, and initiatives throughout all levels of the organization via cascading prepares an effective strategy execution and commitment to execute it by all decision makers. An effective strategy execution implies the effective utilization of the available resources where they have the most significant impact. Once the strategic plan is developed, the decision makers use the budgeting process to assign the resources to organizational units. The resources should be adequate to execute the strategic initiatives to reach the set objectives. The strategic plan and the budgeting process are dependent processes. The finalized plan and the allocated budgets create the foundation for further future analytics, comparing the effectiveness of capital spending across the organization, and measuring actual performance compared to the promises made or expectations set during the planning phase.

Making decisions about the future, including strategic objectives and actions, is a key task in business as well as in sports. A response from hockey legend Wayne Gretzky, answering the question what made him such a great player, was: "Most people skate to where the puck is....I skate to where the puck is going to be" (Jennings & Haughton, 2002, p. 15). Having an improved vision on what is likely to happen can be the competitive advantage that makes a big difference in regards to the effectiveness of strategy execution.

4.2 Decide

Decision making in business has the aim of maximizing the expected value and reaching the best possible outcome. The need for a decision must first be recognized. This can be an ad-hoc response to an alert, or proactively managing, or preparing the execution of the business. The rational model of decision making typically follows a sequence of steps:

- **Definition** and agreement of the problem.
- Assessment of the situation.
- Generation and evaluation of alternatives.
- Selection of the preferred alternative.
- Implementation of the selected alternative.
- Monitoring of the effectiveness of the solution.

This rational model of decision making was questioned by Nobel prize winner Herbert Simon. He framed the term "Bounded rationality" to question the assumptions of the rational model and describe its limitations. Decision makers can disagree on the problem or on the relevance of a problem for an organization, sometimes because they have no shared understanding of the strategic objectives. In addition, decision makers typically have imperfect and incomplete information about the situation, they often do not know all their available alternatives or the consequences of the known alternatives before they choose one. Another limitation is the time for decision making, restricting the gathering of information as well as the time to analyze and process information. Additionally, organizational politics and opportunistic interests can lead to conflicting preferences and suboptimal decisions.

In real life, potential consequences for the decision making might be a tendency to select an easier to identify and achieve, less controversial, or safer alternative in place of the best alternative, the so-called satisficing. Another consequence might be that an individual or team stops searching for alternatives as soon as an acceptable, not the best, solution is discovered. There is never enough time to search endlessly. A pragmatic approach is to stop the search for information when the additional time spent for analytics creates diminishing benefits. This is where business intelligence and analytics impact the richness of information processing. If the information is provided reliably, if access to information is convenient and easy, analytical applications produce rich and useful information, and organizations will then use more analytics because their return on analytics is increased.

As mentioned earlier, organizational politics also impact the decision making process negatively. Often power is used to control information access, the setting of agendas including problems which need to be solved or others which are intentionally given a lower priority, influencing the decision making criteria to select a preferred alternative, establishing coalitions or hiring outside experts. In many of these cases, a transparent strategy creation process involving a maximum number of decision makers to define and agree on the strategic goals of the organization can reduce the above mentioned effects in the decision making process. This is also the reason why some executives in power may not want to support the implementation of business intelligence or analytics since it could limit their capability to exercise their power, leverage established coalitions to their favor, or follow a hidden agenda. On the other hand, this might be exactly the reason for individuals to promote the introduction of business intelligence to uncover decision making practices leading to a suboptimal performance of the organization.

But even if decisions were made in the best interest of the organization and not based on opportunism or hidden agendas, factual information will always be limited and not all information can be provided, even by the best business intelligence systems. Information will always be complemented by gut feelings when decisions are made. An Accenture (2008b) survey of more than 250 executives of large US companies found that major decisions were based on analytics by 60%, while the remaining 40% were more based on judgment. Some of the following reasons were mentioned by the respondents why judgment was so essential:

- Good data was not available (61%).
- For this decision, there was no past data (61%).
- Their decision relied on qualitative and subjective factors (55%).

Independent of the fact that decisions can't be perfect, important decisions should be made the best way possible. But what are the major decisions in business? One of them is certainly the establishment of a strategic plan including the organizational objectives. Stephen Covey in his book, *The 7 habits of highly effective people* pronounces the importance of this process, stating: "'Begin with the end in mind' is based on the principle that all things are created twice. There's a mental or first creation, and a physical or second creation to all things. . .You work with ideas. You work with your mind until you get a clear image of what you want to build. If you want to have a successful enterprise, you clearly define what you're trying to accomplish. You carefully think through the product or service you want to provide in terms of your market target, then you organize all the elements – financial, research and development, operations, marketing, personnel, physical facilities, and so on – to meet that objective. The extent to which you begin with the end in mind often determines whether or not you are able to create a successful enterprise. Most business failures begin in the first creation, with problems such as undercapitalization, misunderstanding of the market, or lack of a business plan" (Covey, 1990, p. 99). A strategic business plan typically consists of the following elements (Grant, 2010, p. 198):

- A statement of the goals.
- A set of assumptions or forecasts about key developments in the external environment.
- A qualitative statement about how the business will be extending its competitive advantage.
- Specific action steps which shall be taken with the associated timeline and an explanation stating what is to be achieved by specific dates.
- A set of financial projections, including a capital expenditure budget and outline operating budgets.

The strategic business plan, and its definition of measurable objectives using clearly defined key performance indicators, sets the stage for later monitoring and evaluation of performance, establishing priorities which help guide the decision making in case of conflicts of interest between organizational units, and also provides the foundation to allocate adequate resources in the budgeting process. The approval, rejection, or modification of these measurable and time-based objectives and plans is one of the main foundations for an effective strategy execution.

When it actually comes to strategy execution, who makes decisions with what kind of significance and how often? Despite the relevance of the decisions made by the top-level management, the majority of all decisions are made by the mid-level managers and knowledge workers across the organization, as displayed in Fig. 4.3.

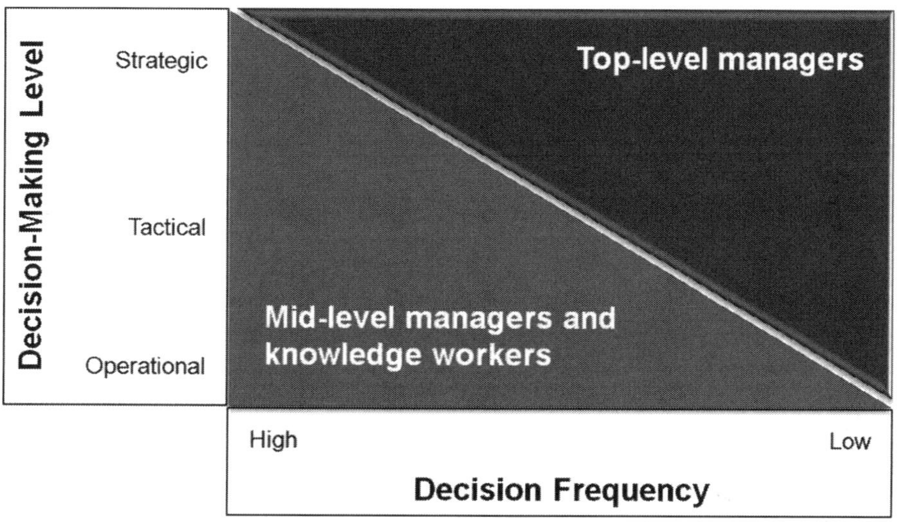

Fig. 4.3 Decisions based on Level and frequency (Adapted based on Stair and Reynolds (2006), p. 484)

If the value of few strategic decisions at the top-level have about the same significance for the organization as many operational decisions at the mid-level or by individual knowledge workers, then it implies that decision makers at all levels should be supported to make well-informed decisions. Analytical applications should not only be provided to the executives.

Another reason to share BI-Frontend applications with all decision makers is to align their decision with the strategy. There are many situations where conflicts arise within an organization and while each party may have valid reasoning, the correct decision for the organization can often only be found by evaluating the different options and their specific contribution to the strategic objectives. One such conflict which can be found in most organizations is the conflict between the front office and the back office. As Buytendijk (2010) states: "The front office represents most customer-facing activities, such as sales, service, and large parts of marketing. The back office represents administration, manufacturing, or other types of production, procurement, logistics, and support functions such as Finance, legal, and

Human Resources. The front office, being market driven, is looking for ways to cater to the specific needs of customers. 'There is always an opportunity to jump on, if only the back office would understand,' they say. The back office has an eye on standardization, looking for ways to create a lean-and-mean operation. 'There simply must be some rules to comply with, if the front office would only grasp that,' they argue. In short, the front office has an outside-in approach, whereas the back office works from the inside out" (Buytendijk, 2010, pp. 50–51). The conflict is a result of different responsibilities and in the end the question is, which aim is more critical: flexibility and an innovation and market-focus; or an efficient, manageable, and scalable organization which is less flexible? Another conflict may be the decision between saving in research and development to optimize the short term profit, e.g., with a focus on the next quarter, or investing in research and development which leads to a negative short term effect on profit but may prepare the organization for more profitable times in future periods. There is no generic solution to these decisions, but with appropriate monitoring and analytics, the key is to learn from past decisions and to improve continuously.

4.3 Act

The final act of management, once the analysis has led to a decision is the execution itself. But who is responsible for making happen what has been decided? What is the exact action that should happen? These aspects need to be part of the decision making. Otherwise, the implementation may not happen at all or deviate from what the decision makers had in mind when making the decision.

Let us take a look at an example where the management control loop for strategy execution was used, including acting in accordance with the decisions made. At Disney, a problem was perceived, the situation was analyzed, alternative solutions were evaluated, an alternative was selected, and finally, also implemented. Based on Disney's own exit polls, the top source of customer unhappiness are long waiting lines. Customers often spend 50% of the total park attendance time just standing in line. In summer time, they often wait 60 min before they take a few minutes' ride. Since a family with two adults and two children can spend US$ 1,000 or more for a day at one of the parks, they may expect more rides and fewer times in line.

Queues develop, even though Disney has designed large rides to accommodate between 1,000 and 2,000 guests per hour. Fung (2010) states that it is not the average number of guests per day that leads to the creation of lines but the variability of their arrival: "If Disney accurately anticipated demand, could it not build sufficient capacity? Did the appearance of long lines reflect negligent design? Surprisingly, the answer to both questions in no. The real culprit is not bad design but variability. Disney constructs each theme park to satisfy the 'design day,' typically up to the ninetieth-percentile level of demand, which means, in theory, on nine out of ten days, the park should have leftover capacity. In reality, patrons report long lines pretty much any day of the year. Worse, statisticians are certain that queues would persist even if Disney had designed for the busiest day of the year. To understand this piece of anti-intuition, we must realize that the busiest-day demand merely conveys the average park attendance, and this number ignores the uneven distribution of patrons, say, from one attraction to another or from 1 hour to the next. Even if Disney correctly predicted the total number of patrons riding Dumbo on the peak day (which itself would have been a tough assignment), a line would materialize unavoidably because the patrons would appear irregularly during the day, while Dumbo's capacity does not change" (Fung, 2010, pp. 6–8).

To design an entertainment park guaranteeing no lines would require extreme levels of overcapacity and a significant increase in cost. Analysis of the average daily visitors would not help the decision makers identify the problem. A drill-down with a view on visitors by hour or minute would help to uncover the times per attraction when the lines build up. It may show that the average visitor follows specific patterns, visiting a sequence of attractions and by using predictive analytics, it may be possible to predict visitor interest above and below capacity at specific times during the day.

An innovative solution to the problem, FASTPASS, was introduced in 1999. On the internet's largest unofficial on-line guide to Walt Disney World (Werner Technologies, 2010) the system is described as follows: "Disney's FASTPASS allows guests to make 'reservations' for a popular ride to avoid waiting in long lines. As you approach the attraction that uses the FASTPASS system, you will see three lines. One is the FASTPASS distribution line (where you get your FASTPASS ticket), the second is the FASTPASS entrance (when you're returning to ride after making your FASTPASS reservation), and the third is the Standby entrance for guests not using FASTPASS. The FASTPASS distribution line features a clock showing what times the tickets are being issued for. A clock with the current time is displayed outside the FASTPASS attraction entrance. The Standby line will have the current wait time posted. Let's see how this all works. It's 11:00am and you want to go on Kali River Rapids but there's a 60 min wait posted outside the Standby line. You take a look at the FASTPASS distribution and see that passes are being issued with a return time of 1:00–2:00pm. You get your FASTPASS and instead of waiting on a 1 hour line, you have two free hours before coming back, bypassing the standby line and getting on Kali with little or no wait. For the attractions, the assigned time will give you a 1 h window to return, so you don't have to run back to be there the minute it goes into effect" (Werner Technologies, 2010).

There is no extra fee to use FASTPASS and using a FASTPASS during peak periods is no different from using it at any other time. On the website AllEars.Net, they describe the system's functioning using a computer system: "The FASTPASS wait time should not be any longer during peak periods, because the computerized system automatically spreads the FASTPASS guests evenly throughout the day regardless of attendance level. The only thing different during peak periods is that since FASTPASS demand is higher the return time (assigned time to come back) will be longer. Therefore, during peak periods when there are more guests in the virtual queue the return time gets extended further out into the day" (RYI Enterprises, 2010).

The introduction really helped to reduce the waiting time for both groups, those using the FASTPASS ticket and those not using it, since the distribution of guests on the bottleneck attractions is improved. But, in addition to this measurable improvement, Disney's management also used scholarly research results on perception management to improve customer satisfaction related to waiting times because study results found that perceived waiting time is not identical to actual waiting time: "Mirrors in elevator lobbies, for example, distort people's sense of the amount of waiting time; we tend not to count time spent looking at our reflection as waiting time. Accordingly, Disney engineers, or 'Imagineers,' devote a lot of effort to shaping patrons' perception of waiting times. Over the years, Disney has perfected the magic of managing perceptions. Take a walk around the park, and you cannot fail to see their handiwork. The waiting area of Expedition Everest, for instance, is decorated as a Nepalese village, with artifacts and flora brought back from the Himalayas; before getting on the rollercoaster, patrons weave through a yeti museum and encounter cryptic messages that generate excitement" (Fung, 2010, pp. 16–20). Another way to improve the perception is to underpromise and overdeliver. This may also be used to signal estimated waiting times that are intentionally showing longer wait times than real.

In summary the interest of hospitality operators is to minimize customer dissatisfaction which can influence the intent to return. This can be done by reducing the actual waiting time, the perceived waiting time, and to make the wait invisible via virtual queues, where customers can utilize the waiting time before they return back at their assigned time. All of these options are used at Disney. Based on Dickson, Ford, and Laval (2005), the key is to find the optimal balance between cost of service and the cost of waiting, and related customer dissatisfaction. To find this balance, they recommend customer surveys to find out what is perceived as an acceptable wait time. They state: "Disney, for example, sets its design day at 80 to 90 percent of expected demand. While this may seem high, this standard reflects a conscious decision to not disappoint its guests even on busy days. That policy also creates a challenge for Disney's marketing department to find creative ways to increase attendance during the nonpeak periods of the year so that the available capacity is used as efficiently as possible. The need to smooth out the peaks and valleys of demand is the reason that downtown convention hotels offer special weekend rates, restaurants offer early bird specials, and airlines offer off-peak discount fares" (Dickson, Ford, & Laval, 2005, pp. 55–56). A result from introducing the virtual queue at Disney World is that guests spend substantially less time in line, spent more per capita, and saw more attractions. The time they saved in lines was either used to visit additional attractions or spent at stores or restaurants. Despite the increased spending, customer satisfaction of the guests could be increased.

This example demonstrates how a smart analysis based on a sophisticated IT infrastructure, in combination with good decision making and a consequent implementation, leads to an effective strategy execution.

Chapter 5
Outlook

John Maynard Keynes, the well known father of Keynesian economics once said: "When the facts change, I change my mind." In this sense, decision making heavily relies on facts and, having shared many new examples demonstrating the potentials of business intelligence, the question you may ask yourself is: "Is my organization equipped and utilizing business intelligence sufficiently? Are there any missed potentials to use this innovation? What is the added value to innovate and use more business intelligence?"

5.1 Innovation Adoption

Based on Rogers' (2003) famous book "Diffusion of Innovations", innovations often happen much later than the related invention. While an invention is the discovery of a new idea, he describes an innovation as an idea, practice, or object that is **perceived as new** by an individual or other unit of adoption. In his words: "It matters little, so far as human behavior is concerned, whether or not an idea is 'objectively' new as measured by the lapse of time since its first use or discovery. The perceived newness of the idea for the individual determines his or her reaction to it. If an idea seems new to the individual, it is an innovation" (Rogers, 2003, p. 12).

The first known mentioning of the term "business intelligence," the invention, happened in 1958 by Luhn (1958). Clearly, the innovation is still in the process of happening. While some organizations recognized the potential of business intelligence several years ago and are using it already, others are still perceiving business intelligence, or at least some aspects of it, as new. For them, business intelligence is an innovation. The adoption of the innovation business intelligence can help to support progress either by leveraging product innovations, e.g., new software solutions, or process innovations, e.g., more effective forecasting, planning, and budgeting by leveraging business intelligence.

B. Heesen, *Effective Strategy Execution*, Management for Professionals,
DOI 10.1007/978-3-642-19205-0_5, © Springer-Verlag Berlin Heidelberg 2012

But why is it that it takes so long for business intelligence or other innovations to be adopted? Some innovations are not even adopted if they are superior. Take the example of your computer keyboard. Most likely you will have a QWERTY (Diamond, 1997) keyboard (see Fig. 5.1) or one of its derivates like the AZERTY or QUERTZ keyboard. The original QWERTY keyboard has the letters Q W E R T Y placed in the top left row. It was patented in 1878 by Christopher Latham Sholes and made popular by the success of the Remington typewriter. Nowadays it is the dominant keyboard design and millions learned typing the sequence A S D F and J K L: on the home row of the keyboard, where the fingers rest at the beginning. Typing on the home row is the fastest and causes the lowest level of strain on the fingers.

Fig. 5.1 Typewriter with QWERTY keyboard

Did you ever ask yourself why the keys are not ordered by the alphabet? Sholes had started out with the key in alphabetical order when he began building his typewriter in 1867 (Wikipedia, 2011b). The problem with this design was that the typewriter jammed when a typist struck two adjacent keys in succession too quickly, causing the second type bar to jam the first type bar before it could fall back into place. To avoid this problem, Sholes used the results of studies to position the letters in a way to reduce typing speed intentionally for those combinations of letters which often caused jamming.

Professor August Dvorak performed motion studies which identified problems with the use of the QWERTY keyboard, like awkward finger motions, common letter combinations being typed with the same finger, or with one hand while the other sits idle. Also, most typing on QWERTY keyboards was found to be done with the left hand and only 32% of all strokes were on the home row, where typing is the quickest and needed the least effort. Dvorak developed the DVORAK keyboard, patented in 1936, to improve the effectiveness. On the DVORAK keyboard, 70% of the English words can be typed on the home row and the reduction of some of the awkward and tiring finger movements not only increase speed but also reduce typing errors. As Jared Diamond wrote in Discover Magazine in 1997: "Typing on a QWERTY keyboard is unnecessarily tiring, slow, inaccurate, hard to learn, and hard to remember. In a normal workday a good typist's fingers cover up to 20 miles on a QWERTY keyboard, but only one mile on a Dvorak keyboard. QWERTY typists achieve barely half the speed of Dvorak typists, who hold most world records for typing speed. QWERTY typists make about twice the errors that Dvorak typists make" (Diamond, 1997). With keyboard-related repetitive-strain injuries being among our most common industrial accidents and with millions using the QWERTY keyboard every day for typing, why is it that we do not leverage the improvement available by the Dvorak keyboard? The jamming problem, which was the reasoning for the QWERTY keyboard we are using, has vanished with the use of computers and printers since many decades. Manufacturers such as Microsoft and Apple are supporting the Dvorak layout. Stickers can be bought to put the Dvorak layout on QWERTY keyboards and Dvorak typing tutors are available (Wood, 2011). What, then, is hindering the adoption of innovations like this one?

According to Rogers (2003), the recognition of a problem or need is often the beginning of an innovation development process that stimulates research into finding a solution or response for the problem or need. Either new market requirements or new technological capabilities typically start the generation of innovations. Once the innovation is available, the innovation-decision process usually consists of the following sequence of steps: (a) knowledge as learning about the existence (awareness-knowledge) and gaining an understanding of the innovation (how-to knowledge and principles-knowledge), (b) persuasion as the development of a positive or negative attitude toward using the innovation, through seeking information that reduces uncertainty about the expected consequences of the innovation, (c) decision as the activity leading toward the adoption or rejection of the innovation, (d) implementation as the step in which the innovation is used, and (e) confirmation as the feedback on the basis of experiences when using the innovation that can lead to reconfirm or reverse the adoption decision (see Fig. 5.2).

Because individuals pay more attention to messages that are consistent with their attitudes and beliefs, selective perception is a factor affecting the adoption process. The following perceptions of the attributes of an innovation were found to be specifically relevant: (a) relative advantage, (b) compatibility, (c) complexity, (d) trialability, and (e) observability. According to Rogers, these five perceived attributes of an innovation can explain between 49 and 87% of the variance of the rate of adoption of innovations.

The **relative advantage** can be measured in economic terms, social prestige, or convenience and it represents the extent to which an innovation is perceived as superior to the current practice. Relative advantage is a ratio of expected benefits versus costs, including economic profitability, increase or decrease in comfort,

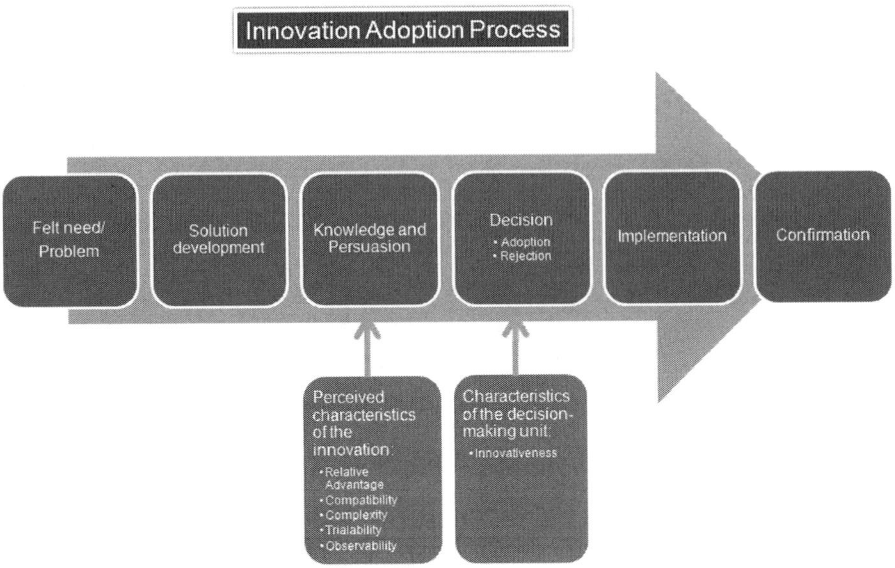

Fig. 5.2 Innovation adoption process (©Bernd Heesen/Prescient. Used with permission)

social prestige, savings or costs of time and effort, and the immediacy of the reward. According to Rogers, "the greater the perceived relative advantage of an innovation, the more rapid its rate of adoption will be" (Rogers, 2003, p. 15). The relative advantage of business intelligence might depend on factors like size of the organization, industry, and the degree to which business intelligence is already used. **Compatibility** is the extent to which an innovation is perceived to be consistent with the potential adopter's needs, socio-cultural values, beliefs, and norms. In cases where the needs are met but the values and norms are not compatible, the adoption of a new value system might be required before the innovation can be adopted; an idea that is incompatible will not be adopted as rapidly as an innovation that is compatible. Rogers stated, "an innovation's incompatibility with cultural values can block its adoption" (Rogers, 2003, p. 241). The perceived compatibility of an innovation is positively related to the rate of adoption. With respect to business intelligence, this can relate to the perceived value of performance measurement and, using key performance indicators in general, the attitude toward sharing information, the leadership style and philosophy within the organization, or the question who should be involved in the strategy creation process. **Complexity** is the degree to which an innovation is perceived as difficult to use or understand. Rogers found that "new ideas that are simple to understand are adopted more rapidly than innovations that require the adopter to develop new skills and understandings" (Rogers, 2003, p. 16). The degree to which an innovation is easy to learn and use has been found to be positively related to the rate of adoption. Consequently, ease of use should be a criteria when implementing business intelligence or introducing the Value Scorecard™. **Trialability** is the extent to which an innovation can be tested prior to full adoption. Testing the innovation reduces uncertainty. If an individual cannot try the innovation, the trial experience from peers can be a substitute. From that perspective, this book with its examples and case studies may help to learn from the experiences already made. Perceived trialability is positively related to the rate of adoption. Another related variable is **Observability**; it is the degree to which the results of an innovation are visible to others. Rogers found that the likelihood for an adoption increases if individuals are able to see the results of an innovation.

Another relevant characteristic measured in innovation research is **innovativeness**. Depending on how quickly the innovation-decision process leads to the adoption of an innovation relative to the other potential adopters, Rogers (2003) classified members on the basis of their level of innovativeness as (a) innovators (the first 2.5% to adopt), (b) early adopters (the next 13.5% of adopters), (c) early majority (the next 34%), (d) late majority (the next 34%), and (e) laggards (the last 16% to adopt) (see Fig. 5.3).

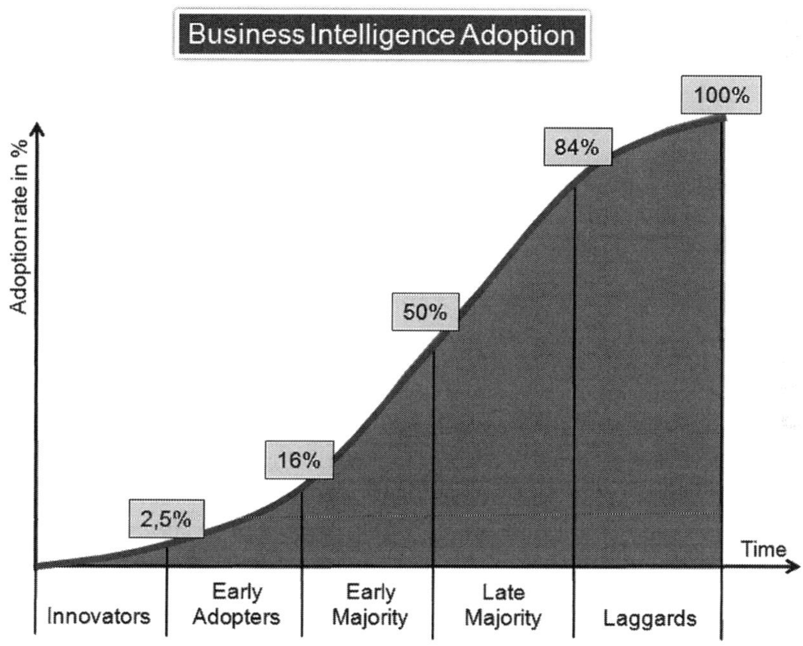

Fig. 5.3 Adopter categorization on the basis of innovativeness (©Bernd Heesen/Prescient. Used with permission)

Additional factors impacting the adoption or rejection decision can be the size of an organization. Since larger organizations typically have more available resources and expertise, they are more likely to adopt innovations. The contextual environment (Souitaris, 2003), e.g., the industry, the intensity of competition, the perceived rate of change of customer needs, and the intensity of external communications, and feedback from business partners as well as the existence of a champion for the innovation were found to be relevant factors as well.

Now, how do these models apply to an effective strategy execution and business intelligence? The innovation adoption process starts with the recognition of a **felt need or problem**. These were addressed in Chap. 1, including the strategy barrier, management barrier, and IT barrier. A set of initiatives were discussed to provide a solution to these problems. This included the definition of measurable strategic objectives as a foundation for the coordination of all organizational efforts and an instrument to gain cooperation from the employees. The Strategic Alignment Process™ was introduced to establish horizontal and vertical alignment. The enablement of Management by Objectives and self-control for knowledge workers on all levels of the organization via the use of Strategic Business Intelligence™ and analytics was discussed. A study published by IBM (LaValle, 2009) in 2009 confirmed that most organizations recognize the opportunity for analytics. It found that they are still very early in the adoption process. Only 14% of the respondents stated to take advantage of new analytics to leverage information to their advantage. The majority, 66% of respondents, stated to recognize the opportunity and getting started, while 20% had not even thought about it. This indicates that the current organizations leveraging business intelligence are early adopters and the majority of organizations still evaluate the potential benefits this innovation could bring to them. One of three respondents described their organization as frequently making major business decisions with incomplete information or information they don't trust. Clearly, some organizations realize a need to innovate.

5.2 Business Intelligence Maturity

The second step in the innovation adoption process is solution development. Obviously, it is not sufficient to recognize a need, like Hans Peter Luhn did in 1958. It requires affordable solutions which are compatible with the problems, are not too complex to be used, and are perceived to gain relative advantage. Organizations interested in business intelligence solutions had to deal with many vendors and their software solutions, some of which were going out of business or being acquired over the years. At the same time vendors optimized their solutions to better meet customer needs. Both, the consolidation of the market and the evolution of software solutions, have helped reduce the overall cost and improve the potential gains for customers. The time for the adoption of business intelligence by the early majority has come. Forrester Research (Evelson, 2011) sees an increasing level of interest and adoption in business intelligence because of more function-rich and robust solutions. Dan Sommer, Principal Research Analyst at Gartner, predicts an increased adoption as well, stating: "BI spending has far surpassed IT budget growth overall for several years, and it is clear that BI continues to be a technology at the center of information-driven initiatives in organizations. Vendors aggressively market their capabilities in this area, so revenue growth is as much a function of vendor push as a demand pull" (Gartner, 2011b). In their press release, Gartner lists the leading five vendors, dominating the business intelligence market as displayed in Fig. 5.4.

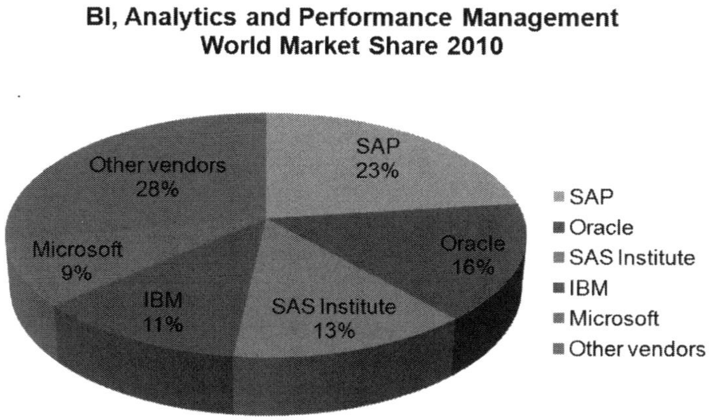

Fig. 5.4 BI, analytics and performance management vendors (©Bernd Heesen/Prescient. Used with permission)

Gartner also envisions the following trends to occur in the coming years, innovations which should impact the adoption of business intelligence (Gartner, 2011a):

- By 2013, 33% of BI functionality will be consumed via handheld devices.
- By 2014, 30% of analytical applications will use in-memory functions to add scale and computational speed.
- By 2014, 30% of analytical applications will use proactive, predictive, and forecasting capabilities.
- By 2013, 15% of BI deployments will combine BI, collaboration, and social software into decision-making environments.

Clearly, the solution development phase, as part of the innovation adoption process, is continuing to make the solutions better fit the requirements of the customers.

5.2.1 Business Intelligence Return on Investment

Under which circumstances should organizations decide to invest in business intelligence? Clearly, the potential value-added gain needs to be higher than the expected cost for the implementation and use of business intelligence. The solutions need to fit the requirements of the organization, and tangible as well as intangible benefits should be expected. Using an ROI (Return on Investment) calculation for each potential business intelligence project, those with the best returns should be implemented first.

An impressive example of the benefits business intelligence can bring to an organization is at Continental Airlines (Watson, Wixom, Hoffer, Anderson-Lehman, & Reynolds, 2006). In the 1990s, Continental Airlines carried approximately 50 million passengers a year worldwide, with more than 2,300 daily departures to more than 227 destinations. There were ten major U.S. airlines, and in the Department of Transportation metrics, used to monitor the industry's performance including on-time arrivals, baggage handling, customer complaints, and denied boardings because of overbooking, Continental consistently ranked last of the ten airlines. The need for improvement was recognized and in 1998, Continental Airlines decided to invest in an enterprise data warehouse to gain faster information to relevant information related to its business and its customers. Benefits were gained in revenue management and accounting, customer relationship management, crew operations and payroll, security and fraud, as well as flight operations. One of the applications was a Flight Management Dashboard, which allowed operations staff to better serve Continental's high value customers. The dashboard allowed operations managers to receive alerts for high valued customers with short transfer times between flights and help them to schedule gate agents and baggage supervisors to assist the customers and their luggage to avoid missing flights. The underlying IT infrastructure was provided by an 8-terabyte enterprise data warehouse integrating two critical primary real-time data sources: (1) the satellite feeds that are transmitted from airplanes, and (2) the central customer database. The purpose of the business intelligence implementation was to increase revenues and decrease costs. Continental Airlines has taken a $30 million investment in hardware, software, and personnel to generate more than $500M in revenue enhancements and cost savings, resulting in a return on investment (ROI) of greater than 1,000%.

The fact that business intelligence can deliver real value is confirmed by the many organizations who participate in the Data Warehousing Institute (TDWI) Best Practices in Business Intelligence contest. The following are facts reported by some of the participants (Eckerson, 2006, pp. 46–47):

- A major airline estimates that it generates $40 million in new revenue and saves $31 million in costs from just four of its 35 analytical applications running in its BI environment.
- A major electronics retailer attributes $1.3 million a year in improved assortments and fewer out-of-stock situations to a BI solution. The same solution also saves $2.3 million a year in inventory, a result of more accurate supplier shipments.

Both, the estimation of the gains and the costs, still remain a challenge as they can only be estimations. For both, gains and costs, it is beneficial to learn from the experiences of similar implementations. This book tries to provide a good number of examples to help you in this process. The transfer, how this may apply to your own organization, is still required.

5.3 Limitations to Analytics

Business intelligence can provide timely and correct information for a person to make a decision or if a decision process is standardized, it can be automated or make a proposal. But software itself can only perform tasks that it was told to do by humans. And even if it is utilized to perform analysis, the interpretation of the results still remains the task of a person. Business intelligence can only collect information and provide access to information. The intelligence still happens within the brain of individuals, except where some intelligence was embedded in software, e.g., pricing, credit fraud detection, to automate prescribed routine decisions.

But even with analytical applications providing relevant information, the decision process might be compromised by limited time to gather or analyze information before a decision needs to be made, by the lack of data on comparable situations, e.g., if this situation has not occurred before, when decisions rely on subjective factors or those that can't be easily measured, or if historical information is misleading.

One example where information was misleading is Australia's cane toad (Commonwealth Scientific and Industrial Research Organisation, 2011), which was released in 1935 by the Australian Bureau of Sugar Experimental Stations to eat French's Cane Beetle and the Greyback Cane Beetle, whose larvae eat the roots of sugar cane and kills or stunts the plants. Cane toads were previously successfully deployed in other countries but proved unsuccessful in controlling the beetles in Australia. Rapid mating and deadly toxins helped the toads spread in number to more than 1.5 billion and killing snakes, lizards, water birds and even crocodiles. But they were not only unsuccessful in controlling the beetles, they also became a pest themselves, leading the Australian government even to release a Policy on Cane Toads (Australian Government: Department of the Environment, Water, Heritage and the Arts, 2009). The facts from previous successful deployments of the toad led to a wrong decision to introduce them in Australia because the contexts were different.

While bounded rationality (see Sect. 4.2) provides additional reasons for suboptimal decision making, generically, the availability of more current and reliable information increases the chance for faster and better decisions in an organization that has a performance culture.

5.4 Performance Culture

What is the benefit of creating a performance culture? Leo Pujals, founder and CEO at TelePizza S.A. in Spain, asks the question: "Can you imagine sitting in a gymnasium and watching a basketball game where no score was kept? It would be boring watching people go up and down the floor shooting baskets with no idea of who was winning and who was losing" (Jennings & Haughton, 2002, p. 210).

In his opinion, keeping score not only helps to provide valuable information to make smarter business decisions, but it can also create fun and excitement at work because measuring helps to recognize good performance. Now, obviously, it also helps to recognize bad performance. In a performance culture, this would be used as a motivation to learn via an analysis of the situation and take corrective action to improve future performance. In a non-performance culture, it may be perceived as a threat to those who do not perform well. The same facts can therefore be perceived very differently.

The uncovering of problematic performance also starts an organizational dialog about the reasoning and how to avoid the recurrence of the same problem in the future. This can even include a debate about the adequacy of the planned performance. Was the targeted performance too optimistic and based upon unrealistic assumptions? As Robert Kaplan and David Norton stated: "Senior executives debate and argue among themselves about the objectives and measure on the organizational scorecard and the cause-and-effect linkages on the strategy map defining the strategic hypotheses. These meetings build an emotional commitment to the strategy, to the scorecard as a communications device, and to the management processes that build a Strategy-Focused Organization" (Kaplan & Norton, 2001, p. 362). The organizational dialog, defining the organizational goals, analysis and interpretation of performance and subsequent decisions help align all efforts with the strategy.

A performance culture is no guarantee for success at all times. It just increases the likelihood of being successful. It is similar to sports where athletes cannot guarantee their success. All they can do is to have a commitment to excellence, permanently monitoring their performance, and trying to learn from it via analysis, and accepting failure as part of the learning and improvement process. Over time, improvements can be expected and those with a performance culture are likely to be more successful than those without one. As Julie Bell and Robin Pou describe it: "In most cases, you cannot be 100 percent confident in the outcome because you do not have complete control of all the variables. Instead of being confident in the outcome, we will look at being confident in the process that creates the outcome. This way of thinking will allow you to be confident today and be confident about achieving future goals" (Bell & Pou, 2009, pp. 50–52).

Establishing goals and permanent reflection and learning are an excellent combination. But if the goals are based on the wrong measures, the systematic does not produce the optimal results. Therefore, the key element on the business perspective of the World of Strategic Business Intelligence™ (see Fig. 5.5) is to select performance indicators, which are best suited to measure the strategic objectives of the organization. An important element of a performance culture is the continuous reflection on whether current measures are adequate or should be replaced.

Even established measures should be reviewed, as the example of the measurement of the wealth of nations shows. Indicators like the Gross Domestic Product (GDP) or GDP per capita are typically used to measure the wealth of nations. The fact that GDP does increase when more scarce resources like oil or coal are used or increases when parents hire nannies instead of taking care of their own children are

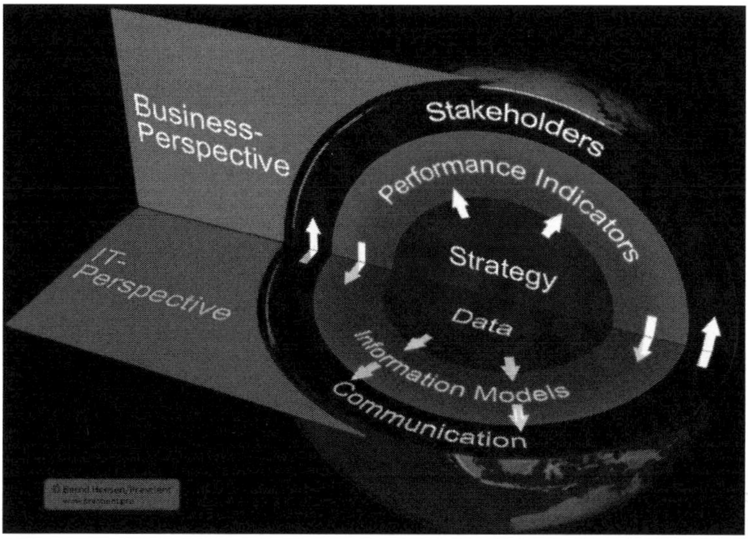

Fig. 5.5 World of Strategic Business Intelligence™ (©Bernd Heesen/Prescient. Used with permission)

just a few scenarios which contribute to question the adequacy of GDP as a measure for wealth. In their book *Mismeasuring our lives: Why the GDP doesn't add up* (Stiglitz, Sen, & Fitoussi, 2010), The Nobel Laureates Joseph Stiglitz and Amartya Sen together with Jean-Paul Fitoussie explain why GDP is a flawed indicator for economic performance and social progress in their opinion.

The New Economy Working Group (2011) correctly states "We Get What We Measure." They request a transition from using GDP as a measure of wealth to a more balanced reflection of human, social, and environmental factors in addition to the monetary measurement. The nuclear catastrophe in Japan clearly demonstrates that the environmental and long-term aspects, even if in conflict with economic or short-term interests, cannot be ignored. The idea of a more balanced measure also sparked the idea to develop the Human Development Index (HDI) (United Nations Development Programme, 2011), which is calculated by the United Nations Development Programmes since 1990. It reflects three performance indicators: life expectancy at birth, mean years of schooling, and GDP per capita. The intent from the initiator of the HDI, the Pakistani economist Mahbub ul Haq, was to establish a new indicator for wealth measurement to shift the attention of policymakers from their concentration on economic progress to human well-being (Wikipedia, 2011c). Another initiative with the name *Valuing What Matters* is undertaken by the New Economics Foundation (2011a), who introduced the Happy Planet Index (HPI) (New Economics Foundation, 2011b) in 2006 to measure the environmental efficiency with which, country by country, people live long and happy lives. It is founded upon the idea that most people want to live long and fulfilling lives and the country which is ranked the best allows its citizens to live long and fulfilling lives, while avoiding to infringe on the opportunity of future people and people in other countries to do the same. The rankings of the countries based on GDP, GDP per capita, HDI and HPI are deviating significantly as displayed in Fig. 5.6. The figure shows the rankings for the largest ten economies based on GDP (World Bank, 2011a), GDP per capita (World Bank, 2011b), HDI (United Nations Development Programme, 2009), and HPI (New Economics Foundation, 2009) in 2009.

	GDP	GDP per capita	HDI	HPI
United States	1	18	13	114
Japan	2	32	10	75
People's Republic of China	3	125	92	20
Germany	4	26	22	51
France	5	25	8	71
United Kingdom	6	29	21	74
Italy	7	35	18	69
Brazil	8	83	75	9
Spain	9	36	15	76
Canada	10	28	4	89

Fig. 5.6 Ranking of the ten largest world economies in 2009

As citizens we should make sure our governments use measures which really reflect what we care about. If we carry responsibility for a group, we should equally make sure that our measures reflect what we care most about.

Despite measures having to be selected carefully, a performance culture also heavily depends on learning. As Ikujiro Nonaka wrote in his landmark book *The knowledge-creating company:* "In an economy where the only certainty is uncertainty, the one sure source of lasting competitive advantage is knowledge. When markets shift, technologies proliferate, competitors multiply, and products become obsolete almost overnight, successful companies are those that consistently create new knowledge, disseminate it widely throughout the organization, and quickly embody it in new technologies and products" (Nonaka, 1998, p. 22). To accomplish these tasks, an organization needs to establish an adequate Strategic Business Intelligence Framework™ which enables the application of Management by Objectives 2.0™ to create organizational alignment with the organizational objectives and, in consequence, to an effective strategy execution.

Key attributes of a performance culture were also described by Jim Collins in his book *Good to Great*: "All good to great companies began the process of finding a path to greatness by confronting the brutal facts of their current reality. Creating a climate where the truth is heard involves four basic practices: 1. Lead with questions, not answers. 2. Engage in dialogue and debate, not coercion. 3. Conduct autopsies, without blame. 4. Build red flag mechanisms that turn information into information that cannot be ignored. Retain absolute faith that you can and will prevail in the end, regardless of the difficulties, *and* at the same time confront the most brutal facts of your current reality, whatever they might be" (Collins, 2001, p. 88). This analytical process, including the resulting dialog, can now be supported by business intelligence. Even the red flag mechanisms can be established via automated alerts.

5.5 What Next?

As Dwight D. Eisenhower once stated: "Leadership is the ability to decide what is to be done and then get others to want to do it." If you are now realizing the potential benefits of business intelligence to support a more effective strategy execution, then it might be your task to lead your organization into a new direction.

Getting this done may be a demanding task, but a worthwhile one. As Charles F. Kettering stated: "We work day after day, not to finish things; but to make the future better . . . because we will spend the rest of our lives there."

The Management Control Loop for Strategy Execution also applies here with the sequence: analyze, decide, act. It is key for organizations not only to have a brilliant strategy but to actually execute it well. Let me share with you the following dialog from Lawrence MacGregor Serven, which he published in 1999, but still applies today: "Question '1: three frogs are sitting on a log. One decides to jump off. How many are left? You might think two, but the answer is three. One had decided to jump off, but he hasn't jumped yet. Question '2: three companies have poor earnings. One decides to revitalize key product lines, strengthen distribution channels, and become customer intimate. Now how many companies have poor earnings? You get the idea: deciding and doing are two different things. The imperative today is to excel at both. High performance requires effective strategy and flawless execution. This is a lesson a lot of companies miss" (MacGregor Serven, 1999, p. 10).

To give you an example of how flawless a strategy can be executed, let me use the metaphor of using a navigation system to drive a car from its current position to a targeted position, in analogy to executing a strategy to change the organization's position from where it is today to its targeted position. The navigation system has embedded intelligence in form of the street maps and it utilizes the global positioning system (GPS) to know its current position. When you drive into the wrong direction, the navigation system alerts you by voice with instructions how to get back on track towards your targeted position, e.g., to turn around. Business intelligence can help organizations reach their goals, similar to a navigation system assisting with driving directions. The system first supports you with identifying your current position and holds a history of past routes taken (Bi-Frontend: Current and past analytics). Then you can enter your target position, which should be defined prior to using the tool. You can use the tool's experience for planning purposes also (BI-Frontend: Future analytics), e.g., to receive a performance forecast after entering a couple of variables, e.g., which route to take, which KPIs to focus on (e.g., shortest distance, fastest, least expensive, etc.) or what kind of accelerators to use (e.g., travel by foot, bike, car, etc.). Once you start moving, the performance is automatically tracked (BI-Foundation) and alerts (e.g., traffic warnings) might require a decision (e.g., accepting or declining the automatic rerouting to avoid a traffic jam). During the complete trip, the performance is tracked and the dashboard (BI-Frontend: Current analytics) displays the expected arrival time, which is continuously updated reflecting current speed as well as expected delays. The tool only helps to improve decision making but it never takes over control of the car. The driver remains in control at all times. If the driver deviates from the recommended route, the system automatically recalculates the best possible directions to reach the final goal. If business intelligence can help you with a more effective strategy execution similar to a navigation system helping you with reaching the target, the question you may want to answer yourself is: How much longer do you want to drive your existing automobile the way you do when you realize that new systems are available and can help you to improve your performance? Can you afford to continue to do business the way you do, knowing that your competitors might already prepare to use strategic business intelligence systems to improve their performance? Do you consider your analytical capabilities as a strength or a weakness when comparing your organization with your competitors? What is your plan of action?

I invite you to take the **Strategy Execution Effectiveness Survey™** now! The survey will help you to assess your organizational effectiveness in regards to strategy execution. Right after completing the survey, you will have access to a summary of all survey responses, which allows you to compare your performance with those of other organizations. In addition, you can download the compiled survey findings from the book website http://www.strategicbusinessintelligence.com The compiled survey will outline best practices and provide recommendations for improvement. By entering the coupon code **u3b8fp** on the first page of the survey, you are entitled to receive a more detailed industry specific survey analysis report in addition to the standard evaluation.

Now it is left to you to help your organization. I hope this book has provided you with some useful new ideas.

Chapter 6
Case Studies

As explained in Sect. 5.1, the adoption of innovations is significantly affected by its attributes: (a) relative advantage, (b) compatibility, (c) complexity, (d) trialability, and (e) observability. The purpose of the case studies in this book is to help you get additional insights about the relative advantages and benefits these organizations were able to gain from implementing measurement systems and business intelligence. Triability of an innovation and the observability of the results of an innovation adoption reduce the uncertainty for potential adopters. The trial experience from peers and the effects of their implementation can be a substitute. I hope you will find the following case studies useful from that perspective as they demonstrate how performance management systems can impact the effectiveness of strategy execution.

The following seven international Case Studies from Daimler, Tetra-Pak, Würth, Germany's Federal Employment Agency, City of Aix-Les-Bains, Giesecke & Devrient, and Midwest Bell show how the organizational performance can be improved. These organizations span four continents and reflect organizations of different sizes and industries:

- Tetra Pak's journey to Business Intelligence maturity.
- Improvement in After Sales Support via Remote-Service at Daimler AG.
- Implementing a Balanced Scorecard to Improve the Performance of Public Administration: The Case of The City Aix Les Bains and Its Social Cohesion Policy.
- Improving Strategic Alignment with CRM and Analytics at Würth: Excellence in Sales.
- How Business Intelligence is Leveraged at the Federal Employment Agency of Germany to Increase the Effectiveness of Activities to Prevent and Reduce the Duration of Unemployment.
- Development of an Operational Reporting Platform at Giesecke & Devrient to Enable Quicker, Better-Informed Decision Making.
- Midwest Bell's Execution of a Hidden Strategy Causing Conflict of Interest and Resistance.

B. Heesen, *Effective Strategy Execution*, Management for Professionals,
DOI 10.1007/978-3-642-19205-0_6,

6.1 Tetra Pak's journey to Business Intelligence Maturity

Authors	
Christopher Rowley	Director Business Intelligence and e-Business Systems Tetra Pak Global Information Management 19 Gul Lane, Singapore 629414, Singapore christopher.rowley@tetrapak.com
Paul Hawking	Institute of Logistics and Supply Chain Management Victoria University 300 Flinders Street, Melbourne/Australia paul.hawking@vu.edu.au
Organization	
Name Industry Size (# employees) Website	Tetra Pak Packaging 21.000 http://www.tetrapak.com
Scope of Success Story	
Geography Functional Area KPIs	Global Information technology User adoption, Response time, Reports accessed
Overview	
This success story describes Tetra Pak's global Business Intelligence journey.	
Business requirement	
Reports meeting global business performance measurement requirements, replace fragmented corporate reporting applications environment, and improve response times for reporting.	
Solution	
Consolidate the financial reporting system based on a centralized SAP ERP and SAP Business Warehouse infrastructure. Establish BI governance via a BI Competency Center.	
Benefits	
Comprehensive support for decision makers with current information and appropriate response times. More decision makers benefit from improved information access.	

6.1.1 Introduction

This success story describes the Business Intelligence journey of Tetra Pak. The journey took different paths as Tetra Pak was confronted with a range of hurdles. A company's Business Intelligence journey often reflects their Business Intelligence maturity. This success story will discuss Tetra Pak's Business Intelligence initiatives, hurdles, learnings, and how these are represented in a Business Intelligence maturity model.

Tetra Pak won the Gartner Business Intelligence Award of Excellence in Asia Pacific in 2009 (Gartner, 2009b).

Companies today have come to realize the importance of providing accurate, relevant, and timely information – information that allows their organizational personnel to engage in effective decision-making practices. Aristotle Onassis, the famous Greek shipping tycoon once commented that "the secret of business is to know something that nobody else knows" (Lorange, 2001, p. 32). Evans and Wurster in their paper on Information Economics stated that "...information is the glue that holds business together" (Evans & Wurster, 1997, p. 72). Clearly, the consequences of treating information as a strategic resource and corporate investment can result in companies gaining industry-wide advantages that are reflected through increased reputation and profitability (Loshin, 2003, p. 11).

Accenture interviewed 163 executives from large enterprises around the world to identify how companies were using Enterprise Resource Planning (ERP) systems to improve business performance and the specific practices that resulted in sustained value creation (Davenport, Harris, & Cantrell, 2003). They found that the implementation of an enterprise-wide information system resulted in sustained value creation; however, some corporations realized far more comparable benefits than others. A more extensive follow-up study involving 450 executives from 370 companies identified the factors that drove value from their ERP system, as well how companies used these systems to enhance competitiveness and differentiation (Harris & Davenport, 2006). One of the key findings from this study was that improved decision making was the most sought-out and realized benefit. Related to this finding was that the top-performing companies aggressively used information and analytics to improve decision making. These findings are supported by Gartner, a leading business analyst firm, who conducted a worldwide survey of 1,500 Chief Information Officers and identified Business Intelligence (BI) as the number one technology priority for companies, followed by ERP systems (Gartner, 2008a). This is reflected in the forecasted BI vendor revenue expected to be $7.7 billion by 2012 (Gartner, 2008b).

Although BI is seen as a priority for many companies to survive in a competitive market, there is uncertainty as to the path to follow. Companies utilize BI in different ways, with varying levels of success. Companies often fail to realize expected benefits of BI and sometimes consider the project to be a failure in itself (Adelman & Moss, 2002; Atre, 2003; Chenoweth, Corral, & Demirkan, 2006; Hwang, Ku, Yen, & Cheng, 2004; Johnson, 2004). Gartner predicted that more than half of the Global 2,000 enterprises would fail to realize the capabilities of BI and would lose market share to the companies that did (Dresner, et al., 2002). A survey of 142 companies found that 41% of the respondents had experienced at least one BI project failure and only 15% of respondents believed that their BI initiative was a major success (Information Management and SourceMedia, 2003). Moss and Atre (2003) indicated that 60% of BI projects failed due to poor planning, poor project management, undelivered business requirements, or of those that were delivered, many were of poor quality. A number of authors believe that in many BI projects the information that is generated is inaccurate or irrelevant to the user's needs or, indeed, delivered too late to be useful (Ballou & Tayi, 1999; Strong, Lee, & Wang, 1997).

Experts have attempted to map BI usage and best practices to provide a roadmap for companies to move forward and maximize the benefits of their BI initiatives. One approach for these roadmaps has been the development of BI Maturity Models (ASUG, 2007; Eckerson, Performance dashboards: Measuring, monitoring, and managing your business, 2006; Hamer, 2005; Hewlett-Packard, 2009; Watson, Ariyachandra, & Matyska, 2001). The BI Maturity Models identify practices incorporating different stages which are associated with a company's BI progress and growth. Although there are many BI Maturity Models each of them differ in the practices and stages characterizing different levels of maturity. This case study will discuss one of the BI Maturity Models and its applicability to a company's BI practices.

6.1.2 BI Maturity Model

SAP (2010a) is the leading Enterprise Resource Planning (ERP) systems vendor and for the past decade has provided a Business Intelligence solution as an extension of their ERP system. The Americas SAP User Group (ASUG, 2010a) is the largest SAP user group in the world with more than 85,000 members from 2,000 companies. ASUG developed a series of benchmarking studies to assist its members to better understand the implementation and usage of ERP systems and associated solutions such as BI. In 2007, ASUG in conjunction with SAP developed a BI benchmarking initiative and has had more than 100 companies participate in the initiative (ASUG, 2010b). The key questions which the study was intended to answer were:

- How do companies leverage BI to drive business performance?
- For which business process is BI most critical?
- What are the key performance indicators of an effective BI environment?
- How much do top-performing companies invest in BI?
- What are the best practices that companies can adopt to drive effectiveness and efficiency of their BI environment?

Key metrics were designed to capture information to answer these questions. These details were compared to details from other participating companies as well as industry standards, allowing a range of BI benchmarks to be created. Part of the benchmarking derivation process was the mapping of companies to the ASUG maturity model. The ASUG Business Intelligence Maturity Model (Table 6.1) allows BI maturity to be classified by the following practices: Application Architecture, Standards and Processes, Governance, and Information and Analytics. Each of these practices is differentiated in four stages which describe different aspects of BI maturity.

Table 6.1 ASUG Business Intelligence Maturity Model

Stage	1	2	3	4
	Information dictatorship	Information anarchy	Information democracy	Information collaboration
Information and analytics	Requirements are driven from a limited executive group	KPIs and analytics are identified, but not well used	KPIs and analytics are identified and effectively used	KPIs and analytics are used to manage the full value chain
Governance	IT-driven BI	Business-driven BI evolving	BI competency centre developing	Enterprise wide BI governance with business leadership
Standards and processes	Do not exist or are not uniform	Evolving effort to formalize	Exist and are not uniform	Uniform, followed, and audited
Application architecture	BI "silos" for each business unit	Some shared BI applications	Consolidating and upgrading	Robust and flexible BI architecture

ASUG (2007)

Each year Gartner recognizes companies with their BI Award of Excellence that demonstrate results and innovation in business intelligence and performance management initiatives. Winners of the award are consistently referred to by Gartner analysts as best practice examples of the results that can be achieved with this technology with particular focus on business strategy, performance management, people and processes, analytical applications, BI platform, and the information management infrastructure (Gartner, 2008c). It is reasonable to expect that a company which achieved such an award would be very mature as per the model. The next part of the text will present the BI operations of Tetra Pak, the 2009 BI Award of Excellence recipient.

6.1.3 *Tetra Pak*

Tetra Pak began in the early 1950s as one of the first packaging companies for liquid milk. Today Tetra Pak is the world's leading food processing and packaging solutions company. Privately held, as of January 2009, the company had 74 sales offices, 53 factories, 21,640 employees and 2008 net sales of 8.8 billion Euros against production of 141 billion packages. Tetra Pak products are sold in more than 150 markets (Tetra Pak, 2010).

Tetra Pak made a first attempt to implement an SAP (2010a) Enterprise Resource Planning (ERP) System in 1994. Similar to many other companies, Tetra Pak's ERP system implementation was not as successful as they would have liked, and so the company decided to start again with a new approach.

In 1999, Tetra Pak was faced with a number of issues. The value chain extending from Tetra Pak's suppliers to its direct customers, retailers, and eventually consumers was rapidly consolidating, with pressure on prices and margins throughout the chain. Competition from plastic bottles, other carton package suppliers and "non-system" package suppliers was increasing. Nonetheless, Tetra Pak's uninterrupted growth story continued, with operational complexity growing in the global environment, pointing to a need for ERP to support a more efficient and effective global supply chain. In addition, there were fears about the year 2000 as some of the legacy systems were 20 years old.

In order to continue to thrive, Tetra Pak launched the biggest investment in its history – a global business process implementation program based on SAP solutions. The initiative was called the ISP program. Its goal was to rollout standard global business processes underpinned by SAP to all major markets, factories, and central organizations.

The ISP program rollout plan started with a small market to generate a quick win. Next in line were a few large central organizations where successful implementations allowed realization of large financial returns. The third cluster of markets to be implemented included two of Tetra Pak's largest markets representing a significant slice of Tetra Pak's worldwide sales. This implementation was rather challenging. The final result was successful, but the implementation required 13 months instead of the planned 7 months, with a corresponding cost overrun. Despite these setbacks, the implementation delivered a set of standard business processes that were running effectively in two major markets, and which were automated by SAP solutions.

The implementation of the data warehouse was a relatively small component of the overall ISP program. During the early phases of the ISP program, Tetra Pak had a sharp focus on automating the transactional steps in its core order fulfillment processes, and one impact was that the data warehouse was not the top priority. The data warehouse was designed to be a large repository of business data based on the premise that if data was collected and stored in one location then the business users would access it for their business information needs.

However, data warehouse usage was rather low. A major reason for this was that the technical architecture selected was not sufficiently reliable – every night, it required an extract from ERP into a staging area, followed by transformation and load into the data warehouse, followed by synchronization to regional data marts, and ending with refreshed reports on the end-user PCs. The lesson learned was that middle managers want daily information on their desktops in a reliable way first thing every morning.

In 2005, the Finance Global Business Process Owner, the VP Group Financial Control, and the IT Delivery Director realized that after several years of multi-million euro investments, the current data warehouse was not providing the expected benefits and arranged a meeting with the Chief Financial Officer (CFO) to discuss the various options. The CFO agreed there needed to be a change of direction and in 2006 a new Business Intelligence (BI) initiative was commenced. The project was referred to as "Business Warehouse" to differentiate it from the previous project.

In order to guarantee reliability, Tetra Pak decided to simplify the technical architecture. Information would be extracted from ERP and loaded into SAP's Business Warehouse (SAP BW (SAP, 2010b)). End users would use Internet Explorer to access reports based on SAP Business Explorer web component, and it worked.

The Business Warehouse project had two early make-or-break milestones. The first was to replace a legacy financial consolidation system by getting the global legal financial accounting data into the SAP BW system and ensure its correctness. The second milestone was to replace the legacy financial consolidation and management accounting system with Cartesis,[1] provide management information reports in SAP BW based on the fully consolidated management level information, and ensure that the financials reconciled exactly with other key performance indicators (KPIs) including business process performance measurements. At this point, the implementation team turned its attention to its own internal processes, delivering quarterly releases with impeccable quality, reliability, and business content.

After both of these milestones were achieved, business usage of the "Business Warehouse" started to grow dramatically. However, there was one remaining technical problem concerning the response time for reports. While in some cases, the response time was acceptable at less than a minute, other responses took up to 20 min, which was often unacceptable.

Fortunately, SAP, in conjunction with their hardware partners, IBM and HP, developed a "bolt on" infrastructure solution to improve the performance of reporting. The SAP Business Warehouse Accelerator (SAP, 2010c) (BWA) utilizing blade computing technology has been reported to improve reporting by up to 200 times faster (IBM, 2008). In early 2009, Tetra Pak implemented the BWA to improve their reporting performance. The reporting response time was reduced from an average of 20 s down to 5 s. The last hurdle to achieve the holy grail of a "single source of truth" for Tetra Pak business information was cleared.

As part of the Business Warehouse project, Tetra Pak considered there were three important phases to their BI journey. The first phase was about getting the necessary infrastructure and data in place to provide some quick wins, while at the same time providing a foundation for future development. Prior to the implementation of the Business Warehouse project, Tetra Pak had a fragmented corporate reporting applications environment. The second phase required implementing proper BI governance along with a robust and predictable new report development process – from collection and prioritization of requirements, to creation and deployment of reports, to training of end users in the business content. A standardized reporting template was developed which included charts, data tables, filters, and the ability to change the dimensions for analysis. All reports were developed based on this template and thus once a user was familiar with the functionality and navigation of one report they could then apply this knowledge to any other report. The only

[1] Cartesis was acquired by Business Objects and Business Objects was acquired by SAP in 2007 (Wikipedia, 2010a).

training that was required was in relation to the business content of the report and its applicability. The governance standardization enabled a best practice approach to ensure a successful BI solution. The final phase was to build upon the foundation laid down by the first two phases to extend the coverage and usage of BI to comprehensively support management and the business.

A major factor of the BI initiative's success was due to the agreement by senior management as to the role of BI within Tetra Pak. There were at least two aspects to this. First, Tetra Pak has its "business performance equation" which states that "Business Performance = Process × People × Tools." Over the years, Tetra Pak has obtained many measurable improvements in business results by making sure that their processes are well designed, that the processes are executed by competent people, and that the appropriate steps in the business processes are automated using tools. BI systems are tools to automate the provision of information to the right people at the right business process step. BI reports often provide measurements of business performance and business process effectiveness. Second, Tetra Pak has shown that a good business strategy implemented through sound business processes which are continuously improved by business process improvement projects including process, people, and IT tools components improves business performance. BI's role is a crucial one – measuring the business performance improvements, the business process improvements, and the effectiveness of the business process improvement projects.

In simpler terms, Tetra Pak agreed on why it needed BI. Like any company, it needed consistent facts about customers, products, suppliers, past performance, and future forecasts – a single source of truth. They needed to measure business performance and business process effectiveness. Finally, as the ISP program was the single largest investment in the company's history, until an effective BI system was in place, Tetra Pak was not able to fully exploit the business information hidden in its ERP system, and therefore was not obtaining full benefits from the investment.

As part of the Business Warehouse project, Tetra Pak consulted with Gartner in an attempt to identify "best practices." One recommendation was the establishment of a Business Intelligence Competency Centre (BICC). A BICC is responsible for developing the overall strategic plan and priorities for BI. It defines the requirements, including data quality and governance, and helps the organization to interpret and apply the insight to business decisions (Gartner, 2006). Tetra Pak considered that a BICC was essential if it was to achieve an enterprise view of the data and reporting requirements.

To fully capture the company's requirements, Tetra Pak's BICC was comprised of two structures. The first structure consisted of:

- Global Business Process Owners/Global Business Process Drivers (GPO/GPD): This group was responsible for designing, implementing, and continuously improving Tetra Pak's global business processes. As Tetra Pak is convinced that IT tools mainly serve to automate steps in their business processes, Tetra Pak decided that Global Business Process Owners are the only people who are allowed to request and prioritise IT projects. This resulted in IT having a very focused role, which led to much higher effectiveness and efficiency.

- Business Information Management (BIM): This consisted of five full-time senior business analysts who had a good understanding of the business and the capabilities of BI.
- Global Information Management (GIM): This project team consisted of between 15 and 25 people and provided the technical BI expertise. The BIM and GIM worked closely together with common goals.
- Global Information Management Service Delivery Team (GIM SDT): This group involved approximately 12 people and was responsible for ensuring the availability and an ongoing support for reports once they were developed.
- Market Cluster Finance Leaders, MIS Coordinators and BI Superusers: This group involved about 100 people in part-time roles. They were responsible for deploying BI reports to those business staff who could benefit from them. Their role was to act as change agents and encourage the adoption and use of the BI solution.

The BICC is overseen by a steering committee made up of senior management and their ongoing support is considered essential to the success of the BI initiative.

A priority of the BICC is not just to gather requirements and develop reports but also the deployment of those reports and the realization of their value. The process of gathering requirements, developing reports, deployment, and report value realization has been documented to ensure that the process is standardized, repeatable, and clearly understood across the company. This has enabled the process to be refined and improved. A timeline for the report development and deployment process was developed and publicized. This facilitated business areas planning and scheduling their reporting requests. Reports are rolled out quarterly.

Tetra Pak's approach to BI has enabled them to gain a high level of success for their BI initiative. In December 2008, they had approximately 1,800 active users representing about 9% of the employees. By June 2009, the number of active users had increased to 2,600 (12.5%). By April 2010, Tetra Pak decided that report usage would be the new measurement of value and found that more than 260,000 reports were requested in Q1, with end users performing more than 900,000 navigations. Tetra Pak believes that usage is an accurate proxy for value because only when users perceive the BI system to be of value, they use it actively.

To ensure that Tetra Pak's approach to BI is best practice they developed a "BI Effectiveness Scorecard." This scorecard consists of a number of assessable components including:

- Business case and vision: (1) Single source of truth, (2) business analysis across borders, processes, businesses, (3) analysts move from data gathering to real business analysis, (4) reduce total reporting cost.
- Executive support: CFO provides visible public support.
- Alignment to business strategy and business processes: Only Global Business Process Owners can request BI or CPM projects.
- Alignment and working practices, business, and IT: Business Transformation Process aligns strategy, process, and organization. Business owns scope prioritization and outcomes.

- Extended BICC: Central team with both business and technical expertise. Network from the center Business Transformation Officers and Market MIS Coordinators provide the link to adoption.
- Predictability and- robust and effective delivery methodology: Compliance to IT project and service processes as a subset of Business Transformation process.

Tetra Pak believes that their BI approach has satisfied the above criteria. However, the above scorecard only reinforces that the correct approach has been implemented. A further scorecard, the "BI Value Scorecard" was developed to quantify the BI impact on the business. This scorecard including measures is displayed in Table 6.2.

Tetra Pak has noticed that due to their approach to BI and the value generated that different areas of the business are placing greater demands on the BI group for new initiatives. This increased demand for BI is reflected by the last measure in the above scorecard.

BI is used to measure business performance, business process performance, and the effectiveness of the business process improvement projects, including business process re-design projects. When Tetra Pak runs business process improvement

Table 6.2 Business Intelligence Value Scorecard

Measure	Score	Comment
Global Enterprise-wide adoption – the ultimate measure of BI success – % of employees as active BI users	>10%	More than 10% of employees are active users, expect to reach 15% in 2009. About 90,000 reports and 300,000 navigations per month. 20% of employees are registered users
% coverage in BI of business processes and business performance measurements. Single source of truth across borders, processes, businesses	100%	Business performance measurements are available for all business processes and all business units. Expanding coverage within processes and units. Used in all markets and in the center
Response time	5 s	Worldwide: all management reports in 15 s or less, average navigation step below 5 s
Reliability, consistency, and quality	7 AM	All managers have fresh data at 7 AM their time worldwide. Information is correct and broadening. Adoption makes sure it stays correct
Easy to use – low training cost	High user adoption	Information portal based on geography, business roles and business processes; standard layouts make it easy to understand and use
Enables next steps – new major business information initiatives	Global information projects	Successful major new information projects – brand information back to our customers, worldwide alignment on sales forecasting

projects above a specified size, they are referred to as Business Transformation Projects. BI allows Tetra Pak to measure improvements. For example, one project reduced lead time for certain capital equipment from 140 to 47 days, and another reduced lead time for packaging material from 15 to 5 days.

Accordingly, BI is considered essential to business sustainability and growth at Tetra Pak. In fact, a central BI system, a single source of truth, has become a part of daily life for more than 12% of Tetra Pak's employees.

In relation to the ASUG BI Maturity Model, Tetra Pak would be considered a very mature company. KPIs and analytics are used extensively to manage the entire business. The BICC has enabled the company to develop enterprise wide governance and BI leadership while at the same time implementing standardized processes and standards to support the BI initiative. This standardization also applies to their BI architecture. These BI practices are aligned with the highest level of maturity in the ASUG model, Information Collaboration.

6.1.4 Conclusion

In conclusion, the reader may want to consider the following quotations from the Gartner's press release about the BI Excellence Award. Speaking at the SAP Australian User Group Summit, Christopher Rowley, Tetra Pak's Singapore-based director of customer management and corporate reporting systems, said that ensuring that the business, not the information technology (IT) department, had ownership of business intelligence and took responsibility for the outcomes was essential to success (Gartner, 2009b):

- We decided some time ago that there would be no more IT projects, only business projects. The first driver for our BI implementation was quite simple to measure and improve our business process performance. Secondly, like any business, we need the facts about our customers, products and suppliers, a single source of truth, to enable better forecasting.
- We have not found any silver bullets. You need to have the right people in place to deliver the project and ensure quality and consistency. You need to ensure that the system has a fast response time and is easy to use so that people adopt it. And you need to ensure that the system will support new business information projects, for example, delivering useful information back to our customers.

Mr. Bertram, Gartner managing vice president and chair of the 2009 Gartner BI Summit, said the quality of the presentations from the finalists were outstanding and demonstrated global best practices (Gartner, 2009b). He further stated that "this award program shows that successful BI can be done. Despite the obvious differences in scale, industry, and business strategies, the approach of all three finalists was remarkably similar. BI must be driven by the business, not IT; it must present a single version of the truth; and it must be easy for end-users to adopt. The organization must also be committed to change, often deep cultural change, for real improvements and benefits to be realized."

6.2 Improvement in After Sales Support via Remote-Service at Daimler AG

Authors	
Michael Jungbauer	Manager After Sales Support Daimler AG 002-R822-GSP/OIS, 70546 Stuttgart/Germany michael.jungbauer@daimler.com
Prof. Dr. Arndt Borgmeier	Professor Aalen University Beethovenstr. 1, 73430 Aalen/Germany arndt.borgmeier@htw-aalen.de
Organization	
Name	Daimler AG
Industry	Automotive
Size (# employees)	256.000 (worldwide)
Website	http://www.daimler.com
Scope of Success Story	
Geography	Germany, Austria, USA
Functional Area	After-Sales Support
KPIs	Process velocity, service process cost
Overview	
Daimler AG was able to improve customer service while reducing cost at the same time by introducing Remote Service in the After Sales Support.	
Business requirement	
Further develop operational excellence and superior customer experience.	
Solution	
Implemented a Remote Service in the After Sales Support.	
Benefits	
Improved Mean Time to Repair and reduced process cost.	

6.2.1 Introduction

After the introduction of the mass manufacturing in the 1920s, the lean production in the 1980s, the automobile industry is currently experiencing a fierce competition over market shares. An impeccable customer service before, during, and after the purchase can contribute to an improved customer satisfaction which consequently can lead to an increased customer loyalty and profitable growth for an organization.

This success story will focus specifically on the After-Sales Support at Daimler. In 2009, a pilot program successfully introduced the use of a Remote-Service solution in Germany, Austria, and the USA. The Remote-Service was introduced to complement the traditional service. Remote-Services are defined as industrial, product related services, that support an underlying technical system (here: automobile). They are provided using real-time bidirectional telecommunication, e.g., in form of a remote diagnosis of an automobile via the internet.

The introduction of the Remote-Service leads to a faster solution of the repair problem and a reduced number of customer visits to a garage. Remote-Services have the potential to create benefits for both parties, the service providers as well as the service customers. The user of Remote-Services, typically a repair shop can, for example, benefit from a faster diagnosis of vehicle malfunctions leading to a reduction of the service costs. The service customer benefits from the service consuming less time.

6.2.2 The After-Sales division at Daimler

The After-Sales division of Daimler (Global Service & Parts, GSP) is responsible for Mercedes-Benz Cars, Daimler Trucks, Mercedes-Benz Vans, and Daimler Buses and includes a variety of brands as displayed in Fig. 6.1.

The After-Sales division of Daimler (Global Service & Parts, GSP) is responsible for Mercedes-Benz Cars, Daimler Trucks, Mercedes-Benz Vans and Daimler Buses and includes a variety of brands as displayed in The After-Sales business units supply the service companies and workshops with parts as well as necessary technical, workshop, parts and customer information and workshop equipment. The After-Sales business units also provide extensive support for the workshops to assist them with the maintenance and repair of vehicles. This support is intended to enable a faster repair and maintenance for the customers, ideally within a single customer visit.

6.2.3 Measuring the Improvement of the Customer Experience

Since one of the strategic goals is providing a superior customer experience the question would be how to measure it. The satisfaction of customers depends on their service expectations which differ from person to person and are influenced by personal needs, beliefs about what is possible, perceived service alterations, and situational factors.

A challenge with customer Service is to ensure a focus on the key areas and use meaningful Key Performance Indicators (KPIs) to measure the performance. The focus must be on those KPIs that will deliver the most value to the overall strategic objective, e.g., quality, cost saving, customer satisfaction, etc. In regards to any single business intervention, the improvement should be measurable.

Time is a critical success factor for service organizations, specifically when customers have to be physically present to receive the service or have expectations about how long a particular service should take. One of the problems with services

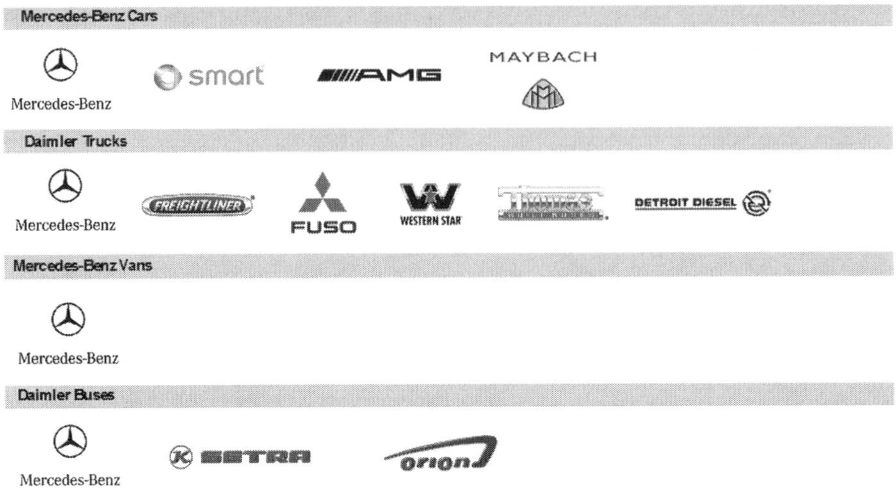

Fig. 6.1 Daimler brand portfolio (Daimler 2010, p. 4)

are that they cannot be stocked for sale while the necessary facilities, equipment, and labor needs to be kept available and this creates cost also when it is unused. Therefore it is a challenge for service organizations to match demand with the appropriate capacity without having customer waiting periods to be too long during peak periods. In these days, customers are increasingly time sensitive, and speed is often a key element in good service. In competitive markets, service managers are therefore continually looking for ways to improve their service without compromising the quality of the service. Another reason why time is a key aspect with services is because it is an important denominator to determine the cost of the services performed.

The contribution of the introduction of Remote-Services, presented here, was measured by several KPIs. One leading indicator was the Mean Time to Repair (MTTR), the average time between the occurrence of an incident and its resolution. Another leading one was the average process cost per service incident. Customer satisfaction as a lagging indicator, indirectly affected by the leading indicators, was measured as well.

6.2.4 Enabling a Solution for the After-Sales Support via Remote-Service

The central tools for the worldwide support with vehicle repair and service are workshop information and diagnosis systems in particular. Diagnosis systems are used for the identification of vehicle problems and crucial when it comes to technologically complex vehicles. While the vehicle is connected to the diagnosis system via cable (LAN) or a wireless connection (WLAN) all existing error codes can be analyzed and fixed immediately.

Workshop information, a combination of information about replacement parts and a description of the repair process as well as individual information about the vehicle, can be used to solve a vehicle malfunction based on the diagnosis. This process helps to speed up the problem solving, ideally allowing to provide the service within a single workshop visit of the customer.

In cases where the workshop could not solve the problem on its own, centralized support was offered for 2nd and 3rd-level support to solve more complex issues. The service problem was typically reported on the phone, sometimes supplemented by a fax with a computer printout. A direct access of the centralized support personnel to the diagnosis and workshop information systems was not possible because of technological problems. Uniform standards and general accepted solutions were missing, so that an abundance of different Remote-Service concepts were pursued by the workshops. Consequently, Daimler had to develop and implement its own Remote-Service concept in order to improve the situation. The technical requirements of a Remote-Service solution for Daimler were:

- Standardized tool
- Web browser based
- Web link to the Remote-Service solution (SSL)
- Net connection over xDSL, LAN/WAN or WLAN/WAN, Internet
- Integration of Daimler Corporate network (DCCN) possibly, UMTS
- Independent use of IP addresses
- No individual user administration for the workshops
- Automatic software installation and updates

These requirements were based on the information gathered in the workshops and the requirements of the Daimler AG, e.g., security aspects. Once the Remote-Service solution was implemented, the telephone contact between the workshop and the support level was complemented by the Remote-Service access, following the process steps as displayed in Fig. 6.2.

6.2.5 The Service Process

To explore the potential uses of Remote-Service in the After-Sales sector a detailed understanding of the service process is helpful. Basically, the service can be divided into six consecutive process steps (see Fig. 6.3). The delay of one process step therefore causes a delay of the overall process and thus all process steps are on the critical path.

The support accompanies the entire process. The support organization operates in different layers (see Fig. 6.4). All levels are connected by a problem management

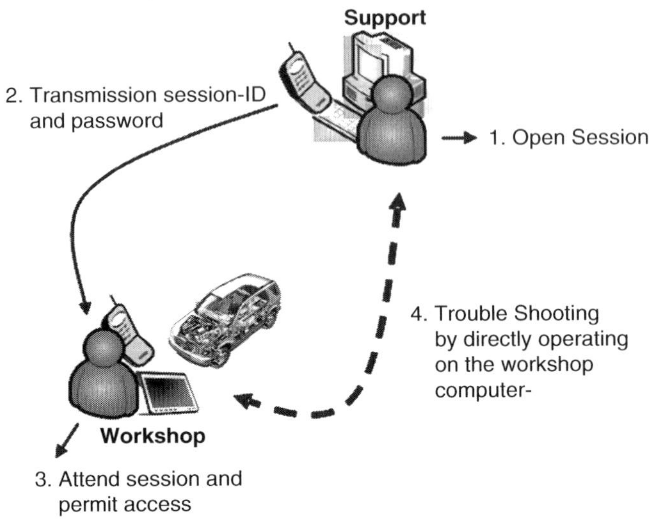

Fig. 6.2 Access by remote service

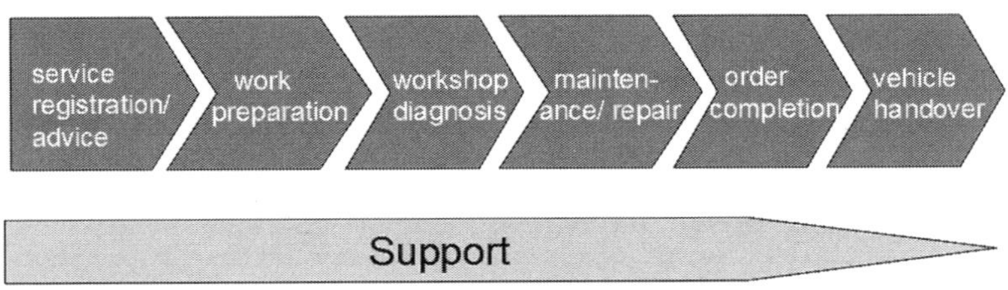

Fig. 6.3 Service process and accompanying support

system, so that the further processing in the subsequent levels, if the problem could not be solved already, is supported via this system.

Remote services with direct access to the information of the diagnosis and workshop system reduce the number of time-consuming call-backs (loops) and thereby reduce process duration (see Fig. 6.5). A positive side effect of the new workflow is that the support requester in the workshop participates and assists in the production of the service by providing his input.

6.2.6 Productivity Improvements via Remote-Services

Three countries (U.S., Germany and Austria) within the Daimler AG were selected in 2009 to pilot the new Remote-Service solution. It proved to be a success. The number of on-site visits to solve complex service problems were reduced significantly which lowered the associated travel and staff cost in addition to the shortened

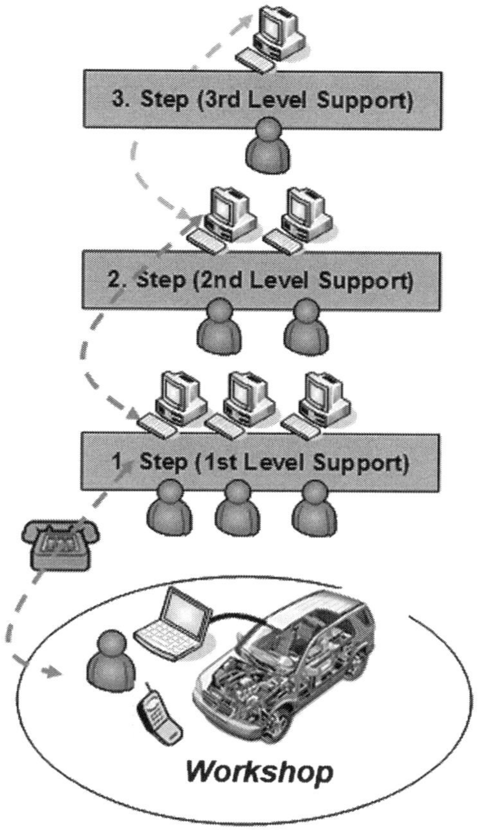

Fig. 6.4 Multi-level support process

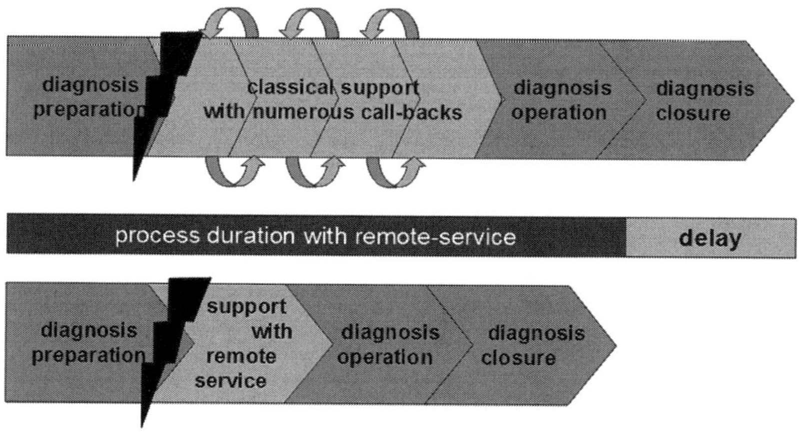

Fig. 6.5 Effects of remote service on subprocess diagnosis

Mean Time to Repair, which led to an additional cost saving (see Fig. 6.6). A quick Return on Investment (ROI) was reached because the upfront investment, e.g., licences, was comparatively low.

For the actual fiscal year 2010 especially, the on-site support costs are expected to be reduced. Now that the improvement has been proven in the pilot countries, it is intended to support the implementation of this process worldwide within the next years.

6.2.7 Conclusion

The introduction of the Remote-Services proved to be an improvement in productivity, improving output quality while reducing cost. The benefits realized by the organization is a reduction of cost and the benefit for the service customer is a reduction in the time to repair.

"Divide et impera" (latin) meaning "share (the benefits from Remote-Services) and rule" the competitive automobile market – we would like to add.

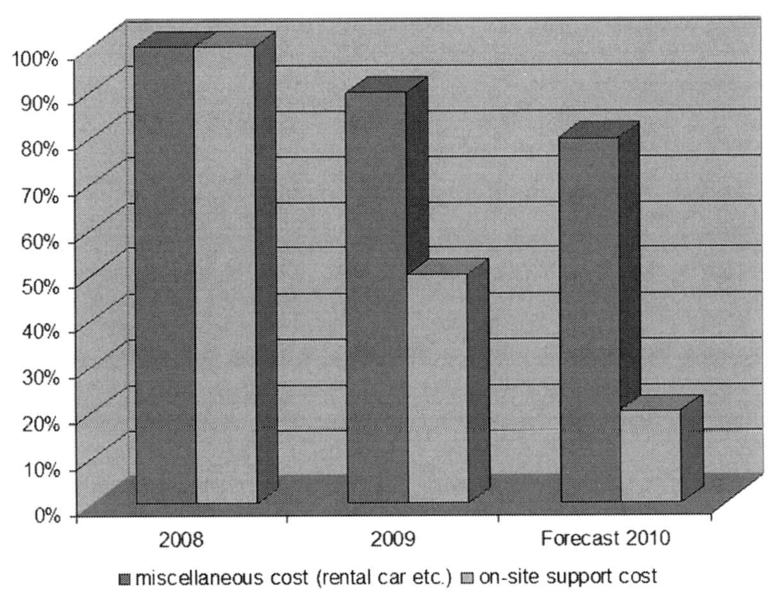

Fig. 6.6 Reduction of cost in the pilot locations (in percent)

6.3 Implementing a Balanced Scorecard to Improve the Performance of Public Administration: The Case of the City Aix les Bains and Its Social Cohesion Policy

Authors	
Catherine Fabbri	Project manager at the office of the General Director (Aix-les-Bains), and Urban social manager at the urban community of Aix-les-Bains (Communauté d'agglomération du Lac du Bourget) Mairie d'Aix-les-Bains, Place Maurice Mollard, BP 348, 73103 Aix les Bains Cedex Savoie-France c.fabbri@aixlesbains.fr
Pascale Fressoz	Director Millenium Enterprises Le Cropt 74230 Thônes/France pascalefressoz@hotmail.com
Organization	
Name	City of Aix les Bains, Savoie, France
Industry	Public Sector
Size (# employees)	597 (27.923 citizens)
Website	http://www.aixlesbains.fr
Scope of Success Story	
Geography	France
Functional Area	Social Cohesion and City Policy
KPIs	Unemployment rate, social housing, social satisfaction
Overview	
Elaborating a territory project based on the Balanced Scorecard methodology in order to improve social cohesion.	
Business requirement	
Create a shared global strategy and an action plan.	
Solution	
Develop and implement the strategic planning based on the 5 axis (economy, healthcare, citizenship, housing, education) with the Balanced Scorecard and the "Nine Steps to Success" methodology.	
Benefits	
Improved social and territorial cohesion, optimized organization, better resources sharing, increased performance.	

6.3.1 Introduction

Today's organizations need to be both strategically and operationally excellent to survive and meet tomorrow's social, economic, and environmental challenges! As mentioned by Drucker (2006b), p. 147, doing the *right things* and doing *things right* involve a good alignment between the strategic and operational dimensions. A statement from Howard Rohm, CEO of the Balanced Scorecard Institute (2010a) summarizes: "It is a balancing act which requires the development of good business strategies and efficient operations to deliver the products and services required to implement the strategies." Making the link between strategy, operations, and budget is moreover a coherence and precision act. Performance improvement and reform pressure on public sector organizations, mandate those organizations continually worry about executing their strategy well. In this context, a modern management tool, used mainly in the private sector, the Balanced Scorecard and its "Nine Steps to Success" methodology (see Fig. 6.8) has been used in the public sector in a city of Savoie, Aix-les-Bains, to become an example at European Level.

Although the City of Aix-les Bains is very attractive, ideally located between lake and mountains in the heart of Savoy in France near Swiss border and renowned for its baths, an important part of the population, living in few districts, are suffering. These citizens are not well integrated from a social and economic point of view and consider themselves as being victims of discrimination.

Social housing represents more than 15.7% of the total housing. Moreover, more than 14% of the citizens live under the poverty level (based on 871 euros in 2007). They would have been more than 21% without family and social allowance funds. A specifically high concentration of persons depending on social welfare is living in districts Sierroz, Franklin, and Marlioz. Those people are considered being in high difficulty according to the rates determined by the French National Office of the Economic Statistics (INSEE) (INSEE, 2010). Besides, this social group causes a large number of incivilities and dissatisfaction to the other residents of Aix-les-Bains thereby strengthening their exclusion and violent behavior.

Aix-les-Bains and the Préfecture de Savoie were not willing to accept this status quo. They were aiming at defining a public policy contributing to "Live Better Together" in Aix-les-Bains. The major axis of this policy known as CUCS (Contrat Urbain de Cohésion Sociale) as defined by the former Minister of Social Cohesion, Jean-Louis Borloo, are the following five pillars of excellence: employment and economic development, healthcare for all, education success, citizenship and prevention of incivility, housing and living environment.

To improve this situation, the City wished to answer the following question: "How can we reinforce the social cohesion and promote equality of chances on the territory in synergy with all the actors and the other related programs?" The mayor of Aix-les-Bains, Dominique Dord, even expected that a social cohesion initiative would improve the effectiveness of the Urban Renovation Program. In order to find the answer to reinforce social cohesion, the steering committee of the new CUCS initiative had the mission to:

- Define strategic objectives
- Mobilize the required resources and set up the implementation task force
- Ensure the good coherence of the project with the other related programs in the territory (Local housing Plan, Local Urbanism Plan, Local Council for Safety and Prevention of Delinquency, Program for Educational Success, Integrated urban Project, etc.)
- Set up actions to be implemented
- Evaluate the results

The steering committee also had to watch the convergence between the European, national, regional, departmental, and local policies which contribute to social cohesion. The European policy included eight specific objectives which did align with those of the CUCS quite well (see Fig. 6.7).

The Social Cohesion Policy has been rapidly reviewed and improved to become a "global integrated urban and territorial project," strongly supported by the European Commission. Aix-les-Bains gained a strong financial support (more than 5.5 millions of euros) from the EU and the Rhône-Alpes Region, FEDERE program, and stand as an example. It has been presented in Paris (to 63 heads of departments) and in Brussels (to leaders of countries), in November 2010, for its capacity to remain global, transversal, and integrated and demonstrate tangible results for the urban population.

European Objectives	CUCS Objectives
Reduce the risk of poverty and social exclusion by a strong commitment in favor of employment, of the accommodation and the equality of chances	Facilitate the equality of chance in each of the CUCS fields of intervention (employment, housing, healthcare, educational success, citizenship)
Guarantee a high level of social cohesion on the whole territory with the respect of the cultural diversity	Support all the actions which facilitate the social cohesion and encourage social mixity
Promote a non discriminatory labor market facilitating participation of women and migrants	Fight against discriminations, in particular for employment and housing
Lead a policy of integration for the migrants and their families	Facilitate the social link for the inhabitants
Support the individuals the most isolated from the labor market to lead them towards a sustainable employment	Strengthen the access to employment and revitalize the economic development
Encourage the participation and the citizenship of the disabled persons	Intervene in favor of public with disabilities

Fig. 6.7 Objectives of the European Commission and of the CUCS

6.3.2 The Implementation Approach

Several questions remained to be answered before getting the initiative off the ground to reinforce social cohesion and promote the equality of chances: How to make the link between strategic dimension "doing the right thing" and the operational dimension, "doing things right" in public administration? How can we make sure that the strategic key elements are aligned with the field work? How, in the eyes of the elected representatives and their executives, should we make the link between performance measures and political objectives? How should we measure financial and nonfinancial elements, such as human capital, internal processes, and citizens requirements and how do we know if the strategic objectives have been reached? Which methodology could be followed to reach the set objectives?

An adapted version of the Balanced Scorecard (BSC) concept, a performance measurement approach developed by Kaplan and Norton (1992) in 1992, was chosen for this initiative. The methodology was called "Nine Steps to Success," developed by Howard Rohm (see Fig. 6.8).

It allows linking the strategic vision of the elected representatives to the operational objectives of the initiative. This approach also helps to face a major difficulty in many implementations – the execution challenge!

Using the Nine Steps to Success approach helped identifying the real issues and challenges, formalizing a vision, identifying the desired outcomes, clarifying specific objectives, the performance measures as well as the initiatives. All this was done to promote the global objective "Live Better Together." We did not focus on the IT side in this first phase of the project, e.g., establishing a business intelligence

Fig. 6.8 Nine steps to make Balanced Scorecard methodology successful (Balanced Scorecard Institute, 2010b)

infrastructure for reporting, knowing that a new IT system would be implemented in a near future.

The objectives of the initiative were defined as:

1. Identify the significant issues and challenges for organizations, diagnose its environment (internal and external), analyse the strengths, the weaknesses, the opportunities, and the threats.
2. Define the vision, the mission, and the values. Move from a culture of "means" to a culture of "results." Define a strategy map including the pillars of excellence (see Fig. 6.10).
3. Define performance measures of relevance from different perspectives: citizens (customers, users, beneficiaries, the other stakeholders), finance, internal process (quality, deadlines, production tools, ecology, communication), and organizational capacity (human resources, information system, infrastructures).
4. Identify the links of cause and effect between performance measures.
5. Define and communicate the required outcomes, specific objectives, implemented actions, performance indicators and cascade them by specifying them at all levels of the organization.
6. Regular evaluations of the level of objectives achievement.

6.3.3 The Use of the Balanced Scorecard to Define and Execute the Social Cohesion Policy in Aix-les-Bains

The initiative was started in November 2006. The consulting organization Millenium Enterprises was selected to assist with the implementation. One hundred and sixty four persons from 83 organizations had participated in 15 workshops between November 2006 and January 2007 to define the CUCS on the basis of five priority axis and three transverse objectives (see Fig. 6.9).

The project kicked off with a diagnostic (based on indicators related to housing, unemployment, incivilities, etc.) and strategic analysis, which had led to a photograph of the situation at that time: an understanding of the needs of the citizens, a gathering of perceptions along ideas of the actors (politicians, actual and future beneficiaries, partners), and an identification of areas of improvement to achieve a better social well-being.

The following strategic foundations and elements of a Social Cohesion Policy for the period 2007–2012 were developed in this process:

Mission: Reinforce social cohesion and encourage innovative and efficient actions enabling access to employment, housing, educative success, citizenship, prevention of delinquency, and healthcare. More generally, improve the well-being of people with greatest level of difficulty and improve the living-better-together concept on the territory.

Vision: A strong engagement to make Aix-les-Bains a city, which shows more solidarity.

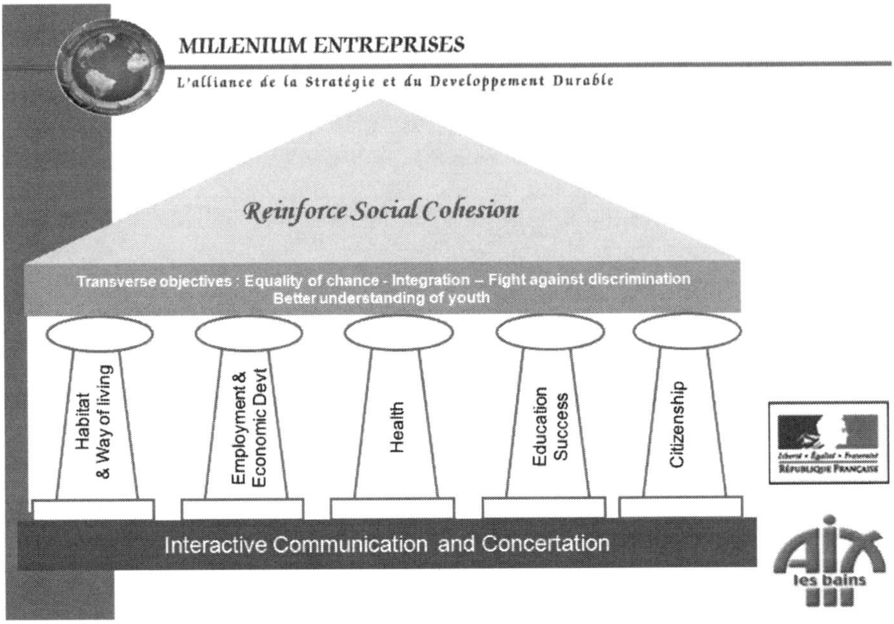

Fig. 6.9 Social cohesion pillars of excellence for a social cohesion strategy

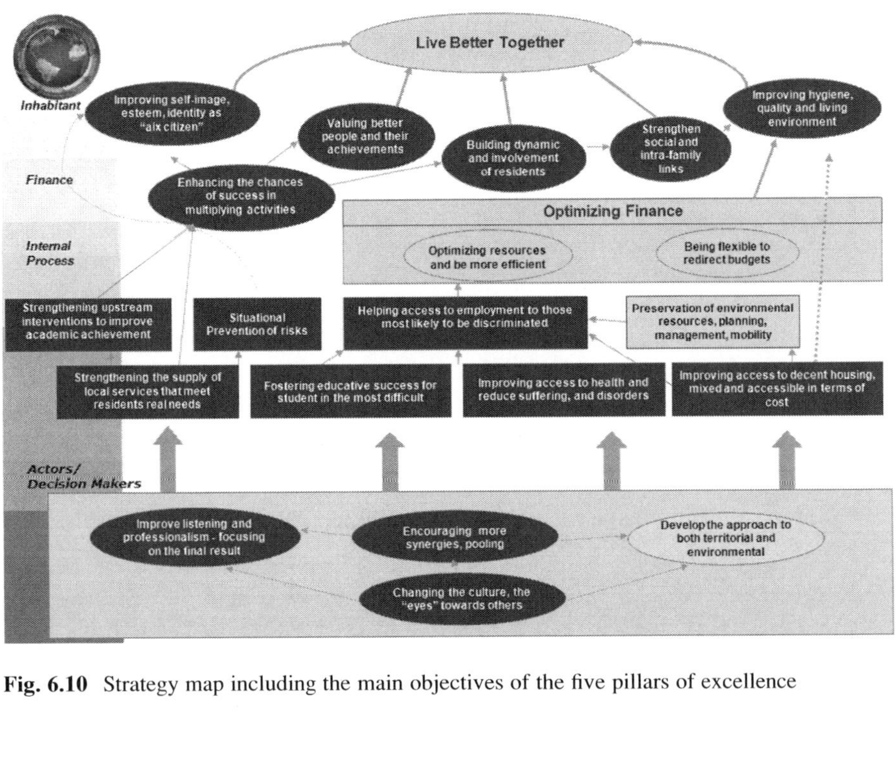

Fig. 6.10 Strategy map including the main objectives of the five pillars of excellence

Values: Proximity, solidarity, respect.
Objectives: Reinforce access to employment and boost economic development, facilitate housing access, and improve the living environment, encourage the educative success, offer a better access to healthcare and suitable responses to the needs of residents, value the citizenship and better prevent delinquency, lead transverse actions for social cohesion.

The main strategic initiatives of the project were defined as:

- Residents perspective:
  - Implication of the citizens as beneficiaries and even more as actors of the implemented programs.
  - Mediation in suburb areas and shelters for the youth and residents.
  - Educational workshops and integration projects to reinforce citizenship.
  - Personalized support for business creation and for encouraging entrepreneurship and new initiatives. Economic autonomy.
  - Nearby services, integrated facilities, funds for micro-loans.
  - Sports and arts: a chance for all (football class with special working schedule, rugby, sport initiation, sensitization to music, etc.).
- Finance perspective:
  - Pool of services.
  - Physical and financial monitoring of actions.
  - Mobilization of European funds to improve financial sources.
- Internal process perspective:
  - Reporting, monitoring, performance management, evaluation of programs which contribute to social cohesion. Organization (steering committee, technical group, working group).
  - Communication plan to inform residents regarding the use of resources (water, electricity, recycling).
  - Develop, consolidate, and quantify the offer related to insertion.
  - Set up a place dedicated to housing access.
- Organizational capacity perspective:
  - Sensibilization of the execution and decision-making actors regarding discrimination.
  - Training program for management team and staff at reception desk in contact with people in high difficulty.
- Organize a transversal way of working between services.

This process allowed developing, formalizing, and validating a real action-oriented plan for the territory. The methodology helped to:

- Align vision and mission with citizens' expectations and the daily work of elected representative and managers of local authorities.
- Manage the execution of the strategy.
- Assess operational efficiency improvement.

The developed CUCS (Contrat Urbain de Cohésion Sociale) was signed in March 2007, and immediately upon the signature, the implementation had started with a continuous monitoring and evaluation of the objectives dedicated to benefit social cohesion.

6.3.4 Strategy Map of Social Cohesion Including the Five Pillars of Excellence

In the public sector, it is often easier to measure efficiency of a single project rather than comprehensive strategy of public policy. The question at hand was how to measure a social cohesion objective with the aim of equal opportunities and "Live Better Together" as displayed in Fig. 6.10?

The following performance measures were defined:

- Global perspective:
  - Social satisfaction on the image given by districts to the residents.
- Citizen perspective:
  - Delinquency rate.
  - Families benefiting from social housing funds.
  - Unemployment rate (per category: youth, women, etc.).
  - People benefiting from financial support (Minimum Income).
- Finance perspective:
  - Sharing human and financial resources.
  - Increase of new financial sources (Communauté d'Agglomération du Lac du Bourget: CALB, Fonds Européen de Développement Régional: FEDER, etc.).
- Internal process perspective:
  - Perception of the residents regarding the city services offers (nearby services, improvement of housing, healthcare, educative success, employment, education, sportive and cultural activities, access to rights, mediation, living environment.).
- Organizational capacity perspective:
  - Number of internal actors dedicated to social cohesion.
  - Number of training programs reinforcing management competences and reception of public in great difficulty.
  - Number of actors trained to become sensitive to discrimination.

While it is important to identify a performance measure for each individual objective it is also essential to identify an indicator for the overall objective. The consulting firm Millennium Enterprises had recommended to the City of Aix-les-Bains to analyze and compare "the well-being in the city and in the districts" in order to evaluate the performance measurement for "Live Better Together" versus the overall goal of social cohesion. This was intended to identify the differences between some districts area and the rest of the city. It was agreed to establish an overall goal of Social Cohesion and use a Social Cohesion Index to measure the social well-being.

This Social Cohesion Index can be used to scale the "Live Better Together" between several parts of the town. For example, if the well-being in the city is 3 on a scale of 0 (negative) to 3 (very good) and that the well-being in districts area is 1.5, then the objective is to increase the value in the districts area by 1.5; therefore, the level of well-being will be the same in the city and districts area, no matter the place of residence.

Measuring the performance in different areas can help to better identify the progress of implementations policy. Identify differences between different groups, e.g., the city and the districts area, can help to set better quantifiable targets to achieve. Consistency in how KPIs are measured is the foundation of making such comparisons. As rightly mentioned by Dominique Dord, Deputy and Mayor of Aix les Bains, the impact of urban policy will have a positive effect on all city residents (a feeling of security, etc.), and vice versa the impact of citizens' behavior will have a positive effect on suburbs residents (change of image, etc.). The two are interdependent which shows the importance of measuring them together.

6.3.5 Results

Two years after initiating this important project, a global evaluation was conducted in 2009 in order to measure the first social satisfaction index. This assessment was undertaken by the firm ARGOS (2010), an independent party not involved in the project to identify changes noticed by the residents, their image on their own districts, and the expected points of improvement.

The following newly implemented indicators, often intangibles, were measured on a scale of 0 representing "negative" to 3 representing "very good". They can be considered as a base of reference for future evaluations.

The outcomes can be summarized as follows:

- Positive outcomes: The people living in Puer and centre ville have a very good and good image of their districts, respectively.
- Chances for improvement: The people living in Sierroz, Franklin, and Marlioz still suffer from the image of their districts. They register the worst deficit in term of image (Fig. 6.11).

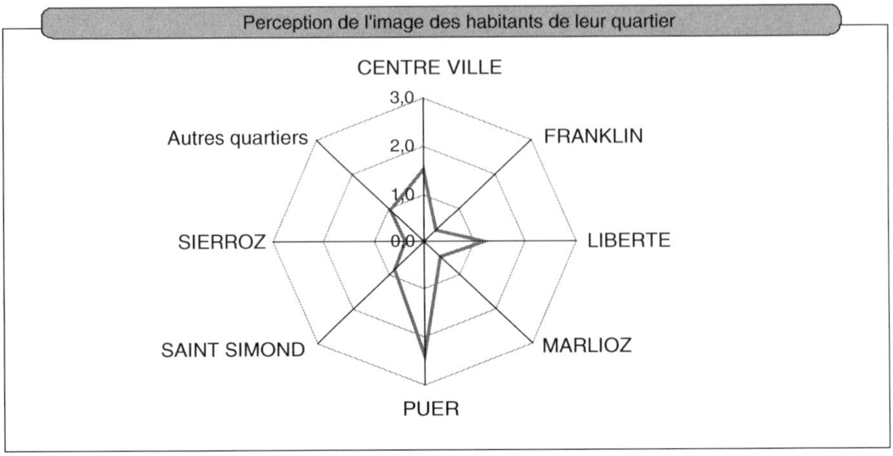

Fig. 6.11 Perception of the citizens regarding the image of their own districts

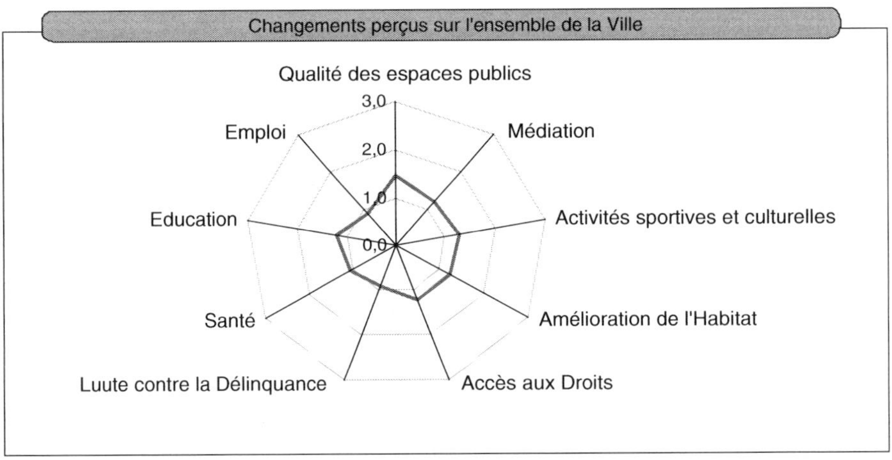

Fig. 6.12 Perceived changes in the city regarding the major areas of work

The outcomes can be summarized as follows:

- Positive outcomes: Relevant progress was perceived in the quality of public spaces, sport and cultural areas, improvement of housing, mediation, and education.
- Chances for improvement: The most important source of dissatisfaction was related to unemployment and delinquency (Fig. 6.12).

The outcomes can be summarized as follows:

- Positive outcomes: The residents have a very good perception of City services thanks to their nearby services as sport and cultural activities, improvement of housing and educative success.

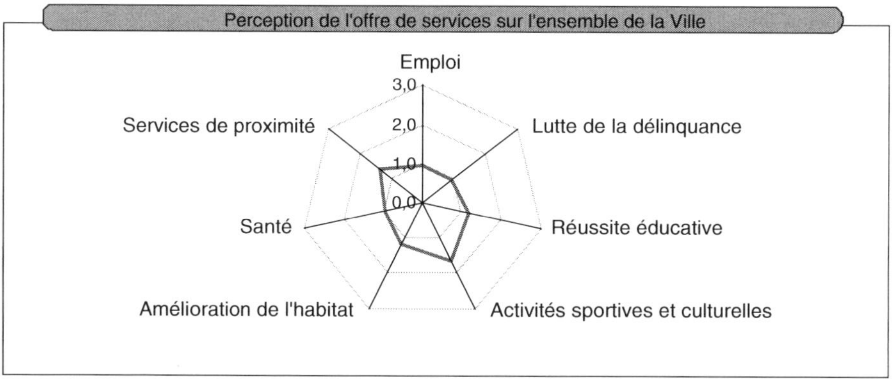

Fig. 6.13 Perception regarding the city services offers

- Chances for improvement: They have a lower perception regarding the services related to healthcare, employment, and delinquency; however, none of them have been judged as having a bad quality (Fig. 6.13).

A significant improvement could be measured in the reduction of people in need of financial support (previously RMI – Minimum Income, now called RSA – Active Solidarity Revenue), which changed from 5.42% of the population at the end of 2007 to 3.94% of the population at the end of 2009. A similar improvement could be measured by the decline of the family allowance funds beneficiaries living under the limit of the lowest income (from 6.2% of the population at the end of 2007 to 5.7% of the population at the end of 2009).

The outcomes can be summarized as below:

- Positive outcomes: The number of financial support beneficiaries has decreased by 1.50% as well as the number of people being under the limit for the lowest income.
- Chances for improvement: We still have almost 5.7% of people under the lowest income. This rate should be improved.

The development of the unemployment rate can be summarized as follows:

- Positive outcomes: The proportion of unemployed women is high with 49% in January 2010; however, it has decreased by 10% comparing to January 2008.
- Chances for improvement: unemployment rate has increased dramatically by 16%, which has been mainly caused by the economic crisis.

Overall, the global performance has been evaluated for 2009 and 2010, based on constant indicators, both in terms of "image of their districts" and "perceived changes." We moved from 1 to 1.14 in terms of image and from 1.16 to 1.3 in terms of "perceived change," an index including all dimensions of CUCS (habitat, education, employment, social mediation, sport and culture, access to legal assistance, health, fight against discrimination), knowing that the global objective for "perceived change" in 2013 is to reach a result of 1.5. This global approach and measurable achievement has been strongly appreciated by the actors and leaders involved on this important urban development policy.

6.3.6 Summary

Despite the very positive context of the project like a good coordination between the City and prefecture, a high commitment of the mayor and his participation at meetings with the citizens and the State's representatives, we experienced some issues during the implementation of the project. The allotted time for the project was very short by starting in November 2006 to be implemented in March 2007. Information and communication meetings planned to be given to citizens and actors of the program have not been set up because prefecture had preferred waiting for the new awaited ministerial policy. Announced for 2009, this new disposal is still not available today.

The Balanced Scorecard method helped to formalize a vision, identify the pillars of excellence, guidelines, desired outcomes, clarify the priority objectives, identify the measures of performance, and the strategic initiatives as displayed in Fig. 6.14.

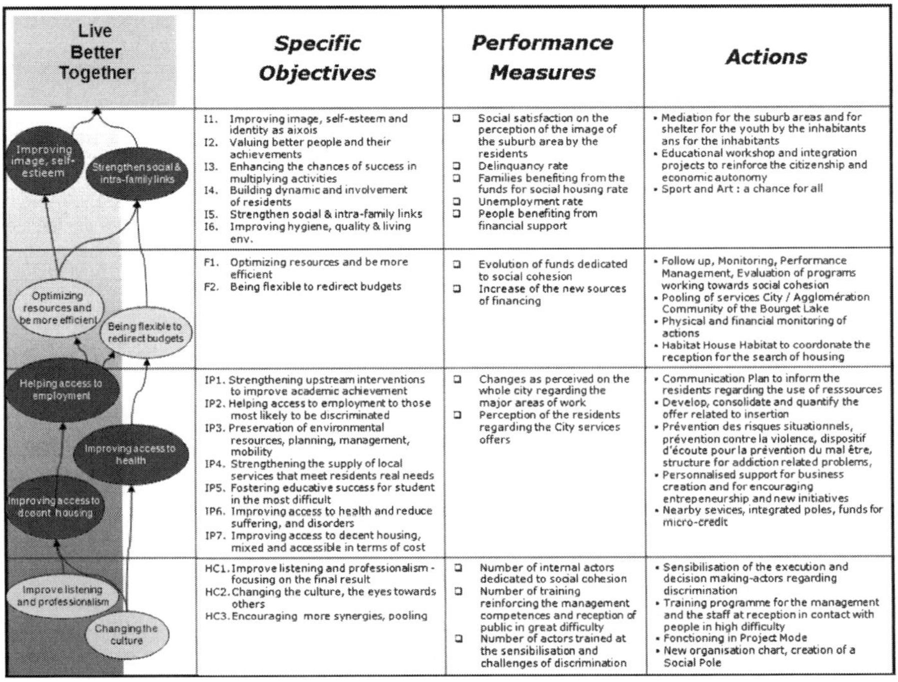

Fig. 6.14 Balanced Scorecard including objectives, performance measures and actions

Within the city of Aix les Bains, the BSC has enabled us to:

- Share a vision and promote cohesion among the players – "Better Work Together." Benefit from a financial and non-financial approach in the evaluation process to measure the tangible and intangible aspects (social satisfaction, image, citizen satisfaction, etc.).
- Build a consensus and practice good governance by involving all actors and generate a long-lasting dynamic.
- Formalize and implement a strategy, deploy objectives and action modes, link measures to the strategy.
- Align strategy with budgets and operations.

Overall, the feedback from participants, co-authors of the public policy of social cohesion, has been very positive. "We had excellent reviews on the methodology used" declared the Director of Urban Policy, considering that it has created a strong dynamic and allowed the players to work better together. The success in the definition phase was based on:

- The richness of the exchange between 164 participants from different social, economic, educational organizations as well as citizens which were present in the different groups.
- A methodology for managing change in a "controlled and balanced" manner which reconciles the economic, social, and environmental objectives in a participative and consensual way.

We consider that the momentum generated, which helped to overcome some issues and obstacles was achieved because of several factors:

- The climate both friendly and dynamic where participants felt valued.
- Skills in terms of know-how of the leaders of the City and Prefecture (human qualities, communication skills, ability to convince, etc.).
- The strong presence of the managers of the Prefecture and their personal commitment.
- The role of "facilitator" by the consultants.
- A high level of compassion by the actors for the cause.
- A commitment to transparency and questioning of existing solutions and real problems.
- The structured approach helping to avoid falling continuously into the analysis and pushing the participants to be constructive and forward looking.

The city of Aix-les-Bains and the Prefecture were able to implement a transparent system of performance measurement promoting "Better Live Together." All this work has enabled the City to respond to the call for projects launched by the European Commission (European Regional Development Fund) in 2007 and carry a "fully integrated urban project" which is a real lever for the development in the territory. This project has been awarded funding of 5.5 million Euros by the European Commission for the timeframe from 2007 until 2013.

6.4 Improving Strategic Alignment with CRM and Analytics at Würth: Excellence in Sales

Authors	
Friedrich Saller	Chief Information Officer Würth Handelsgesellschaft m.b.H. Würth Straße 1, 3071 Böheimkirchen/Austria friedrich.saller@wuerth.at
Christian Schneider	Principal Consultant & CRM Project Manager maihiro GmbH Donau-City-Str.1, 1220 Vienna/Austria christian.schneider@maihiro.com
Organization	
Name	Würth Handelsgesellschaft m.b.H.
Industry	Wholesale
Size (# employees)	670 (Austria), 58,000 (worldwide)
Website	http://www.wuerth.com/web/en
Scope of Success Story	
Geography	Austria
Functional Area	Sales and Telesales
KPIs	Customer visits, orders, customer retention, revenue and profit
Overview	
This case study demonstrates how the implementation of a Customer Relationship Management solution including analytics helped to improve the sales and telesales processes.	
Business requirement	
Improve number and volume of orders places and enable zero-customer reactivation.	
Solution	
Creating a centralized customer data management, enhancement of field force efficiency and customer service, as well as an automated creation of call lists for telesales with the support of a new CRM system.	
Benefits	
Improved decision making via availability of up-to-date information, customer service and increased total customer count.	

6.4.1 *Introduction*

Würth Handelsges.m.b.H. is a full-line provider for fastening and assembly technology for the automotive, wood, and metal industry. The company's philosophy "quality beats price" is expressed by proximity to customers, service, and product quality. As the market has undergone radical changes with decreasing customer and supplier loyalty as well as massively elevated pricing pressure during the last years, effective sales force, sales service, and marketing processes become a key factor for future success and an even extended market share. Würth responded to these challenges by introducing a CRM solution that makes all customer information centrally available and enhances not only the collaboration of internal sales service, customer management, accounting, and logistics, but also allows effective reporting.

This success story describes the business strategy of Würth Austria and the implementation of a Customer Relationship Management system including CRM-Analytics to improve the alignment of operations with business strategy.

6.4.2 Würth Company Profile

Würth Handelsges.m.b.H. is a full-line provider for fastening and assembly technology for the automotive, wood, and metal industry. The core business of the Würth Group is the worldwide trade of fixing and assembly materials, including screws, screw accessories, dowels and plugs, chemical products, furniture and construction fittings, tools, stockkeeping, and picking systems.

Building up the Würth Group is the life's work of Prof. Dr. h.c. mult. Reinhold Würth and it is one of the success stories in the German economic history. In 1945, the parent company of the Group, Adolf Würth GmbH & Co. KG, was founded by Adolf Würth. After the early death of his father in 1954, Reinhold Würth, today's Chairman of the Supervisory Board of the Würth Group's Family Trusts, took over the company. Starting from the early years of the company in postwar Germany, he has turned the former two-man business into a trading group operating worldwide with about 400 companies in 84 countries, a revenue of 7.5 billion Euro, and approximately 58,000 employees.

With around 670 employees, the Austrian company achieved a turnover of 135.2 million Euros in fiscal year 2009. More than 400 field force employees, 7 telesales employees, and over 20 customer centers in Austria handle more than 50,000 customers throughout the country.

Würth's corporate culture is based on core values such as optimism, drive, and high regard for employees, their work and their commitment to the company, and their customers. In early years, the founder of the Würth Group set impulses to proactively contact customers. This led to the establishment of a direct sales organization as a basic principle for Würth's future success.

The company's philosophy "quality beats price" is expressed by proximity to customers, service, and product quality. More than half of the Austrian employees work in that field and are in daily contact with customers. The Würth assortment comprises 100,000 products across the group. Out of 25,000 articles in stock in Austria, 99% can be delivered within 24 h. Würth products can be distinguished by its high quality. More than 250 technicians, engineers, physicians, and chemists worldwide work within the product management and development department and continuously strive for engineering new products and solutions. Around 50% of the turnover is achieved with products which have been developed during the last 8 years which is an indication for the level of innovation at Würth.

6.4.3 Market Environment and Business Strategy

The market for fixing and assembly materials is a typical polypoly, a market with a large number of small buyers and tens of thousands of sellers, none of which can influence prices. Some of these competitors are large companies but the majority is very small. Even ironmongers and sanitary or technical wholesalers are counted among the competitors. Despite this market structure and a market share, i.e., of only around 5% in Germany, Würth is the dominant market leader. Within the next 15 years, the company aims at reaching a market share of around 14–16% worldwide.

Würth differentiates itself from other market actors with a crystal clear strategy of "top quality for an appropriate price." To follow this strategy, customer orientation and top quality in sales are measurable key success factors. Würth therefore conducts customer satisfaction surveys every 3–5 years and, e.g., monitors the details of customer orders. Since the year 2000, Würth globally boosted its number of sales representatives by 60%. The earnings have been growing accordingly and constantly amount to 7–10% within the last years. Following the philosophy of Prof. Dr. h.c. Reinhold Würth, the core competence of Würth is rooted in sales to 95%. It has always been a people-driven business with, e.g., sales representatives who have cared for the same customer for 25–30 years. These tight relationships between sales representatives and customers help to establish high barriers for competitors. Nevertheless, Würth's initial situation before starting the CRM initiative, was characterized by decreasing customer loyalty and massively elevated pricing pressure.

In order to respond to these market changes, to safeguard and to refine the extensive know-how of more than one generation of sales representatives, centrally accessible customer information combined with effective sales and marketing processes have become indispensible factors for future growth. Würth developed a CRM Vision to deal with these challenges as displayed in Fig. 6.15.

6.4.4 Objectives of the CRM Initiative

Employees at Würth had to cope with increasing efforts for administrative processes in sales. Sales visit planning became more and more inefficient due to information silos and inconsistent customer visit documentation. Central availability of all customer information for a better collaboration of internal sales service, customer management, accounting, and logistics became urgent. Moreover, due to

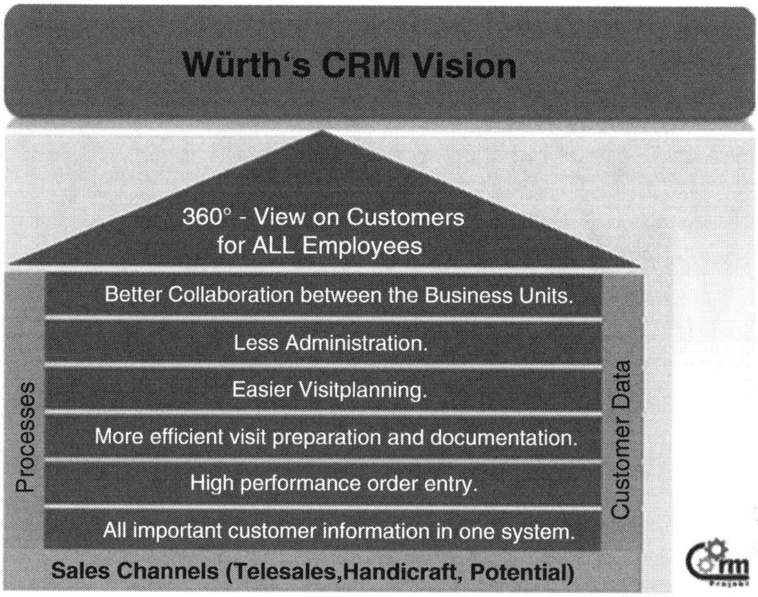

Fig. 6.15 Würth's CRM Vision

an increasing number of Würth products, a high-performance order entry was needed.

From an IT perspective, the existing data and information models possessed deficits. Knowledge about customers and prospects was not centrally available because isolated applications and a paper-based file card system prevented a consistent view on customer data. The telephone system and call center functions as well as the telesales solution with the ERP system needed to be integrated. For telesales, the existing Microsoft Dynamics CRM solution had to be replaced by an integrated CRM solution with CTI (Computer Telephone Integration) and system-based call lists. Through this communication support for processes and a centrally accessible system, customer management, including customer acquisition, customer retention, and customer win-back was intended to be strengthened. Figure 6.16 indicates the anticipated customer lifecycle development including quick new customer development, long customer retention, and efficient customer revitalization.

To measure the success of Würth's CRM initiatives, key performance indicators (KPIs) were needed. They could be differentiated between leading and lagging indicators and have been defined as follows.

Leading indicators like the customers' average number of customer visits or order frequency or the number of first orders can be influenced directly by the sales staff. Therefore customer-related processes have been optimized across all relevant departments so that prospect data can be efficiently maintained within the system. The knowledge about customers is captured and can be provided to all involved employees.

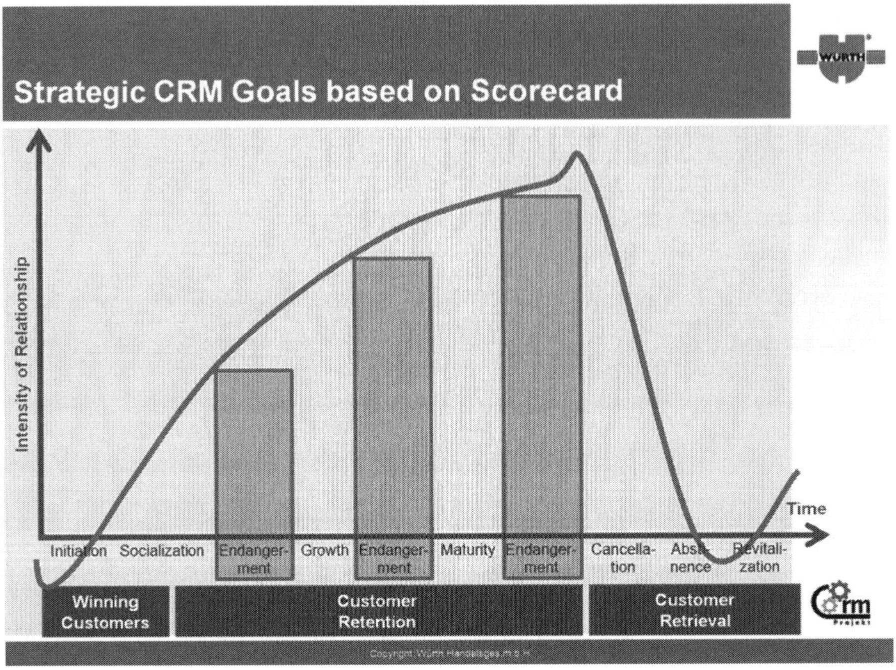

Fig. 6.16 Strategic CRM Goals

Lagging indicators depend on the previously mentioned leading indicators and can be measured with a delay in time. Examples for these are increased numbers in sales and profit. Another lagging indicator is measuring if the customer retention has been increased over time thanks to targeted customer management and marketing activities. The customer fluctuation rate, churn rate, can be measured, which is expected to be reduced in the next years due to the CRM implementation.

6.4.5 CRM for Sales Force, Sales Service and Telesales

The scope of the CRM implementation comprised business partner management (customers), call center and telesales processes, activity management, customer visit management (planning, preparation, execution and documentation), extensive order entry, and creating a complete customer history. Würth started to use SAP Customer Relationship Management (SAP, 2010e) (SAP CRM) in the first phase of the implementation to better support its sales representatives in 2009. Marketing activities were planned to be implemented in the second phase in 2010. Three of the main improvements during the first phase included creating a centralized customer data management, enhancement of field force efficiency and customer service, as well as an automated creation of call lists for telesales.

6.4.6 Centralized View Upon Customer Information

Prior to the implementation, the sales representatives used handwritten filing cards to record the customer data. Now they record the data in the CRM system. The customer infosheet in the CRM system contains more information as the previous infosheet on the handwritten filing cards and is available via a mobile device, the Blackberry, at any time and any place for everybody who needs the information.

Typical Würth customers are, e.g., car repair shops, plumber and electric shops as well as carpenters. Prior to the introduction of CRM, each sales representative used his laptop with a locally installed solution for order entries and noted customer data on paper based customer file cards. Customer information was only available locally and had to be collected from several sources for corporate reporting of KPIs. Würth, moreover, had huge problems with data not being up-to-date. When replicating data, a lot of information had already been out-dated. Thanks to the online SAP Customer Relationship Management application, the data are up-to-date. Data are hosted at the central server and all users have access to the same information. One of the advantages is the immediate and full access to all customer agreements, complaints, credit notes, contracts, and any attached documents such as scanned images. This helped Würth to ameliorate its customer service significantly.

Customers are supported via sales representatives, the sales channel telesales, and the field force, which are visiting customers on site. Depending on the sales channels, a different number of customers are assigned to each of Würth's sales representatives. A telesales employee is the contact person for 600–800 potential customers. A field force employee responsible for handicraft businesses cares for 80–200 customers whereas a field force employee for large accounts is responsible for 20–60 customers. These customers are revisited in varying frequency between twice per week up to every other month. The CRM system helps to plan the schedule based on the customer information and enables an appropriate analysis of the key performance indicators, i.e., number of visits per day, and thereby help to improve a consistent management of the sales pipeline.

6.4.7 Enhancement of Field Force Efficiency and Customer Service

SAP Customer Relationship Management was introduced to improve customer support and field work at the same time. For the field staff, it is necessary to have access to all customer information on site in order to better prepare customer visits. Before starting their visits, sales representatives are enabled to plan the weekly tours by assigning activities for each visit and integrating them in their Outlook calendar. To each visit in Outlook, a PDF with the customer infosheet is attached and includes a view on the customer transaction history. This has been enabled via the integration of SAP and Microsoft Outlook. The new customer information sheet helps to enhance customer consultations and consequently contributes to an improved customer satisfaction. There are multiple advantages of the PDF attachment. General information about the customer and its contact persons are complemented by buying recommendations provided by the CRM system. Potential cross- and up-selling potentials are analyzed via Data Mining, performed on a Business Intelligence system from SAP, which is integrated with the CRM system. This allows to better understand and predict customer behavior. In addition to the customer information, field force employees obtain a proposition list of top seller products in a specific industry sector and see what the customer ordered within the last years. For the employees, this helps to improve the preparation of their visits. The key performance indicator to measure the effectiveness of this improvement is the average revenue per visit.

6.4.8 Automatic Creation of Call Lists for Telesales

Each of Würth's seven telesales employees is in charge of around 600–800 customers and makes up to 60 calls per day. By having integrated SAP Business Communications Management (SAP, 2010f) (SAP BCM) into the telephone system, automatically generated call lists and automatic dialing facilitate daily work considerably. When creating call lists, criteria such as the historic consumer behavior, the last successful call, or the customer classification are taken into consideration. This guarantees an ideal and consistent handling of the entire sales process. Thanks to this support, the telesales department can develop potential and minor customers to more significant customers with less effort and make more calls a day. As a follow up from the contact via the telesales, the field force can visit promising customers and increase revenue.

6.4.9 Effective Reporting of All Data

The new CRM solution combined with SAP Business Warehouse (SAP, 2010b) (SAP BW) also enabled the management of Würth to effectively analyze sales-oriented measures that before could only be estimated. With an analysis of the customers' buying behavior, important conclusions could be drawn.

One of the benefits of the improved reporting was the calculation of the customer value based on current sales figures. This information could be used to properly support the customer segmentation and helped to assign customers to the appropriate departments; while telesales staff cares for smaller customers the more important ones are serviced by sales representatives.

Additional reports allowed to maintain an overview of all customer activities, the impact of marketing campaigns on the buying behavior of customers and the

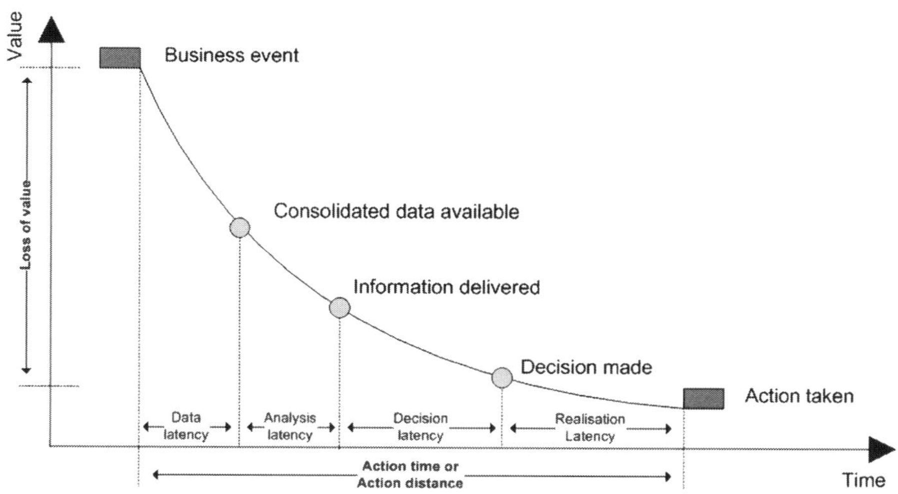

Fig. 6.17 Value of Information (Heesen, 2010, p. 148)

success rate of a reactivation of so-called zero-customers, customers without any order for a long time. Another benefit was the improved cross selling facilitated by data mining and analytical CRM. New reports displayed the impact of sales activities on the orders placed. CRM and ERP data could be compared and contrasted for significant reports showing, for example, the number of customer visits needed for an initial order or the number of visits per 1,000 euro order value.

In the same way, activity analyses of the sales department and the sales area displaying the visit quota according to the customer value classification are available. Customers in remote geographical areas who may not be visited can be analyzed displaying the date of the last visit and the last order. Furthermore, so-called joint customer tours (number of combined customer visits, number of joint travel days) and specific customer management analyses, e.g., reports about the activation of the so-called zero-customers, are available.

To summarize the benefits for the management, an effective reporting solution reduces the action time for decision makers (see Fig. 6.17). The Würth management is enabled to react much faster because all data previously entered by the sales and marketing staff is available in the system and can be analyzed right away. At short notice, faster strategic action is possible if, for example, more favorable competitor prices lead to a loss of orders.

6.4.10 Consulting and Implementation Approach

As consulting and implementation partner, Würth chose the CRM specialist maihiro (maihiro, 2010). maihiro's phased "CRM to Go" prototype-based consulting approach for wholesale is intended to reduce complexity. In the analysis phase of the implementation, the project team already worked with a prototype system tailored to the customer's wholesale industry. This allowed the team to concentrate on the unique key process characteristics. Not having to design a system from scratch reduces complexity, implementation time, and risks.

Successful projects have to reflect the needs and interests of different stakeholders. In the case of Würth, the owners expected an improved financial return; the customers of Würth were expected to benefit from an improved service, so for these stakeholders a positive attitude could be assumed. Nevertheless, Würth expected resistance from some employees who did not know if the implementation might affect their workplace and their daily business potentially negatively, e.g., layoffs, increased expectations from the management, or positively, e.g., improved support for their work. In order to reduce this uncertainty, the project team tried to create a quick success by implementing CRM for the telesales department during phase two of the implementation to demonstrate the reliability and ease of use of the software. After having successfully implemented this functionality as promised, the project was perceived as a success. The second activity to avoid resistance was a proactive communication about the project via a monthly newsletter.

Following the telesales implementation, CRM was introduced to a significant number of sales representatives. The project phase three was dedicated to visit planning and phase four concentrated on the reactivation of zero-customers, by utilizing the so-called segment builder, used for creating target groups within SAP CRM. After identifying the target group of zero-customers, tailored marketing campaigns were executed to make them familiar with new, innovative products to win them back.

Based on the World of Strategic Business Intelligence™ model (see Fig. 2.2), a project affects many stakeholders. These stakeholders may have competing interests. For the project's success, it is indispensable to try to avoid resistance during an implementation. Through the prototype approach, the end users got an early hands-on-feeling for the CRM system and the future processes in the system right away. The process analysis workshops took place with stakeholders from all affected departments, e.g., sales, telesales, and CRM, and status presentations were given at every sales meeting. This helped to decrease the level of uncertainty. As information is the key, company-wide pro-active communication took place, e.g., monthly newsletters informed the Würth staff about the CRM initiative. To strengthen the end-user acceptance during go-live, intensive hands-on trainings for the entire sales staff were performed in advance. These communication efforts led to the acceptance of the new processes and systems.

6.4.11 Conclusion and Perspectives

By introducing CRM and CRM Analytics, Würth was able to increase the efficiency of the sales processes and to make all customer-related information available for all business units throughout the company. Technical highlights were the integration of

SAP CRM with SAP Business Communication for Telesales as well as the introduction of mobile CRM for the field force.

The business value is significant. The benefits are an optimal support and traceability of customer-centric processes between all involved business units, centrally accessible customer information for each point of sale, improved customer service, efficient preparation of customer visits and tour planning, additional cross selling opportunities and measurable customer visit efficiency via analytics based on the SAP Business Warehouse. The mobile use of CRM per smartphone, i.e., BlackBerry, is possible and enables the online access to activities and the documentation of visits.

Würth also monitors the absolute number of customers, who have ordered products during the past 12 months, using the new systems. Thanks to the company's successful CRM initiative, around 38,706 active customers have been counted in May 2010. This is the highest number of customers that has ever been recorded since the foundation of Würth Austria in 1962.

Another measurable benefit of the online CRM solution is that the delay until the order is placed in the system could be reduced significantly and the delivery could happen up to 12 h earlier because of this change. The KPI used to measure this progress is the percentage of articles which can be delivered within 24 h. Currently 99% of the 25,000 stocked articles can be delivered within 24 h.

Ultimately, Würth continues to follow an ongoing process improvement. At the end of this project, another one will follow. The only consistency is change.

6.5 How Business Intelligence is Leveraged at the Federal Employment Agency of Germany to Increase the Effectiveness of Activities to Prevent and Reduce the Duration of Unemployment

Authors	
Erich Maierhofer	Head of Coordination Office for Business Intelligence Requirements Federal Employment Agency Regensburger Straße 104, 90478 Nuremberg/Germany Erich.Maierhofer2@arbeitsagentur.de
Thomas Paal	Head of Business Unit Business Intelligence Federal Employment Agency, IT System House Regensburger Straße 104, 90478 Nuremberg/Germany thomas.paal@arbeitsagentur.de
Organization	
Name Industry Size (# employees) Website	Federal Employment Agency of Germany Public Sector >100,000 http://www.arbeitsagentur.de/
Scope of Success Story	
Geography Functional Area KPIs	Germany Unemployment Job vacancies filled, Duration of unemployment, Ratio of integrations, #Benefit recipients, Benefits paid
Overview	
The Federal Employment Agency (Bundesagentur für Arbeit - BA) is the labor market's biggest service provider. To maintain its position as #1 service provider in this market the BA decided in 2002 to establish a new governance control and reformed its processes and organizational structures. The case study demonstrates, how the use of KPIs was used to avoid and reduce unemployment. The reader will understand the framework used to define KPIs and how they are utilized for reporting and analytics. The technical infrastructure of the business intelligence solution at the BA has proven to be a reliable platform to provide the official statistics regarding the German employment market and corporate controlling at the BA.	
Business requirement	
Define a new governance control which enables the strategy execution to be more efficient and effective by planning and monitoring the relevant Key Performance Indicators.	
Solution	
Establish an integrated data warehouse for the employment agency to support the required business intelligence tools and applications.	
Benefits	
Improved efficiency and effectiveness of operations at the BA.	

6.5.1 Introduction to the Federal Employment Agency

The Federal Employment Agency (Bundesagentur für Arbeit – BA) is the labor market's biggest service provider (Bundesagentur für Arbeit, 2010). As a public body with self-governance it acts independently within the framework of applicable law. The BA is composed of the headquarter in Nuremberg, 10 regional directorates, 176 employment agencies, and approximately 610 branch offices. The Federal Employment Agency offers a broad range of services on the labor and training market for citizens as well as companies and institutions. The main duties of the Federal Employment Agency are placement in training places and workplaces, vocational guidance, employer counseling, promotion of vocational training, promotion of further training, promotion of professional integration of people with disabilities, benefits to retain employment, and compensations for reduced income, e.g., unemployment benefit or insolvency payments.

The economical crisis of 2008, which was the worst within the history of the Federal Republic of Germany, had great impact on the financial situation of the BA and its operational tasks. Nevertheless, the BA was able to cope with these challenges. A major foundation for this was the governance control established as part of the reform of the employment agency which enabled the strategy execution to be more efficient and effective. The data warehouse of the employment agency created the necessary IT infrastructure to support the required business intelligence tools and applications.

6.5.2 Use of BI-Tools Within the BA

Business Intelligence is used to support the management of three main areas within the BA. First, official employment statistics and reporting, second research of the labor market, and third, corporate controlling. This case study will exclusively focus on the use of BI-Tools within the area of corporate controlling. Special features of the BA, e.g., the special attributes of the employment market, which are not relevant in other industry sectors, are omitted. The intent is to allow readers to transfer the presented concepts of this case study to their own organization. The focus in the first part of the case study is the application of BI-Tools to support business execution while the second part describes the technical aspects and the implementation process.

6.5.3 The Governance Control of the BA

The governance control of the BA is characterized by a management by objectives and unequivocally defined individual responsibilities in all business units. The BA expects efficient and effective decentralized decision making and acting from all managers and employees within their areas of responsibilities. One of the prerequisites to enable this management model is information transparency and availability supported by efficient information technology. Modern service organizations such as the BA create transparency by sharing information, some of which is reported via key performance indicators (KPIs). These KPIs are used in regular performance evaluations to assess the level of goal attainment in each of the strategic business segments. The functions of the BA are divided into six business segments and each segment has a unique set of key performance indicators. The key performance indicators are used to monitor the level of achievement compared to the plan. Standardized reporting is used within the entire organization to visualize the results. The success of using BI-Tools for management control depends on how well the following three components are aligned with each other:

- Definition of content (what).
- Organizational procedures (how).
- Technological implementation (whereby).

The definition of content defines what is needed to achieve the defined targets. What is needed to measure the strategic objective of "avoiding unemployment" and "reduction of the duration of unemployment?" Which data from operations can be used to define adequate measures? Which information should be made accessible for which employees?

The organizational procedures should be able to facilitate the realization of the defined objectives. How should the organizational units be defined to allow efficient and effective performance? Which procedures can facilitate the cooperation and alignment of business units and the IT-department? Which individuals and committees should be involved during the planning process to define the objectives? What are the competences employees need to comprehend all relevant business aspects and to be able to use the available information systems? What support do employees need to fill in competency gaps and increase their strength?

The technological implementation defines which means are used from an IT perspective to support the organizational performance. To fulfill these important tasks it is essential to act efficiently and effectively while taking innovative aspects of information delivery into consideration. The three components, definition of content, organizational procedures, and technological implementation have to be optimized within a limited budget.

6.5.4 Key Performance Indicators as Parameter to Determine Strategic Direction

It is essential for successful controlling to obtain transparency. This can be achieved by an operationalization via key performance indicators. Key performance indicators are the central means to define the contents and therefore represent the "what" of the governance control of the BA. The determination and definition of the key performance indicators is conducted above the level of individual business units, making unequivocal definitions essential. The determination and definition of the key performance indicators are realized by the organization's corporate controlling department. Key performance indicators are by the majority quantitative data, used to condense the complex reality. They inform about quantitatively measurable performance (Weber & Schäffer, 2008, p. 167).

The strategic policy goals of "avoiding unemployment" and "reduction of the duration of unemployment" can be verbally expressed intelligibly, and since unemployment is one of the biggest problems in society, people will generally agree. Unemployment means a reduction of production, income, and human capital, increases in the gap between social classes, and can mean great psychological stress for unemployed adults and adolescents who feel useless and without a perspective. It is far more difficult to describe the strategic objectives based on measurable key performance indicators. The following figure (Fig. 6.18) explains the assignment of six key performance indicators to their respective strategic objective. The abbreviations in the right column (I, Va) indicate the sphere of influence on subordinate objectives of the six business segments.

The primary goal is to avoid the occurrence of unemployment. Therefore, the goal is to find suitable new employment opportunities for terminated employees during the period of notice, before they are actually dismissed ("Job-to-Job"). The key performance indicator for this goal is the ratio of job-to-job integrations to job-to-job customers (Integrationsgrad Job-to-Job).

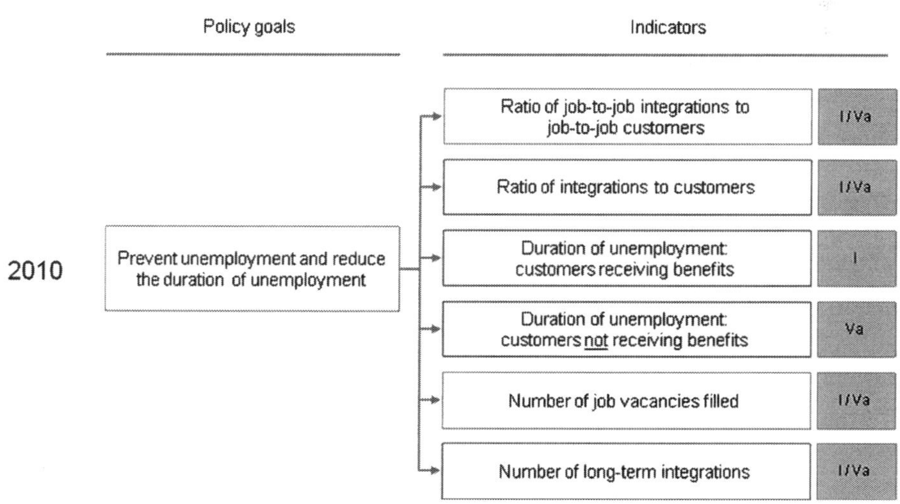

Fig. 6.18 Policy goals and (target) indicators

If unemployment cannot be avoided, then the goal is to keep it as short as possible. The key performance indicator to measure the achievement of this goal is the duration of unemployment for customers receiving or not receiving benefits.

A high rate of job-to-job placements and a short duration of unemployment reduce the amount of unemployment benefits that need to be paid, lower the necessary unemployment contributions for employers/employees, and increase the dues income for the BA.

For all potential customers of the BA, the total integration in the employment market shall be maximized (ratio of integrations of customers). Another objective is the sustainability of the integration. The goal is that the arranged new contracts of employment are sustainable and have a long duration. The key performance indicator to measure the sustainability is the number of long-term integrations. The assessment happens 6 months after the start of the new employment relationship by checking if the employment relationship is still existing.

Matching demand and supply in the employment market is another task of the BA. The key performance indicator used to measure the degree of fulfillment for this objective is the number of job vacancies filled.

The different KPIs are finally integrated in a systematic fashion via an analysis tree, in which all Explanation Indicators and Analysis Indicators are linked to the top-level targets (Target Indicators). Figure 6.19 displays the analysis tree for the KPI "Duration of unemployment of customers receiving benefits" (abbreviated aDfA LE). The duration of unemployment of customers receiving benefits is measured in the number of days it takes an unemployed person from the day they register their unemployment in one of the 786 offices until they get a new employment contract.

A similar analysis tree exists for every Target Indicator, which is updated every reporting period, for duration of unemployment of customers receiving benefits monthly. The following information, as displayed in the example above, is extracted from data cubes for reporting: short name of the indicator (grey field), current value, deviation between current and planned value in percent, deviation between current value and the value from the previous year in percent, and ranking in the regional cluster.

For Explanation and Analysis Indicators the current values are always displayed in the lower left of the KPI box. The development of the KPI over time is displayed as the deviation from the current value to the value of the previous year in the lower right of the KPI box. All KPIs in the analysis tree with a direct connection to the Target Indicator represent factors of influence and are called Explanation Indicators. Examples for Explanation Indicators in the above figure are: Duration of unemployment up to now LE, aDfA LE-Integrations1, aDfA LE-Other outflow, Outflow in total LE, Integrations 1-LE, Other outflow LE and all KPIs related to the customer profile. Explanation Indicators can be further explained via Analysis Indicators, which are indented to the right in the analysis tree so that users of the diagram can easily recognize the meaning. Further discussion of the labor market will be omitted at this point. The indicators were determined through statistical methods.

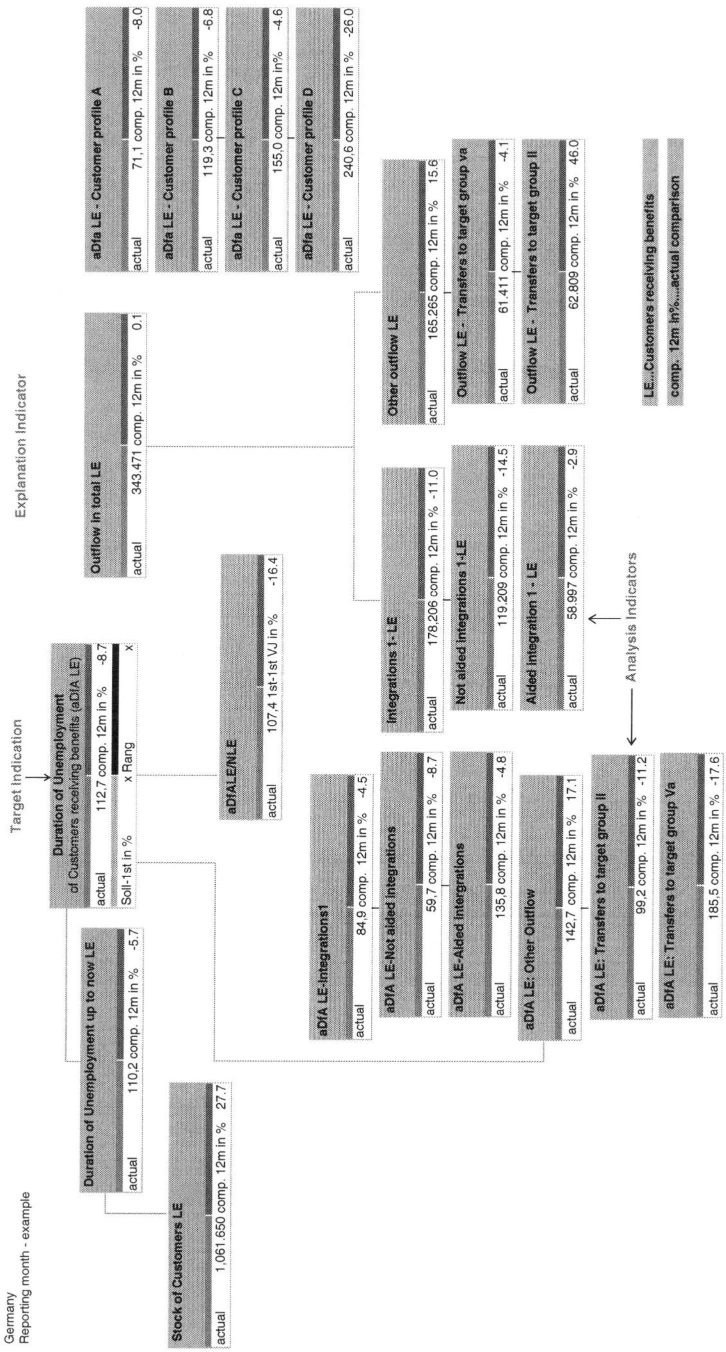

Fig. 6.19 Target indicator and interdependent indicators

The described form of data representation allows the users in the headquarters, regional offices, and employment agencies a fast overview of the current Target Indicators and the most relevant factors of influence. To avoid misinterpretation, users need a working knowledge of the definition and build of the key performance indicators. If uncertainties exist, users have the possibility to view the actual definition of the KPIs (metadata) in the KPI catalogue via a hyperlink directly from the analysis tree diagram. The analysis tree is only one of many reporting outputs generated by the Executive Information System (EIS). The EIS itself is only one component in the Model of the architecture of the data warehouse of the BA (see Fig. 6.21) to inform users.

The following Fig. 6.20 displays a screenshot of the web-based EIS and allow to see some of its elemental functionalities. The user leverages the left side of the screen for navigation and the remaining part is used to display the standardized reports.

The navigation list offers three important options for selection: First, the reporting period. All KPIs are made available on a monthly basis on fixed dates. Second, selection of the organizational unit to be analyzed. All standardized information can be retrieved for each business unit (e.g., headquarters, regional directorates, employment agencies) at the same point of time. Additionally, information can be retrieved by operative subunits, e.g., teams with more than three

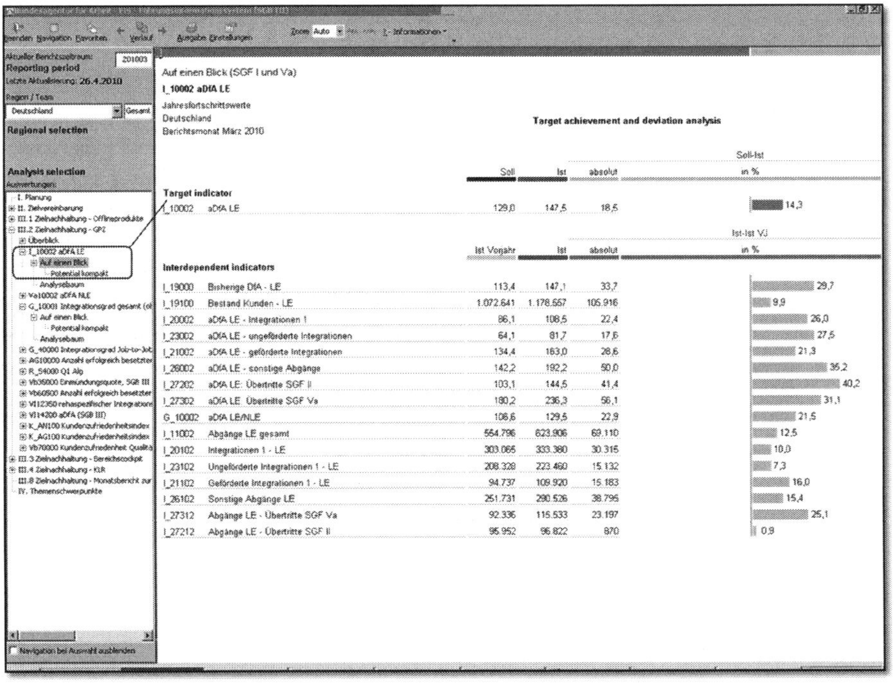

Fig. 6.20 Screenshot of EIS

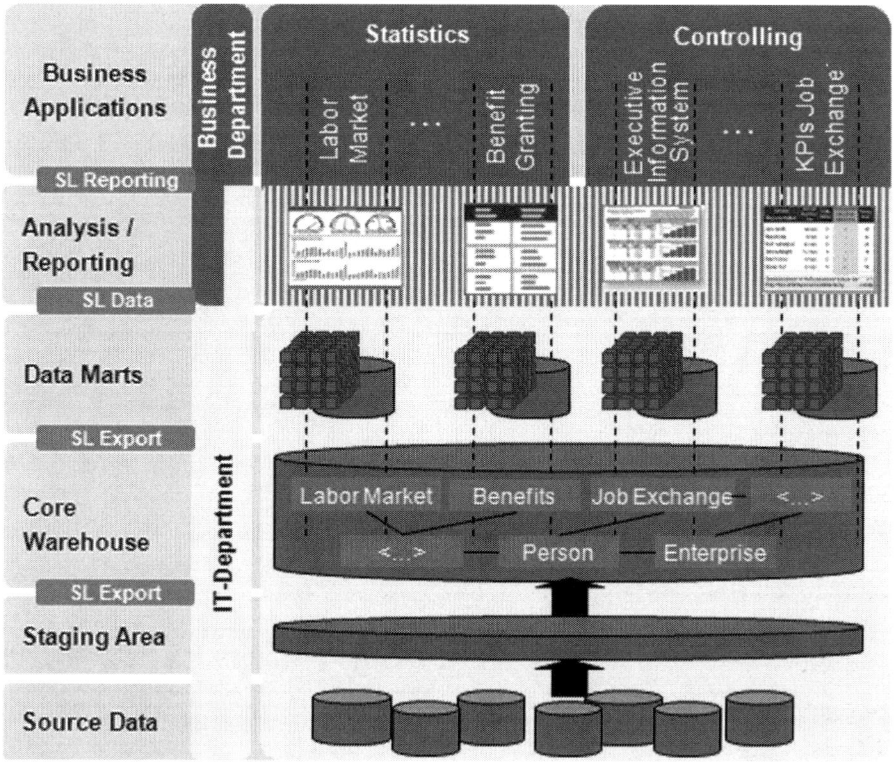

Fig. 6.21 Model of the technical architecture of the data warehouse of the BA

employees. Third, the type of standardized report specifying the type of content to be displayed. Figure 6.20 shows the Target Indicator aDfA LE, duration of unemployment for customers receiving benefits, with its planned and current value as well as the corresponding deviation in percent. A list of the relevant Explanation and Analysis Indicators is displayed below the Target Indicator. Because the data is visualized via bar charts, the user is able to recognize changes promptly and gets indications for further analyses. For this purpose, the user can use the navigation list on the left which offers extensive selection options, or power-users utilize the additional BI-tools of the data-warehouse. The complex data marts with a multitude of navigation dimensions are one of the widely used BI-tools (see Fig. 6.21).

6.5.5 Professional Use of BI-Tools

Within the corporate controlling, Business Intelligence Tools represent tools to support the information processes, which provide the necessary data for planning, controlling, and reporting for the different levels of decision making based on the defined controlling methods. BI-tools are intended to support the measurable attainment of set goals within all strategic business units. The professional supply of information shall help to

- Provide transparency on the path toward the strategic objectives
- Provide the required information in a timely fashion and with high quality
- Guarantee a high level of standardization for report layout and report content
- Minimize manual work during the determination of complex connections related to the labor market by offering a strong integration of click applications
- Support all members of the organization in their aspiration toward goal achievement by making all relevant information available

6.5.6 The Data Warehouse

Since 2002, The BA uses a data warehouse (DWH) as the core of its extensive dispositive system for collecting, processing, and evaluating labor market data. The focus is on the availability of statistical data concerning the labor market in Germany as well as data used for the corporate controlling of the goal achievement for the BA. In 2009, more than 10,000 users, among them about 300 power-users, executed an average of 500,000 random queries per month by using the reporting cockpits. The execution of more than 90% of the queries took less than 2 s.

Additionally, the data warehouse is used as a data resource for the monthly reporting on the situation of the labor market on federal level as well as on county and community level. For the preparation of its official labor market statistics, the BA has its own data center and printing facilities, which produces up to 140,000 standardized reporting brochures per month.

6.5.7 The Architecture of the Data Warehouse

The architecture of the data warehouse, which was established between 1998 and 2002 is primarily designed to fulfill the requirements for the official statistics. These are characterized by specific processing (e.g., benefits statistics, unemployment statistics) across all levels of the data warehouse architecture (see Fig. 6.21) at loading, at the core warehouse layer, the specific data marts (e.g., financial benefits) to the cubes, upon which the standard reporting and the cockpits are based. In 2006, the data warehouse architecture was extended to also reflect the reporting requirements from corporate controlling. The necessary architectonical changes toward an integrated and normalized data model within the data warehouse were conducted within the past years, according to predefined business and data protection rules.

The data sources for the data warehouse are the transactional systems for the job placement, granting benefits, the overall master data about individuals and operations as well as the business applications. Required data is mirrored on the loading layer, a selection process extracts the relevant objects and attributes, and transforms and loads the data in the core warehouse layer (DBMS: Informix (IBM, 2010b), Net volume of data: 45 TB). This process is conducted daily, weekly, or monthly dependent on the need for up-to-datedness of the data.

To guarantee short response times for the users for individual evaluation within the different departments, specific data marts and up to 600 user group specific cubes are prepared monthly based on the available data from the data warehouse. The most complex data marts consist of up to 10 facts, 100 dimensions, and a data volume of 3 TB. As evaluation tools, the products from SAP/BO (SAP, 2010g) are used for the OLAP analysis, the products from Micro Strategy (Microstrategy, 2010) for the relational analysis directly on the data mart, and the tool TN Planning (Thinking Networks, 2010) for planning. The departments can access data and reports through defined service delivery points (Leistungsübergabepunkte, LÜP).

6.5.8 Modeling and Realization of Controlling Indicators

In Sect. 6.5.4 we introduced examples for controlling indicators. This chapter will show how professional requirements are used as the foundation for the technical modeling and implementation.

The functional design usually consists of a textual description of the semantics of the KPIs including the associated rules for calculation or transformation based on the transactional data. If possible, first hints regarding the semantical connection of the objects and attributes in the integrated data warehouse layer are provided in the form of a conceptual data model.

For the technical modeling of the objects, attributes, histories, and dimensions on the data warehouse layer, the Entity-Relationship-Method (ERM) is used. The data flow and the transformation rules between the loading layer and the integrated data warehouse are modeled with the method of Structured Analysis (SA). The documentation is performed with the support of tool Innovator (MID, 2010). This methodical procedure has the advantage of creating a high transparency about available information on each layer. This enables the modeler to compare the current model with the targeted model when receiving new requirements.

Figure 6.22 displays the model of the object BI-Person with its attributes (e.g., age, gender, education, residence), its time spent (e.g., in employment, education, rehabilitation) and the received benefits (e.g., payments received from/to). The implementation of the integrated data warehouse layer is identical to this model. Necessary changes required for technical optimization by the developing department lead to a supplementary adaption within the ERM or SA model. Thus, an up-to-date documentation is guaranteed.

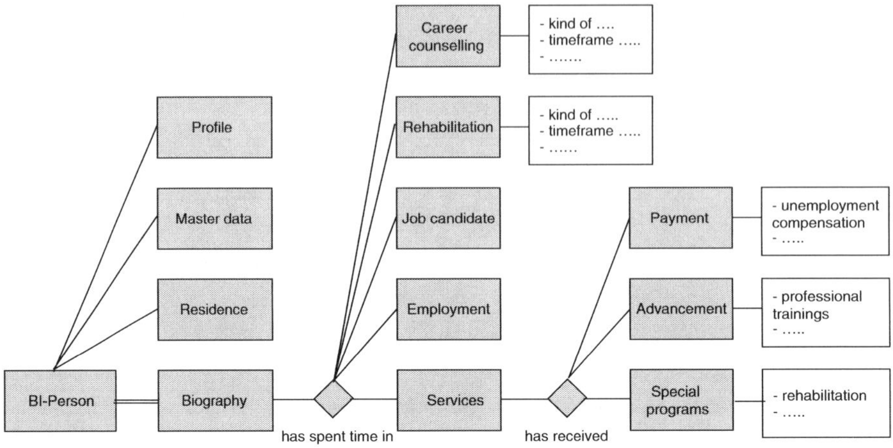

Fig. 6.22 Model of biographies

For the use within the controlling department, the data are edited in subject-specific data marts (e.g., unemployment insurance, rehabilitation). A data mart can consist of up to 50 KPIs. The calculation of the attributes of a person and the actual KPIs is technically separated. The table for indicator Integration-2 only consists of an anonymous personal ID, the reason for termination and the respective date. The anonymous personal attributes are calculated centrally and added uniformly to all controlling data marts. This guarantees that all calculations regarding the person related dimensions are identical system-wide.

User specific cubes (e.g., internet user, extranet user,) are developed as extracts from data marts to improve performance of the systems and fulfill the required response times at the cockpits. An indicator such as Integration-2 can be evaluated via more than 20 dimensions (e.g., age, regions, duration of employment, duration of unemployment).

Prior to starting to establish the strategic objectives for the next year, all relevant KPIs from statistics and controlling are combined in a single cube. The cube is utilized by corporate controlling for a review of the current year and by the planning department for planning the next year.

6.5.9 Operation of the Data Warehouse

The IT System House at the BA holds the sole responsibility to meet the demands of the BA for the development and the operation of the data warehouse. A team of more than 100 employees implements up to 400 change requests every month.

Besides the layered systems architecture, an additional layered software engineering concept is applied to differentiate the phases design, acceptance, editing, and deployment. The infrastructure used includes several Solaris servers (Oracle, 2010) (DWH), approximately 180 Windows SQL-Server (Microsoft, 2010) (Data Marts, Cubes) and about 80 Informix (IBM, 2010b) database instances (DWH). This infrastructure made sure that performance was not a problem most of the time. The dispositive data of the past 5 years are stored in the data warehouse and can be used for reporting when needed. Contrary to many operative procedures, historic data need to be available in consolidated format for the entire period. Many attributes need to be maintained including their history.

6.5.10 Availability of Data

For the relational and multidimensional reporting a differentiation between regular users and power users allows to control the availability of functionality and depth of data. There also exist different users roles, e.g., for the monthly release of data and special measures to protect the data prior to the monthly press conference where the results are presented to the public.

Quality control is conducted before releasing the monthly controlling indicators to the users. This procedure is supported by a QS-portal, where the organization maintains their respective status, all corrections for KPIs happening between reporting periods, including the validation rules, the validation protocol, and potential action that need to be taken.

6.5.11 Conclusion and Outlook

The expected objectives for the use of the data warehouse were achieved. During the past 8 years of daily operations of the data warehouse, the system developed to a level of maturity where it functions reliably. A raising number of users prove the acceptance of the system.

Looking back, it is evident that the biggest technical problems were caused during loading and transformation of the transactional data in the normalized layer of the data warehouse. To reduce the complexity and to facilitate maintenance, we plan to standardize all interfaces from an architectonical angle. The more than 20 data source systems will have to provide their data in an event driven and semantically interpretable format. This approach will further increase the efficiency of the data warehouse at the BA.

6.6 Development of an Operational Reporting Platform at Giesecke & Devrient to Enable Quicker, Better-Informed Decision Making

Author	
Ute Riemann	Business Process Architect Giesecke & Devrient GmbH Prinzregentenstrasse 159, 81607 Munich/Germany ute.riemann@gi-de.com
Organization	
Name	Giesecke & Devrient GmbH
Industry	Technology
Size (# employees)	3.800 (Germany), 10.000 (worldwide)
Website	http://www.gi-de.com/
Scope of Success Story	
Geography	Germany
Functional Area	Business processes across the organization
KPIs	Operational level measures
Overview	
The case study provides an insight how to design and introduce an operational reporting that supports the day-to-day activities of Giesecke & Devrient to enable quicker, better-informed decisions. It emphasizes the linkage of process change and implementation to the overall reporting strategy and setup.	
Business requirement	
Establish an operational reporting infrastructure to provide current facts about key performance indicators.	
Solution	
Integrated design of business processes in conjunction with establishing a Steering Model for operational reporting requirements and thereby creating the foundation for a business intelligence system providing a consistent and convenient access to critical performance indicators on all levels of the organization.	
Benefits	
Developing and introducing processes together with the appropriate reporting resulting in an improved monitoring of performance indicators and better decision making based on more reliable information availability.	

6.6.1 *Introduction*

Can a new process landscape be rolled out successfully without also replacing the operational reporting systems needed to monitor the performance indicators for the changed processes? This case study relies on the hypothesis that support by an

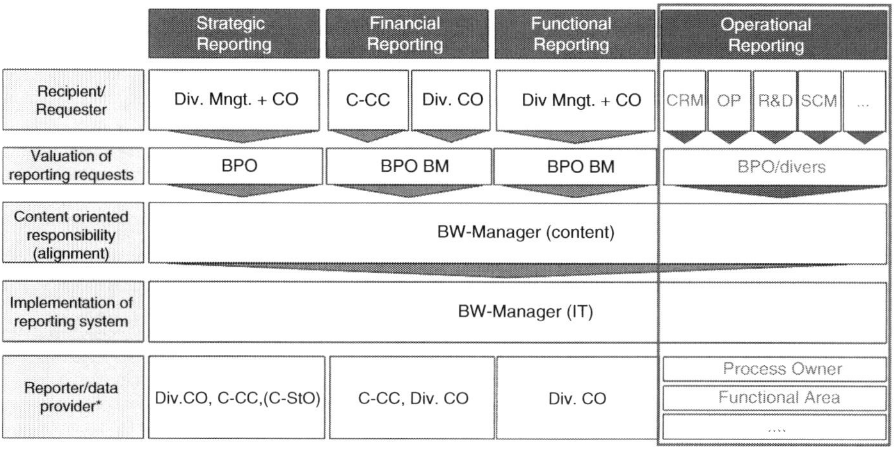

Fig. 6.23 Reporting structure Giesecke and Devrient (2010)

integrated system landscape promotes the global harmonization of reporting and enhances the transparency of the decision making.

This case study about Giesecke & Devrient describes the implementation of a new process landscape and the operational reporting system. It provides an insight how we managed to implement an operational reporting system improving the day-to-day activities of Giesecke & Devrient. This is done on an operational level with the target to enable quicker and better-informed decisions by presenting an operational excellence driver metric that is linked to the company's strategy. The focus of this case study is on operational reporting as displayed in Fig. 6.23.

Since we had a consistent understanding of WHAT we would like to achieve we needed to define the approach on HOW we can make this happen:

- Develop new processes while replacing poorly integrated reports with limited fit to the new processes
- Provide decision makers at all levels of the organization with reliable and current information
- Improve transparency of reliable key performance indicators to improve business decisions
- Allow to track, measure, and view key performance indicators on all levels of the organization

Please note that some key figures, systems and processes presented here are fictional ones for non-disclosure reasons. However, the general approach and the issues presented are representative and cover the findings during the implementation at Giesecke & Devrient. This case study should be of value to all those who want to understand how to link business process design with the design of an operational reporting system used to measure the performance of the business processes.

6.6.2 Current Situation and Issues

Giesecke & Devrient (G&D) has changed significantly over the past years based on new business requirements. The core processes have become more complex but G&D continued to operate within the same basic organizational structures. To prepare the company for future growth opportunities and competitive challenges, G&D initiated the CHANGE program in 2007. The program focuses on the development of global processes and steering tools, including integrated decision support systems, which support the organizations' strategy based on an adequate IT system landscape. It strives toward business excellence and is intended to drive G&D's further growth and competitive ability.

One of the deficiencies which had grown over time at G&D was the increased demand for operational reporting. Changes in the business processes and their information collected had demanded and caused changes in the supporting operational information systems. Similar business processes in different business units could not be fully harmonized. The result was a heterogeneous information systems infrastructure. Aggregating or comparing key performance indicators for management reporting from these heterogeneous systems were difficult or not possible in a timely manner. Managers' information needs on various hierarchical levels to support their decision making were not met. It became obvious that this needed to be changed and an adequate operational reporting should be established at G&D to provide current facts about key performance indicators and thereby create more transparency within the organization. This implementation was considered essential to further improve the business of G&D.

Operational reporting is a detailed form of reporting and provides real time data on the transaction level with information tailored to the needs of the respective decision makers. In order to provide a high level of transparency, the operational reporting needs to display the relevant performance indicators without delay and measured consistently across the organization in different levels of granularity, e.g., aggregations based on organizational levels or type of product. Only under these circumstances, management will be able to monitor the performance and take appropriate action after analyzing the information according to the management control loop (see Fig. 4.1).

An integrated operational reporting solution needed to be implemented. The approach we followed was based on the following three pillars:

1. **Business process design with performance indicators**
   This "process" pillar has led to a set of defined (a) end-to-end processes, (b) their related key performance indicators, and (c) new operational reporting requirements for each of these processes to make sure that the process performance can be measured adequately. The key challenges were to make sure that we identified the right performance indicators for each process.
2. **Reporting governance**
   In order to enable management reporting the business processes, performance indicators and their subsequent monitoring via reporting needed to be

harmonized across the organization. To meet this requirement, Giesecke & Devrient created the Steering Model for operational reporting (see Fig. 6.26).

3. **Data Warehouse structures and dimensions**
   Based on the multi-dimensional reporting requirements collected, we needed to consider an approach to implement a robust and appropriate operational reporting system considering primarily near-time data to provide the right information at the right time. We decided to implement a SAP Business Intelligence (SAP, 2010b) system.

6.6.3 Business Process Design with Business Use Cases

To set the stage for a new view on processes triggered by business requirements and to avoid sticking to old functional pillars an integrated (cross-functional, organization wide), end-to-end view on processes and corresponding reporting requirements was needed. Therefore, we defined the so-called "business use cases."

The approach of defining the business use cases helps to provide a software-independent description of business processes both in textual form and via Unified Modeling Language activity diagrams (Frankl, 2010). Different groups of stakeholders as well as business process analysts can use the business analysis model to understand how the business currently works (as-is) and to analyze the effects of changes to the business (to-be). The finalization of a shared understanding and documentation of business processes facilitates the formation of a consensus where there may have existed multiple, possibly conflicting, stakeholders and stakeholder expectations. This process helps to make sure that the implemented processes (not all processes are automated by systems) meet the business goals. It creates an integrated business view and allows to document significant integration points as "glue" between the processes and to derive the relevant operational measures. The business use cases establish the foundation to start a structured IT Build phase and thereby maximize the benefits generated by introducing business processes which are aligned with the business needs.

The identification of the business use cases from the business perspective is the essential starting point in the process optimization and the development of an integrative process landscape. Describing the business use cases in different levels of detail helps to understand the big picture (level 1) of the business and on the transactional level (level 5) as well (see Fig. 6.24).

The business use cases are a key to understand business process requirements to run the respective business and to drive the performance indicators and operational reports. The business use cases represent all customer-oriented activities in regards to requirements, market orientation toward, e.g., new products, in the most effective way. They are a systematic approach to develop an integrated process design and link relevant business processes together. The identified business use cases do not only support a structured build phase but help to push the prototyping, derive business-driven test cases, and process-oriented trainings.

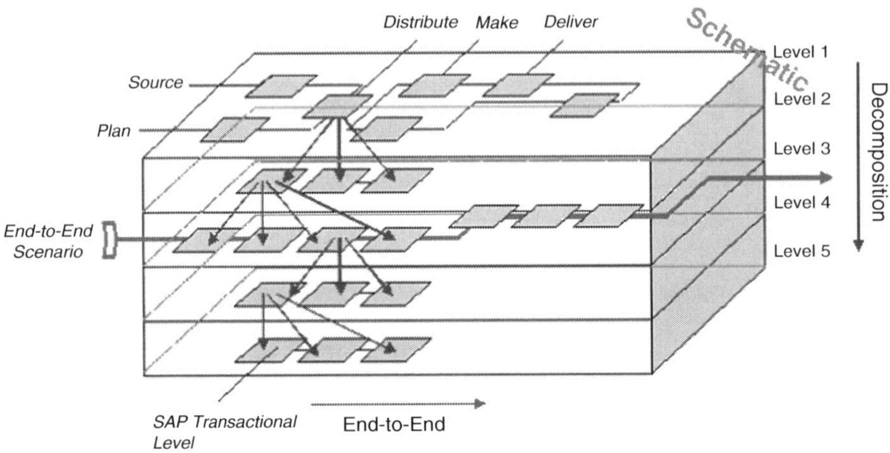

Fig. 6.24 Business use cases level of detail

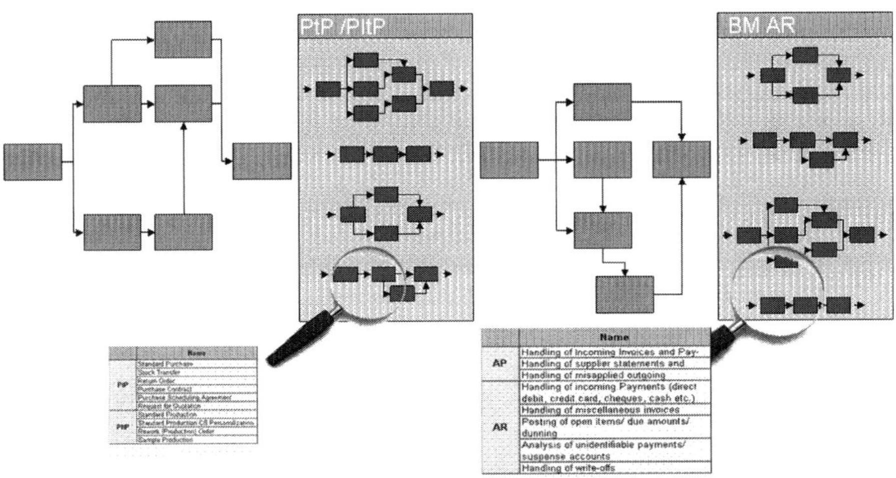

Fig. 6.25 Performance indicators per process step

The process landscape describes the business view across different functional areas and allows documenting the relevant performance indicators for each process step as displayed in Fig. 6.25. In order to monitor the performance of the organization, these indicators need to be incorporated in the operational reporting to support adequate decision making on all levels.

6.6.4 Reporting Governance

After having designed the processes, we were able to assign the respective performance indicators per process. As a first step, we identified the currently used performance indicators per process and per division (As-Is). We differentiated these performance indicators in those established and used by the strategy department as Key Performance Indicators (KPIs) within Giesecke & Devrient to measure corporate performance and Process Indicators (PIs) relevant for at least one department within the company.

It became obvious that different departments used slightly different performance indicators for similar purposes, complicating the aggregation for corporate reporting. To avoid this problem in future we developed the Steering Model for operational reporting (see Fig. 6.26) to identify on which levels business processes and related performance indicators needed to follow a corporate standard or division specific derivations were accepted. This helped to harmonize key figures and established the basis for efficiency measurement and operational reporting.

Besides collecting the performance relevant information for reporting via IT-systems, we also needed to answer some of the following questions:

- What information should be available to whom?
- What is the format of the data stored?
- Where is the information coming from, single or multiple sources?
- Is there a need to convert the source into a shared unit of measurement, a coding or a specific format?

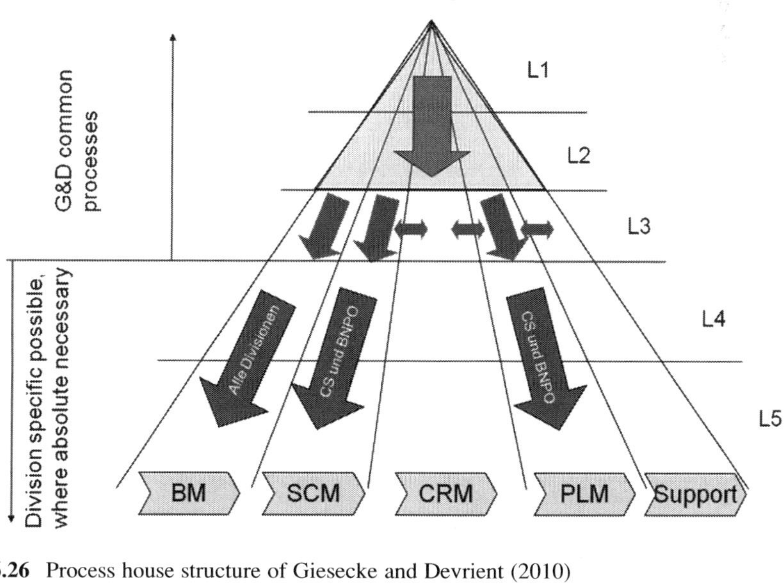

Fig. 6.26 Process house structure of Giesecke and Devrient (2010)

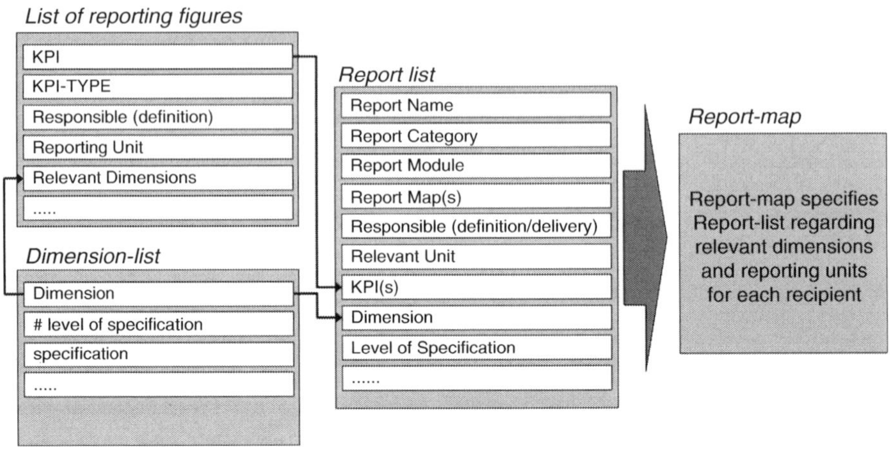

Fig. 6.27 Link from reporting figures to reports (Giesecke & Devrient, 2010)

Based on this collected information, e.g., on KPIs, dimensions and reporting needs we were able to develop a stringent approach for reporting as displayed in Fig. 6.27.

To document the detailed information, following a structured approach, we collected all information related to performance indicators in a central table format. Besides others, we collected the following main attributes such as: Perspective, Target, Impact/Relevance, Definition, Unit, Source, Census Frequency, Supplier.

The following example demonstrates some of the key information collected for each performance indicator (see Table 6.3).

6.6.5 Data Warehouse Structures and Dimensions

The findings also show that the operational reporting requirements driven by processes are caused by the following factors as displayed in Fig. 6.28.

While documenting the business use cases, we decided which performance indicators to use. In order to collect the relevant information a data model including all performance indicators was designed and implemented in the Business Intelligence system. This design included the extraction from various source systems, the mapping of the receiving information object in which the information should be stored, and depending on the case some transformation rules. We used an SAP BI system for this purpose.

Another business requirement collected during the analysis of the business processes were the detailed reporting requirements including the different navigation options used by end-users, e.g., the dimensions they wanted to use to select (slice, dice) relevant chunks of information and organize the output (group, sort). Utilizing this information from all processes prior to the design of the reports in

Table 6.3 KPI details for On Time Delivery (OTD)

Indicator name	On Time Delivery
Processes (level 1–3)	• Order-to-cash • Order management • Customer order processing
KPI based approach	• Definition of KPIs per site, product/solution/industry plans • Aggregate information relevant for each report • Summarize goal achievement(s) per report • Analyze achievements • Decide based on indicators within analysis
Description	On Time Delivery against committed delivery date
Owner/receiver	Operational manager/operational head
Calculation	Number of shipped orders that have not been delayed compared against the committed date/date requested by customer divided by total number of shipments
Measurement unit	Percentage of OTDs
Target value	Proportion of OTDs vs. 100%
Threshold	in%
Update frequency	Monthly
Drill down dimensions	Production sites

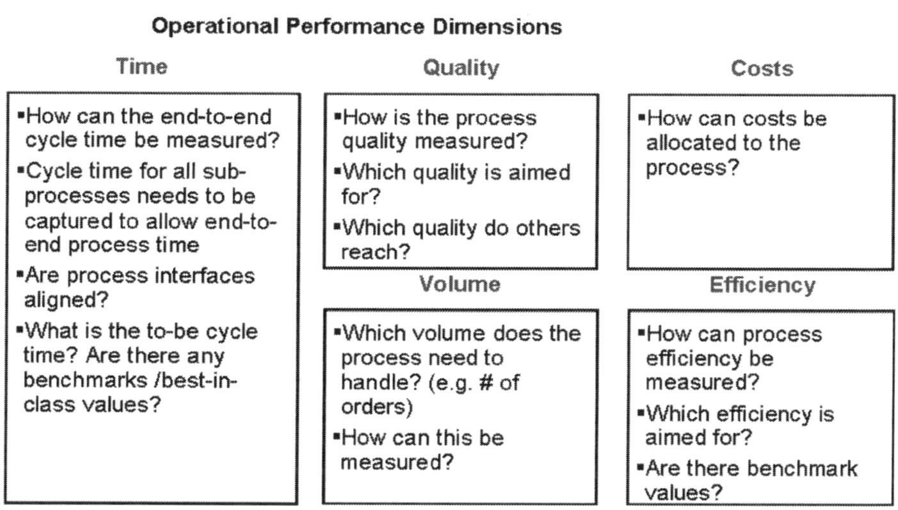

Fig. 6.28 Example for operational performance dimensions

SAP BI, we clustered the data into information objects and provided the required reporting dimensions which could later be used for easy reporting.

The definition of the reporting dimensions is used to pre-define the level of granularity for which data can be stored in an information object. Since the data are reported in different levels of detail it is essential that the data are loaded for

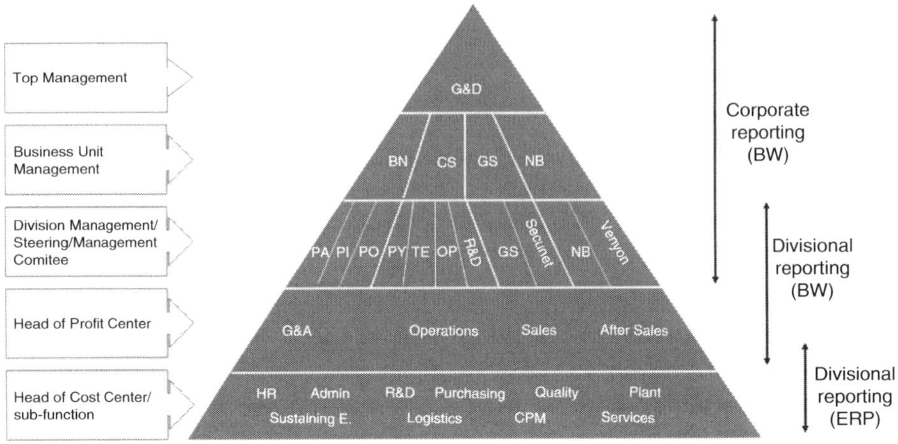

Fig. 6.29 Reporting pyramid according to Giesecke & Devrient organizational structure (Giesecke & Devrient, 2010)

different levels of granularity in each dimension. Based on the shared and standardized definition and use of performance measures throughout the organization, the aggregation and comparison is possible for different entities. The reporting governance guarantees data consistency.

Within the SAP BI system, the info cubes were established in a way that corresponded to the business requirements gathered. Based on the reporting requirements, we were able to create report layouts by displaying the performance indicators on the desired level of granularity (degree of fineness). Based on the steering model that is applied at Giesecke & Devrient (see Fig. 6.26), the dimensions and performance indicators were either defined globally or locally. Subsequently the appropriate dimensions were offered for reporting. Figure 6.29 displays the five organizational levels used for reporting.

6.6.6 Conclusion

Designing the layout of information objects, info cubes, transformation processes, queries and reports is a lot of effort. Changes in the design of the information structures of a BI-system require substantial rework in modeling and report design. Therefore it is critical to gather all relevant requirements related to the performance indicators and their reporting properly and consistently. To avoid unnecessary complications, we established a reporting governance structure and used a centralized rather than a decentralized approach for our BI backend system. Let me share the following lessons learned and pitfalls to avoid with you, based on our experience:

- Collect the specific performance measures for the business processes while you document the business use cases along with their reporting requirement since these are the foundation for your design of the business intelligence system's information objects and dimensions.
- Business requirements change continuously, so processes require maintenance of KPI definitions as well.
- Closely link the teams responsible for process improvement with the operational reporting team during the implementation of a business intelligence solution. In order to be able to support decision makers on all levels of the organization with the best possible reporting the selection of the right data sources, data structures needs to be linked to the processes and steering model.

We truly believe that for a successful process and IT-alignment, it is necessary to connect the process- and reporting-centric development and their system architectures including the definition of relevant performance indicators and their respective use in operational reporting. The architecture of the IT system landscape can then be established to match the business requirements. We believe that the value of using a comprehensive "enterprise architecture" can be maximized by combining the business process and reporting requirements in one joint architectural approach!

The benefits we gained from this initiative were:

- Increased reliability of business process performance measurement due to commonly defined processes and performance indicators and utilizing a Business Intelligence system to capture the KPIs and make them available to the decision makers on all levels of the organization.
- Improved monitoring of operational targets and better decision making based on more reliable information availability.

6.7 Midwest Bell's Execution of a Hidden Strategy Causing Conflict of Interest and Resistance

Author	
Chris Roberts, Ph. D.	Director, School of Hospitality Leadership DePaul University 1 E. Jackson Boulevard, Chicago, IL 60604/USA crober31@depaul.edu
Organization	
Name Industry Size (# employees) Website	Midwest Bell (real name hidden to protect identity) Telecommunication 87,000 N/A
Scope of Success Story	
Geography Functional Area KPIs	United States of America Sales Revenue
Overview	
Strategic intent kept secret internally and compensation programs not aligned to reflect goals.	
Business requirement	
Coordinate strategic information and action across the organization.	
Solution	
Sharing rationale and intent of strategy with all levels of the organization; aligning compensation program at multiple levels to reflect strategic intent.	
Benefits	
Coordinated effort by employees to understand, support and implement strategies, leading to better organizational performance.	

6.7.1 Introduction

Jose Mendez was the manager of the Business Service Center (BSC) in the capital city. He had been with the company for 18 years and he had never seen morale so low and his group's performance so far off expectations. It had been a long, frustrating year so far, and it was only the first of August. Jose did not look forward to the end of the year. He felt frustrated because of what he and many of his peers felt were confusing senior management decisions. The eight supervisors he managed felt the same way, and even many of the service representatives questioned the wisdom of current operations. Service representatives were being rewarded, even encouraged, to lower company revenue. It just did not make sense and his questions to upper management went unresolved. He did not know how he was going to salvage the situation. Jose leaned back in his office chair and stared out the window at the state capitol building, reflecting upon the events of the past that led him to this low point.

6.7.2 Promoted Through the Ranks

Jose started with Midwest Bell as a repairman for residential services. He had initially gotten the job because his uncle was a manager in the engineering department. Jose had spent 2 years riding a truck, stopping at people's homes to replace broken phones, splice damaged wires in household walls, and climb poles to repair broken lines. Jose liked the variety of the work, and had enjoyed getting out and about in the community. Sometimes the shifts were not too desirable, but working on weekends and evenings sure was better than no job at all.

After 2 years he had demonstrated his competency in repair and was promoted into residential installation. Instead of fixing broken equipment and lines, he now was making all of the external line connections to bring new service to a home, feeding wires into walls to install telephone jacks where people wanted them, and delivering the phone equipment people had ordered. It was more challenging, as he had to create the connections to get the dial tone to the new phones, which often meant he needed to solve logistical problems. Placing wire where it would withstand the weather and human interaction always required thought and care. He remembered, as a repairman, how many times he had to reinstall wires that installers had done poorly. As an installer himself, he vowed that he would not make the same mistakes.

He also liked the more regular work schedule. Repairman worked all hours, including weekends. Installation crews just worked during the business week. That regularity allowed Jose to begin taking classes at a local community college. He aspired to earn his bachelor's degree in business one day.

While working as an installer, he got to know many of the service representatives who issued the orders that he handled. After 3 years of working with them, he became quite familiar with their systems and processes, so when an opening was posted for the Residential Service Center (RSC), he jumped at the chance. While it meant leaving the freedom to roam the community to working indoors all day, that did not seem so bad after spending 5 years in the field. Some of those days it was quite cold. He looked forward to working in a different side of the business, and to do it in the temperature-controlled offices of the state headquarters building.

The RSC work was challenging at first. While he had worked with the service orders for many years and thought he was familiar with the routines, he was surprised to learn how much more information he had to learn. Further, talking with customers in a selling mode was much more complicated than in the service encounters he had handled in the past. He had not had to worry about product prices and credit status when he was in the field. Mastering the art of selling while ensuring the customer had the appropriate credit ability was a new skill for Jose. Still, with time, training and practice, he became quite proficient at the job.

After 3 years in the RSC, Jose wanted to transfer to the BSC. The BSC is the Business Service Center. They did the same function as the RSC, but they worked with businesses rather than residential customers. That seemed more challenging to Jose than just placing orders for the basic service that most people wanted for their homes. That basic service had a nickname: Plain Old Telephone Service, or POTS. While POTS was important to the company (it was the bulk of the service orders that were processed each day), the orders were very repetitive and simple. The work of the BSC was considerably more difficult because of the extremely wide range of needs of businesses and the products available to address those needs.

Jose was quickly promoted to the BSC when he applied for an opening. His outstanding performance as a service representative combined with his field experience as an installer and repairman made him highly desirable. With his multiple views of the company, management felt that Jose would be better able to understand customer needs and offer them useful solutions.

The next 3 years in the BSC seemed to fly by. Jose went through many weeks of training sessions in order to learn the complex equipment available to businesses. He found it fascinating and enjoyed solving communication problems for customers. He became so proficient that he was asked to join an account team. The account teams were groups of service representatives who were dedicated to a very large account. The team was lead by an Account Executive from the Marketing Department, and the service representatives were responsible for the daily needs of the account. Jose was assigned to the team than handled the state government telephone needs.

It was not long before Jose's outstanding performance brought him to the special attention of management. Within a year he had demonstrated many positive behaviors, including working well without direct supervision, receiving compliments from the state government staff for his service, and delivering innovative solutions to fulfill customer requests. When a supervisory position in the BSC opened, Jose was the first choice of management. The Account Executive of the state government team was not happy to be losing Jose from the group, but certainly understood the value Jose could bring to the company in the role of supervisor.

Jose was pleased at this promotion and felt that his business classes certainly were paying off at work. It had been only 9 years and he had made the transition from a craft worker to management. He had completed his associate degree and had transferred to the nearby university where he continued to work on his business degree requirements. He had about one more year's worth of coursework to complete in order to graduate. He was very thankful that the university offered many of the courses online, enabling him to make progress toward the degree while continuing to work full time.

During the next 5 years, Jose learned how to supervise others and to master the fine art of handling escalated customer issues. He interacted with many other departments, further expanding his network of contacts and his knowledge of the firm's operations. An opening for the office manager was announced and Jose thought long and hard about applying. He felt a "natural" as a supervisor but was not certain he was ready for the next step. He had completed his undergraduate degree in business management and was in the middle of earning his MBA. While he certainly felt wiser he did not feel he was ready for the next level. Jose decided to wait until he completed his MBA and then would apply for the next opening.

Two years later, his manager was promoted to an opening in another state, and the position was available once again. Having completed his MBA, this time Jose aggressively sought the position, obtaining written recommendations from his peers and other managers. With 16 years with the company, he felt ready both in terms of industry knowledge, management skill, and political network. After a 2-month interview period, to his joy, Jose was awarded the position. He was now a second-level manager, leading one of 15 city-based business offices in the company. Jose was responsible for eight supervisors and 102 service representatives. He reported to a district manager (3rd level manager) in another state who oversaw five BSCs.

Still, with all of that experience and company knowledge, Jose could not understand the thinking of senior management. Two years ago, the company had instituted a reward program for service representatives. They earned points for selling certain company products, and the points could be accumulated to earn valuable items such as computers, furniture, kitchen appliances, garden tools, etc. When the program was announced for this year, most of the products and rewards were the same as before, but there were a few changes. What appeared to be a minor change was the addition of the "Call Forward/Busy" feature (CFB). That seemingly innocuous addition to the program quickly created a monster for Jose and his fellow managers that would not go away.

6.7.3 *The Company*

Midwest Bell (MB) was one of the original 23 Bell System operation companies in the United States. With over one million employees in the Bell System, AT&T had to organize itself in different units in order to ensure smooth functioning. It was simply too big to operate as one company. Because much of the company's operations were regulated by the states, the operating companies were historically grouped around state borders. Midwest Bell was comprised of seven US states in the heartland of the nation.

Similar to all of the telephone operating companies (Telcos), MB provided both residential and business communication services in its territory. It also provided "carrier services" to the many long distance companies (carriers) so that their customers could access their long distance networks seamlessly. While "carrier services" is an important revenue source for the company, its level of activity was fairly consistent and predictable. A separate group was responsible for handling the service requests of those long distance carriers.

The business services division of the company was a key revenue stream. The range of products included modular telephone systems for small businesses (up to ten lines) and PBX systems for larger operations. In addition to providing telephone equipment for homes and offices, the company also provided the telephone lines and a large number of software options such as Call Waiting, Call Forwarding, 3-Way Calling, etc.

The company had established an approach to the market place that priced business services at a different rate than residential services. The thinking behind this approach was centered in the value received from the telephone services. Residential customers used the telephone to make personal calls and other non-commercial uses. Business customers, on the other hand, used the telephone to generate money. Therefore, MB had proposed to the regulators that business use of telephone services should be worth more than for residential customers. Thus, the pricing for services was 2–6 times greater than for residential usage.

One of the standard business services was the "rollover" feature. This was the feature where a call to a business would literally roll over from the main number dialed to any idle, additional line. Many firms would have multiple telephone lines. Each line was assigned a unique number, allowing the company to bill charges for services and long distance calls accurately. However, the firms did not want their customers to have to learn all of the various numbers, but wanted their customers to just dial one main number to reach them. The rollover service met that business need. To compensate for the automatic service, customers were charged US$6 per line/per month. Therefore, a business with five lines would be billed for five rollover elements, or US$30/month.

The rollover service was initially a mechanical wiring arrangement in the nearby telephone central office that served that area. Prior to the implementation of computerized switching equipment, all lines were organized manually in the central office. That is, a work order to install the rollover feature was issued by the BSC to the central office where a technician would manually wire the lines together, allowing the automatic rollover to operate if the first line in the sequence was in use. If the second line were also in use, the system would check the third line, etc., seeking an available line to route the call. Only if all lines in the sequence were in use would a busy signal be sent back to the original caller.

But here was the crux of the current situation. The company had introduced the new feature of Call Forward/Busy (CFB) in the previous year. It was a software feature that was easily programmed in the central office computer system and did not require the manual wiring by a technician. The features operated together. If a number dialed was in use (Busy), the line automatically was forwarded to another line within the same set of lines.

The monthly cost for the service was US$1 per line, considerably less than the standard rollover monthly charge of US$6. Service representatives were encouraged to place the new product, and they could earn award points for each line they added the new feature.

The BSC representatives quickly saw the easy sale prospect. In short, they could tell business customers that they could lower monthly bills by replacing the rollover feature with the new CFB feature. Business customers could save US$5/line/month! That was US$60/line in a year. That business customer with five lines could save US$360/year. True, there was an installation charge of $10/line plus an order charge of $25, but the monthly savings quickly absorbed the total one-time installation charge of US$75. It was indeed an easy "sale" for the service representatives and they were quickly earning large numbers of award points. It was a "sale" only if you define it as lowering someone's bill; however, in the perspective of the service representative, it was a sale as it earned award points.

6.7.4 *January*

Unfortunately, managers were not on the award program and did not earn points. They each had revenue objectives for the year, and they each could earn a bonus if they exceeded those revenue objectives. The award program was initially warmly embraced, as it was a useful tool for encouraging the sale of specific company products. Service representatives saw it in their own self-interest to focus upon the products that earned the most points. As an incentive tool, the program was effective in driving sales behaviors. When it had been announced that the program would be renewed for the current year, both managers and representatives were excited. The program had become an integral part of the representative's income stream, and they looked forward to the prizes they could earn. Managers liked the program because it did drive sales behavior. It seemed a win–win for all involved.

The sales goals for each unit were announced at the same time. There was a modest increase in revenue attainment from the previous year, but the increase seemed reasonable to Jose and well within what he believed were the capabilities of his staff. He compared notes with his fellow managers in other offices and learned they had similar increases. Therefore, Jose felt the goals for the year were both fair and attainable. With the award program as an incentive tool, he started the New Year with an optimistic perspective.

6.7.5 *February*

When the month report for January was issued during the second week of February, Jose had the first inclination that he had a problem. Total revenue billed was up just a small percentage of 1.3%, but he noted the large quantity of CFB that had been ordered by customers (4,571). He saw the corresponding decrease in rollover units (4,493). The number of CFB units ordered was almost identical to the decrease in rollover units. Jose thought he understood what was happening. After reviewing the award program details, he confirmed his suspicion. Indeed, sales representatives were placing the CFB product and were earning award points. Unfortunately, they were also reducing the total billing for the month because they were replacing the older rollover with CFB. Again, Jose noted his total billing was up slightly, so the impact was not that apparent. Still, he wondered if it was just a result of the new additions to the award program or something else. He decided to keep his thoughts to himself and see what transpired in the next month.

6.7.6 March

The sales report for February was late in its distribution, and when Jose finally received his copy of the report, he became alarmed. Overall, the total billed revenue had dropped, with a decrease of 2.4%. His year-to-date percentage was now at 98.9%. All of the gain from January was wiped-out and he was actually behind the starting point on January 1st. His bonus was directly impacted by billed revenue. He certainly was not going to earn a bonus at this rate. Fearing he understood the root cause of the decrease, he quickly found the entries for both rollover and CFB. The numbers had tripled from the January report! More than 14,000 units of CFB had been sold and 13,571 units of rollover had been removed. It was clear to Jose what was happening. Sales representatives had discovered an easy method of earning award points. Jose decided he needed to discuss this with his supervisors to see what they knew about the issue.

At the regular staff meeting on the following Monday afternoon, Jose brought up the revenue report as the first item for discussion. Several supervisors immediately responded. Mary reported that she knew of several reps (industry jargon for service representative) who were gleefully talking with customers, placing quick orders by presenting the CFB product as an important monthly savings while improving service. Bill mentioned that he had been routinely monitoring a few reps and had heard where they initiated the sales discussion for CFB. He not only was not concerned as it was a featured new product, but he had given the reps positive comments in their reviews because of their self-initiated behavior! Bill had no idea that they were actually lowering billed revenue and harming the organization. Maria had not noticed the activity but wondered what any of them could do about it. It seemed to Maria that management intended to drive the placement of certain products and structured the award program accordingly, and if the BSC reps were doing just that, what was the problem?

Jose countered that the sales activity was lowering total billed revenue, which was moving the group in the opposite direction of their annual goals. He reminded the supervisors that bonuses were tied to exceeding annual revenue goals, so reversing the trend was important. The supervisors acknowledged his point, but again asked what they could do about the BSC reps selling activity. Jose had no useful response, but said that he would pursue this with the district manager (the 3rd level of management).

After the meeting, Jose returned to his office and immediately fired off an email message to his boss. Hilary Wong was a fair boss, but often difficult to reach. She seemed to be very focused on some of the top-level, strategic management activity in the company, so she was not in her office on a regular basis. She had also let Jose and her other direct reports know that she did not want to be bothered with detailed issues. Hilary felt those types of problems were the responsibility of the 2nd level managers. She only wanted them to bring forward larger issues worthy of her attention. Jose had thought carefully about even contacting her while the staff meeting wound down, but felt the trend that seemed to be emerging was indicative of a larger problem, and that Hilary would want to know. He took the risk and sent her the email with the broad strokes of the issue as he saw it.

Not unexpectedly, Hilary wrote back the next day with a response that gave Jose pause. She replied that the award program had been carefully designed to support the company's strategy, and that he was to trust the process. She was sure he could stimulate sales in other product lines to compensate for this issue. After all, she wrote, the company had more than 45 products for business customers. Surely Jose could guide staff in his unit to sell other products! Jose was not pleased with this response, and chided himself that he should have known better. Hilary had shown many times that she was a "company person" and would automatically defend policies and procedures. Jose resolved to work with the supervisors to encourage sales of other products to compensate for the lost revenue of CFB activity.

6.7.7 April

The March sales report that was issued by the 10th of April was again reflecting a negative revenue situation. Total billed revenue for his unit was now down 4.4% for the month. Jose was very upset. He had guesstimated that, by the end of this first quarter, his unit would be 3% ahead of target. He knew that many firms had fresh budgets at the start of the year, and would place orders for service that they had delayed ordering from the end of last year. At another loss of 4.4%, he was actually at 94.5%, or 8.5% behind the goal of where he wanted to be, and 5.5% behind where he needed to be. This was turning into a major issue.

He wondered if he should approach Hilary again, but quickly decided against that. Hilary would likely respond that he was not doing his job by compensating through the sales of other products. He certainly did not want to draw her attention to that. He knew that Hilary rarely looked closely at the monthly reports, instead preferring to look at overall summary reports by quarter. Jose decided it was time to consult with his peer managers in other units to see if they were experiencing a similar effect. Of course, he would have to approach this carefully.

Hilary had set up a group situation where the 2nd level managers were actually in competition with one another. Hilary and her superiors set the annual revenue goal, but within the division, the climate was one of striving to out-perform one another. Hilary wanted to look like an outstanding 3rd level manager, and her way of doing it was to goad the 2nd level managers to perform better by pitting them against one another. Hilary reinforced this climate by sending group messages where she would showcase the best performing manager while completely ignoring everyone else. If Jose was going to learn anything about this issue from his peers, he had better be careful what he disclosed. If the other managers learned of his decreasing revenue total, they would spread that word quickly, undermining Jose's position in the group. He felt telling too much would weaken his position in the group, so he would not share too much if he did not have to do so.

Jose did not want a record of this sort of inquiry, so he called Betty, a manager in his group who was fairly friendly with him. The tough aspect of the manager's group was that they were all in different states, which meant they did not physically see one another very often, and their business activities rarely intersected. Thus, talking with Betty was somewhat risky, as she had no real allegiance to Jose or any other manager in their group. Still, Jose knew he needed to do something because the drop in billing was clearly a problem for him.

His call to Betty did not tell him much new information. After exchanging pleasantries, Betty just made safe comments about how it was a new year with fresh challenges, and how her group was making satisfactory progress. That was not very helpful to Jose at all. He did not dare risk making her aware of his situation at this point. He decided to wait another month to see what would happen. But in the meanwhile, he would press his supervisors to continue to encourage BSC reps to sell other products.

What he also observed was the great feeling among the sales representatives. Morale was very high. Several reps had accumulated enough award points to place orders for prizes. They had received them and were showing them off proudly to their peers. A few had new laptop computers and others described the joy of receiving new furniture or equipment for their homes. Jose often saw employees clustered around the prize booklet in the break room. The program certainly was effective in creating incentives for the BSC reps.

The strategy of selling CFB in place of the rollover had spread across the entire office. Now all 60 reps were aggressively selling CFB. While Jose was glad to see morale so high, he also was very concerned about total billed revenue. He feared that his unit was on a slippery slope from which there was no retreat. He saw his yearly bonus evaporating. His morale certainly was not as positive as that of the BSC reps in his unit. He wondered if the supervisors had any sense of the magnitude of this issue.

6.7.8 May

The new month had barely started when the entire group of supervisors ambushed Jose. He had just walked in for the day and they were all waiting outside of his office. It seemed they had finally caught on to the magnitude of the CFB issue and were quite concerned. They expressed that they had been encouraging BSC reps to place other products, but that the "easy" sale of CFB was their focus. True, other customer needs were being met, but the only actual upgrade selling was coming from CFB. They knew the April sales report had not been issued yet, but already, they forecasted that Jose would see another decrease in total billed revenue.

Maria said that she had been attempting to counter the sales blitzing of CFB, but she did not have a useful response when the reps pointed to the award program. A few reps seemed to hear her express a concern about lowering the total income for the company, but the vast majority of reps were more interested in the personal gain they could achieve through the award points program.

Ken echoed Maria's comment, and added that he had explained to a number of reps that if they kept going this way, the company would not be able to afford keeping so many reps on staff. That seemed to shock a few reps and their conversation ended, but he felt that reps continued to sell CFB anyway. Ken felt helpless to do anything, too. He said that he saw his bonus disappearing and was getting depressed about it all. Jose asked that they do their best to encourage reps to place other products. The supervisors left his office grumbling, and Jose felt helpless to help them too.

When the April sales report arrived, Jose was stunned. The number of CFB units placed as 25,610 and the number of rollovers removed was 24,868. The trend was clearly established and the impact upon revenue devastating to his annual goal. The impact of this activity was to reduce billed revenue by 7.6%, bringing his annual progress toward the goal to 86.8%. He knew a call from Hilary would be forthcoming, and he prepared for it. He did not want to sound like he had lost control of the sales force, so he had to make a persuasive case about the negative impact the reward program was having upon total billed revenue.

The call from Hilary came within the hour of Jose's receipt of the report. She demanded to know what was going on and what he planned to do to fix the situation. Hilary reminded Jose that not only was his bonus on the line, but so was the bonus for the entire unit. She said that his unit was not the only one struggling but she certainly wanted to know how he was going to reverse the negative trend.

Feeling defensive and helpless but not wanting to have Hilary sense either feeling, Jose attempted to explain what he felt was the root cause of the negative billing trend. Hilary interrupted his explanation to say that she had heard of this before, and that it was just one minor product. She said that a $5 reduction in billing for one line certainly could be recovered by the sale of a new line or the addition of other software features (such as call waiting or 3-way calling). Hilary felt that his unit was taking the easy way out and not making the sales effort that was expected. Jose was told to work harder to get BSC reps to do their job and to not worry about the awards program. Overall, the program was quite effective in driving behavior and was appreciated by the staff. Jose was not to start interfering in such a good program. After all, product management and human resources staffs in the corporate office were experts in sales and compensation. They certainly knew what they were doing. Jose was not to question them, but instead was to spend his energy on increasing sales of all of the products. Hilary ended the call by saying she looked forward to a positive report next month.

Jose had no idea what to do. The supervisors were looking to him to guide them. He had turned to his boss for assistance and been told that things were fine, and he was to just do his job. What else could Jose do at this point?

He decided to call a staff meeting with the supervisors. He outlined the basic response from Hilary and asked them to generate ideas to stimulate more sales. They reported that a number of reps were wary, understanding that a sustained effort to lower customer bills would result in less jobs. But beyond that, many reps still kept selling CFB. The supervisors were not very excited about the ideas they developed, feeling most were either already in place or were not likely to succeed, and left the meeting grumbling under their breaths. Jose knew they were not happy, and their morale was low, but he felt just as frustrated. Plus, it just dawned on him that Hilary had not sent out a monthly "brag" report to announce the top performer in 2 months. He had been so focused upon this problem that he had not noticed. He wondered if this meant that other units were having difficulties, too.

6.7.9 June

Either word of the shortfall of the annual goal had spread through the office, or the BSC reps were more mindful of the impact of their actions, but the issue was now openly debated. A number of reps declared they would not sell CFB unless specifically requested by a customer because of the negative impact upon the company. Other reps told the first group that they were silly, and that the company knew what it was doing. Certainly the company would not design an award program that actually harmed revenue. This second group was quite defensive and encouraged others to just mind their own business and focus upon earning award points. Tensions had risen in the office, and morale had dipped once again. The uncertainty, reflected in both the monthly results as well as in the attitudes of the supervisors, contributed to the lowering of morale. Many BSC reps expressed that they did not think that the company was well run anymore. Jose did not blame them, but he knew it was his responsibility to change their thinking. The problem was that he did not know what to do.

The May sales report showed a continued drop in billed revenue, although the decrease was slightly lower. Annual billing had fallen to 85.0%, a decrease of 1.8%. Maybe, Jose thought, the bulk of the conversions were over and the situation would stabilize. Still, 15% lower than his goal was a depressing thought. Even if he instituted redoubled efforts to encourage sales of other products, he doubted that the unit would reach the annual revenue goal.

Feeling ready to give up, Jose swallowed his pride and again called his peer manager, Betty. Immediately, he could hear concern in her voice and when he mentioned CFB, it seemed to unleash a torrent within Betty. She just began to rapidly describe the impact upon her results and started complaining about the reward program. Betty said that her results had her progress listed at 85.2% for the year. She was thinking the company would ask her to return part of her salary instead of receiving a bonus. She felt that bad.

Jose revealed to Betty his situation and agreed the source of the problem was in the award program. He also told Betty of his conversations with Hilary. They decided to call the other 2nd level managers to see if others had similar results, and assuming they did, would work together to form an action plan.

While Betty checked with the other 2nd level managers, Jose decided to speak with his supervisory group once again. This time, when he broached the topic, his supervisors expressed anger and disgust with senior management, and depression about their effectiveness. They reported that most BSC reps openly made comments about the "stupid leadership" of the company and about how it was going "down the drain." Because they did not have an effective rebuttal, all the supervisors could do was offer platitudes such as "it would all work out in the end" or similar trite sayings. The mood on the sales floor was dour and a number of reps expressed fear that they were selling themselves out of a job. That new laptop or sofa no longer looked so attractive when compared to future employment.

Betty called Jose back to report that all of the other 2nd level managers had similar results. They had agreed to an immediate conference call to devise an action plan. Betty bridged Jose right into the call and the group discussed the situation. They decided that Betty would represent them by contacting Hilary, laying out the full range of the problem that each was suffering, and then asking her to escalate the matter up the line. They agreed to another conference call at the end of the day to see how Hilary responded.

Betty created another conference bridge at the end of the day and reported that Hilary had not returned any of her calls and had not answered her email message. While that was not completely unusual when Hilary was traveling, it was not typical. Still, the group decided it was appropriate to give Hilary a reasonable amount of time to respond, so they adjourned and counted on Betty to give them regular updates.

Jose received no word the next day, or even the next week. It seemed that Hilary had not responded at all, and had then left on her 2-week summer vacation. They would not have any response until the first of next month at the earliest. That was disappointing and discouraging to all.

6.7.10 July

Results for June were no different from previous months, which made the situation worse for all. By now, the news about revenue attainment was an open secret throughout the entire office. Some BSC reps were actually harassing their peers when they heard someone offer CFB to a customer. Factions had formed, with those very concerned about the impact upon the company actively watching and reporting out loud anyone who wrote up an order for CFB. Those less concerned were either being browbeaten into compliance with the first group, or they were hiding their work so that they could still earn the award points. Either way, it had become a hostile work environment. Efforts by the supervisors to impact the situation were modest, especially as all of them agreed that the negative impact was dangerous to the company's financial health. It was difficult to promote the company line when they simply did not believe it was the right thing to be doing. The BSC reps easily picked up their attitude, and that just magnified the lowering morale.

The June sales report reflected another 2% decrease in revenue. Jose, Betty, and the other 2nd level managers could not reach Hilary for weeks now. She was either traveling, in high-level meetings, or would get back to them later. It was odd that Hilary would deal with other issues, but she was avoiding any response on this matter. Any communication from Hilary was either via email or voice mail. None of them ever reached her that month via telephone or in person. Not giving up, each manager continued to periodically send Hilary messages, asking for help.

6.7.11 August

Jose leaned back in his office chair, through with his reflection upon the year to date. He had just received an email notice of a scheduled video conference call with senior management. All 2nd level managers and above in the BSC were invited. The topic of the call was not included in the announcement, so they had to guess at the content. But all of the managers felt it had to be the CFB issue. That was the only one important unresolved of which they were aware, and they did not usually have this type of video conference call in the middle of the summer season. Something important was clearly at hand. The meeting was scheduled for two days away, so they only had a short time to wonder and hope.

The call began on time, and was led by Sue Watson, a company vice president (a 4th level manager). Sue had recently been promoted to the position from another Bell System company, so very little was known about her. Still, Jose immediately felt hopeful with such a senior-level manager leading the call.

After introducing all of the 3rd level managers in the room with her, including Hilary, Sue announced that the topic of the meeting would be the issue of CFB and the award program. She then explained that the 3rd level managers had brought the issue to her attention 5 or 6 weeks ago, but that she had needed time to become familiar with the operation and to understand the entire program before acting on this one product's role in the reward program. She now believed she understood the issue and had solutions to resolve it.

First, she acknowledged that the current program setup was intentional, but that the manager's annual billed revenue objectives should have been adjusted to reflect the expected impact. Sue explained that the company was aware of several new competitors' products soon to be offered on the market that included the ability of rollover within those systems. That would immediately negate the need for business customers to pay for their rollover product at all. Senior management believed it would become a standard ability of competing telephone equipment in the future, including the systems sold by their own company. Thus, the strategic intention of management was to transition businesses into the software features of their central offices in an attempt to save some of the soon-to-be-lost revenue. At $6/line, competitors could make a good case for businesses to purchase their systems and pay for the internal ability for the rollover. At $1/line, senior management felt that the competitors could no longer make that argument effectively. Thus, senior management was well aware the CFB was cannibalizing the old, mechanical rollover product revenue stream. Their actions in the reward program were an effort to retain some of the billing instead of losing all of the rollover revenue.

Second, Sue readily admitted that the sales goals of the units should have been adjusted to reflect this approach. She also admitted that senior management should have explained this at the start of the year. They had not, out of a desire to get a jump on the competitors; fearing word of their intent would spur an earlier release of the competing systems. They were aware that confusion could occur, but certainly not to the extent that it did. For that, Sue offered an apology to all managers.

Third, Sue then proceeded to explain the action steps that would be taken by the corporate office to address the issue. Revenue goal relief would immediately be implemented. Removing the past and current billing for both the rollover product and the CFB product would reset all revenue goals. In that manner, managers would only be responsible for the billed revenue of the products not impacted by this strategy. The recalculation would be backdated until the first of the year, and all bonus compensation would be based upon the revised numbers. Sue stated that the financial staff would begin working on that effort very soon, but from her estimates, all units would be either near 100% of targets or above. Jose and several other managers actually cheered at this good news!

Sue next explained that the reward program would continue "as is" but offered suggestions about how to handle the news with the BSC representatives. First and foremost, managers and supervisors were to strongly support the integrity of the awards program. They were to explain to the BSC reps that the program had been recently reviewed and all aspects of it were confirmed. The program represented the intentions of senior management and reps were encouraged to participate as strongly as they had earlier in the year.

Next, Sue suggested that 2nd level managers were to explain the strategic intent of the company in face-to-face meetings. When possible, Sue wanted these meetings to include the 3rd level manager; however, she knew that time was of the essence and that the 3rd level managers could not travel to all office locations that fast. Therefore, each 3rd level would select the office location where he or she felt a visit would be most effective, and work with that 2nd level manager to schedule the group talk. Other 2nd level managers were to move quickly to set up their own face-to-face meetings. During the meetings, managers were to reveal the full intent of the strategy and thank all of the representatives for their good-faith efforts, regardless of which perspective they advocated. Those that were highly concerned about the negative impact upon revenue were to be acknowledged and thanked. Those that continued to sell CFB were also to be recognized and appreciated, explaining to both factions that they each seemed to have the well-being of the company at heart and were struggling with limited information. None of them had jobs at risk, and they were supporting the company's plans by following the award plan.

Finally, Sue wanted the managers to express to the reps that the company preferred if they could keep the strategy information "in-house" at this time. Senior management knew that the word of the strategy would travel through the industry rather quickly, but if they could limit who knew outside of the BSC for now, they could give themselves a few weeks to convert more customers. They did not want to push the competitors to launch the new systems any sooner than necessary. Although the company had the benefit of 7+ months in converting customers, and those new systems would be unveiled fairly soon, the time remaining would be important in terms of protecting revenue.

6.7.12 Program Effort Rejuvenated

Jose exited the video conference call with a huge sigh of relief. He could not wait to call his supervisory group into his office to explain everything. He just knew this information would make all of the difference, and both morale and performance would bounce up quickly. Of course, he wanted to be well prepared for the face-to-face meeting so that he explained the strategy correctly, and to answer all of their questions accurately, but he could not wait to get started. Of course, he did not know just yet if Hilary wanted to be at his group meeting, but he was certain he would hear from her within hours. Sue had made it clear that time was of the essence, and if nothing else, Hilary paid attention to senior management. Within the week, Jose had no doubt that all would be well again in the BSC. He just wished that none of them had to go through this 7-month roller coaster.

As he walked out of his office to gather the supervisors, he wondered what other secret strategies had been developed that his group was resisting rather than supporting, all because management did not want competitors to know, or the systems were not properly aligned, or?

Glossary

Analytics Interpretation of information by individuals to improve decision making. The **Strategic Business Intelligence Framework™** distinguishes different types of analytical applications and their main purpose: (a) Past analytics such as data mining, correlation analysis, and trend analysis should help to gain insights about what happened in the past and digging deep to find short- and long-term correlations between key performance indicators. This may lead, e. g., to an understanding which marketing campaigns for which customer segments were most effective for improving the company image, customer satisfaction, or sales. Via this kind of analysis the organization understands and learns more about their own operations and how to potentially improve the effectiveness. (b) Current analytics include operational reporting and performance monitoring as well as automated alerts. The purpose of these analytics is to align all activities of the organization with its strategy. (c) Future analytics support business planning, budgeting, forecasting, and simulating alternative business scenarios based on predictive analytics and are part of strategy creation. The strategy is defined based on the forecasts and simulations of business scenarios and the strategic objectives are defined during the planning process. Budgets are allocated to enable the organizational units to accomplish these strategic goals. Obviously past analytics and current analytics are supporting this important decision-making process as well. The decisions made during the planning and budgeting process define the strategic contribution of each organizational entity and thereby establish strategies on all levels, which align toward the shared objectives

Alerts They can be triggered automatically and establish a 24×7 surveillance based on individually defined deviations from expected performance thresholds, thereby freeing up scarce management time. Alerts are specifically useful to reduce the demand on management time to monitor performance for diagnostic KPIs.

Alignment An adjustment of components for coordinated functioning.

Business Intelligence Luhn (1958) introduced the term in 1958. He envisioned a flexible automated system identifying information needs and disseminating the

DOI 10.1007/978-3-642-19205-0, © Springer-Verlag Berlin Heidelberg 2012

information efficiently within the organization. In 1992, Howard Dresner (Dresner Advisory Services, 2011) described business intelligence as a set of concepts and methods to improve business decision making by using fact-based support systems. The term Business Intelligence is often used as a synonym for data warehousing or decision support systems, as an IT-solution or an OLAP infrastructure. Such a perception of Business Intelligence as an information technology solution does not put much emphasis on the business perspective of business intelligence. The term **Strategic Business Intelligence™** emphasizes that intelligence based on analytics is applied in a business context to support an effective strategy execution.

Dashboard Management cockpits or dashboards summarize the key facts similar to the cockpit of an airplane or the dashboard of a car. They display the key performance indicators in a transparent, consistent, and timely manner. Management cockpits and dashboards help managers to "drive" their business. They use graphics similar to regular dashboards including dials, gauges, traffic lights, and complement these with charts, maps, and text.

Data Mining A process of knowledge discovery including correlation analysis, pattern and trend recognition by using statistical and mathematical models. Informative data mining methods include clustering, ABC classification, and association analysis. Predictive data mining methods include decision trees and scoring methods based on weighted score tables and linear as well as nonlinear regression.

Data Warehouse Data warehouses are required to store the data from multiple OLTP systems in a multidimensional format to support Online Analytical Processing (OLAP). Codd, Codd, and Salley (1993) defined twelve requirements for OLAP systems: (1) Multidimensional conceptual view enabling users to slice, dice, drill-down, zoom out, (2) Transparency, (3) Accessibility, (4) Consistent reporting performance, (5) Client/server architecture, (6) Generic dimensionality, (7) Dynamic sparse matrix handling, (8) Multiuser support, (9) Unrestricted cross-dimensional operations, (10) Intuitive data manipulation, (11) Flexible reporting, and (12) Unlimited dimensions and aggregation levels. The advantages of using a data warehouse as a foundation for corporate reporting compared to reporting based on OLTP systems are: (1) Improved online transactional processing performance, (2) improved reporting performance, (3) easy access to data, (4) integrated and consistent data from multiple source enabling a single version of the truth.

Key Performance Indicator (KPI) KPIs are metrics used to define objectives and to measure performance. We know, based on our own experience, what is measured is important. Something that is measured might be noticed and may be used for evaluations and decisions. It can have an effect for those that are measured. Something that is not measured is likely to be ignored and therefore of lesser relevance. Naturally, we have to spend our time wisely, where we believe it has the most impact. Now, if something is measured and potentially being used for decision making, it makes sense to focus our efforts on that matter. Consequently, the use of KPIs has an impact on behavior, specifically if the performance is made public and leads to positive or negative recognition by colleagues or is used as a basis for incentive compensation or promotion.

Leading and Lagging Key Performance Indicators Leading indicators have a significant impact on future performance. A change in a leading indicator can have subsequent, delayed effects on lagging indicators. An example is the investment in a new quality improvement program in manufacturing which leads to an increase in manufacturing cost and the number of recognized errors in production (leading indicators) in the short term. Since malfunctions are recognized before the product is delivered to the customer, this leads to fewer customer complaints and returns and an improvement in customer satisfaction over time (lagging indicators). The understanding of cause and effect or correlations between leading and lagging indicators helps to make predictions about the future and focus the effort on those leading indicators which are most relevant to contribute to a positive development of the lagging indicators. Many of the financial indicators such as revenue are examples for lagging indicators, measuring the result of initiatives of the past. Proactive management therefore requires a focus on initiatives which positively impact relevant leading indicators with an expected positive effect on future performance.

Management by Objectives 2.0 (MBO 2.0)™ Management by Objectives (MBO), has been popularized by the management guru Peter Drucker in his book *The Practice of Management* (Drucker, 2006a) since 1954. Thanks to the improvement of IT systems capabilities, it can now be put into practice on a new scale. The availability of new innovative applications facilitating interactive and collaborative dialogue is enabling the revival of Management by Objectives in the 21st century.

Mission "The unique purpose that sets a company apart from others of its type and identifies the scope of its operations in product, market, and technology terms" (Pearce & Robinson, 2009, p. 25).

Performance Management Performance is defined as "the manner in which or the efficiency with which something reacts or fulfills its intended purpose" (Webster's, 1996, p. 1439). The intended purpose of an organization is defined by its vision and mission. Performance management requires to define measurable strategic objectives and monitor performance. Scorecards are used to support decision makers at all organizational levels to assess and manage their performance.

Scorecard "A visual display mechanism used in a strategically oriented performance management system that charts progress towards achieving strategic objectives by comparing performance against targets and thresholds" (Eckerson, 2006, p. 295). A widely used scorecard is the Balanced Scorecard. The **Value Scorecard™** is a special scorecard focusing on a maximum value creation for the organization.

Strategic Alignment Process™ A process to align all organizational members to pull in the same direction, toward the strategic objectives including two major process steps: Preparation for strategy execution and executing strategy. Part of the preparation is: (1) Formulating the strategy, identifying the stakeholder groups and their information needs, (2) establishing meaningful key performance indicators, and (3) measuring and collecting relevant data and integrating the data in information models for reporting. The execution of strategy can be broken down in three tasks: (1) Analyze, (2) decide, and (3) act. In order to support the analysis, the most appropriate communication channels should be leveraged to supply the needed information and enable management on all levels to make appropriate decisions. Acting in accordance with the made decisions should help to improve performance.

Strategic Alignment Remote Control™ An easy-to-use management tool supporting all steps of the Strategic Alignment Process™. It allows managers to access all relevant information in order to focus their attention on the most relevant problems as well as opportunities while exercising strategic control.

Strategic Business Intelligence™ A set of concepts and tools to improve decision making on all levels of the organization and enable an effective strategy execution. Strategic Business intelligence applies the concept of the Value Scorecard™ and leverages information technologies in a Strategic Business Intelligence™ to enable past, current, and future analytics to support continuous learning, strategy alignment as well as strategy creation.

Strategic Business Intelligence Framework™ It consists of a BI-Foundation, including a Data Supply layer, a Data Management layer, and BI-Frontend-Applications to support analytics. It distinguishes different types of analytical applications and their main purpose: (a) Past analytics such as data mining, correlation analysis, trend analysis should help to gain insights about what happened in the past and digging deep to find short- and long-term correlations between key performance indicators. This may lead, e.g., to an understanding which marketing campaigns for which customer segments were most effective for improving the company image, customer satisfaction, or sales. Via this kind of analysis, the organization understands and learns more about their own operations and how to potentially improve the effectiveness. (b) Current analytics include operational reporting and performance monitoring as well as automated alerts. The purpose of these analytics is to align all activities of the organization with its strategy. (c) Future analytics support business planning, budgeting, forecasting, simulating alternative business scenarios based on predictive analytics and are part of strategy creation. The strategy is defined based on the forecasts and simulations of business scenarios and the strategic objectives are defined during the planning process. Budgets are allocated to enable the organizational units to accomplish these strategic goals. Obviously past analytics and current analytics are supporting this important decision-making process as well. The decisions made during the planning and budgeting process define the strategic contribution of each organizational entity and thereby establish strategies on all levels, which align toward the shared objectives.

Strategic Control "Management efforts to track a strategy as it is being implemented, detect problems or changes in its underlying premises, and make necessary adjustments" (Pearce & Robinson, 2009, p. 409).

Strategic Management "The set of decisions and actions that result in the formulation and implementation of plans designed to achieve a company's objectives" (Pearce & Robinson, 2009, p. 3).

Strategic Objective An objective is "something that one's efforts or actions are intended to attain or accomplish" (Webster's, 1996, p. 1336). A goal is "the result or achievement toward which effort is directed" (Webster's, 1996, p. 817). In order to use strategic objectives as a foundation for corporate performance management, strategic objectives should define measurable, time-bound goals.

Strategic Planning A plan is "a scheme or method of acting, doing, proceeding, making, etc., developed in advance. Plan refers to any method of thinking out acts and purposes beforehand" (Webster's, 1996, p. 1480). Strategic planning is a process of defining strategic objectives and appropriate actions to reach them.

Strategy Plan of action to achieve a particular goal. "A plan, method, or series of maneuvers or stratagems for obtaining a specific goal or result" (Webster's, 1996, p. 1880). "Strategy is the means by which individuals or organizations achieve their objectives" (Grant, 2010, p. 16). "Large-scale, future-oriented plans for interacting with the competitive environment to achieve company objectives" (Pearce & Robinson, 2009, p. 3). "Strategy is a plan that aims to give the enterprise a competitive advantage over rivals through differentiation. Strategy is about understanding what you do, what you want to become, and – most importantly – focusing on how you plan to get there. Likewise, it is about what you don't do; it draws boundaries around the scope of a company's intentions" (Harvard Business School, 2005, p. xiv).

Strategy Execution Execution of plans to achieve the organizations' objectives. An effective strategy execution does not only depend on a well-developed strategy but depends on the complete organization to be aligned with this strategy.

Strategy Execution Effectiveness Survey™ A survey available on the book website http://www.strategicbusinessintelligence.com to assess your organizational effectiveness in regards to strategy execution.

Value Scorecard™ A scorecard which is not only balanced but focuses on the attainment of maximum value for an organization. The value chain includes suppliers, the organization and the buyers. The organizational value can be optimized by maximizing the difference between the price the buyer is willing to pay and the cost for all suppliers who provide their work at a defined cost. The overall value created is split between all actors and it is not only important for organizations to add a maximum value but to secure a maximum share of this value for their organization by reducing the cost paid to suppliers and by increasing the price for buyers. The bargaining between the players will determine how the value will be divided. A maximum value appropriation for the own organization therefore requires good negotiation skills as well as knowledge of the willingness to pay and opportunity cost, since these two present upper bounds in the negotiation process. The Value Scorecard therefore focuses on the KPIs in the four essential dimensions: Value, Demander, Supplier, and Internal.

Vision "The act or power of anticipating that which will or may come to be" (Webster's, 1996, p. 2126). "A statement that presents a firm's strategic intent designed to focus the energies and resources of the company on achieving a desirable future" (Pearce & Robinson, 2009, p. 37).

World of Strategic Business Intelligence™ A conceptual foundation to align two worlds and perspectives that too often exist in isolation: Business and IT. Each perspective is broken down in three layers. At the core of the business perspective is the strategy. Keeping in mind that you cannot manage what you cannot measure, the performance indicators need to be used to establish measurable, strategic objectives. These should be used for communication with the stakeholders. On the IT perspective, data is at the core. Data models are used to integrate data from different sources and formats. Communicating the relevant information to the respective stakeholders is supported via suitable communication channels.

References

Accenture. (2008a). *Cultivating high performance through information management: Findings from the Accenture CIO survey 2007: Business Intelligence*. Retrieved November 5, 2010, from http://www.accenture.com/NR/rdonlyres/B500F42A-36A3-469E-87E2-9439DD8AB44E/0/3660_AIMSCIOSurvey_BIfindingsfinal.pdf

Accenture. (2008b). *Most U.S. companies say business analytics still future goal, not present reality*. Retrieved November 16, 2010, from http://newsroom.accenture.com/article_display.cfm?article_id=4777

Accenture. (2010). *Weak analytics capabilities hindering companies' and governments' decision-making abilities, Accenture research reveals*. Retrieved February 19, 2010, from http://newsroom.accenture.com/article_display.cfm?article_id=4935

Adelman, S., & Moss, L. T. (2002). *Data Warehouse project management*. Boston, MA: Addison Wesley.

Adidas group. (2011). *mi adidas*. Retrieved February 11, 2011, from http://shop.adidas.de/miadidas

Adkins, T. C. (2006). *Case studies in performance management: A guide from the experts*. Hoboken, NJ: Wiley.

Aidmatrix. (2010). *About us: The right aid to the right people at the right time*. Retrieved December 14, 2010, from http://www.aidmatrix.org/aboutus/index.htm

AIODM. (2010). *Alliance Internationale pour les Objectifs Du Millénaire*. Retrieved 11 September 2010, from http://www.aiodm2015.org/

Alexander, S. (2008). *Volkswagen nutzt BI mit System [Volkswagen uses BI system systematically] (Computerwoche 44/2008)*. Retrieved November 03, 2010, from http://www.computerwoche.de/heftarchiv/2008/44/1225096/

Amazon. (2011). *Amazon.com*. Retrieved February 09, 2011, from http://www.amazon.com/

Andler, N. (2008). *Tools for project management, workshops and consulting: A must-have compendium of essential tools and techniques*. Erlangen: Publicis.

Andreyeva, T., Long, M. W., & Brownell, K. D. (2010). *The impact of food prices on consumption: A systematic review of research on the price elasticity of demand for food*. Retrieved January 16, 2011, from http://ajph.aphapublications.org/cgi/content/abstract/100/2/216

ARGOS. (2010). *Argos: Expert en aménagement du territoire, développement économique et social et évaluation de politique publique*. Retrieved December 02, 2010, from http://www.argos-consultants.fr/

ASUG. (2007). *ASUG/SAP Benchmarking Initiative: Business Intelligence/Analytics*. American SAP Users Group Annual Meeting. Atlanta, GA, USA.

ASUG. (2010a). *American SAP Users Group*. Retrieved August 05, 2010, from http://www.asug.com/

DOI 10.1007/978-3-642-19205-0, © Springer-Verlag Berlin Heidelberg 2012

ASUG. (2010b). *ASUG and SAP Benchmarking and Best Practices program*. Retrieved August 05, 2010, from http://www.sap-for-utilities.com/VCR/vcr_documents_847235098374590345/BenchmarkingBrochure_FINAL.pdf

Atre, S. (2003). *The Top 10 critical challenges for Business Intelligence success*. Retrieved August 05, 2010, from http://www.computerworld.com/computerworld/records/images/pdf/BusIntellWPonline.pdf

Australian Government: Department of the Environment, Water, Heritage and the Arts. (2009). *Australian government policy on cane toads*. Retrieved February 20, 2011, from http://www.environment.gov.au/biodiversity/invasive/publications/cane-toad/pubs/cane-toad-policy.pdf

Axson, D. A. (2010). *Best practices in planning and performance management: Radically rethinking management for a volatile world*. Hoboken, NJ: Wiley.

Balanced Scorecard Institute. (2010a). *Balanced Scorecard Institute*. Retrieved September 12, 2010, from http://www.balancedscorecard.org/

Balanced Scorecard Institute. (2010b). *How to create a Balanced Scorecard*. Retrieved September 11, 2010, from http://www.balancedscorecard.org/BSCResources/TheNineStepstoSuccess/tabid/58/Default.aspx

Ballou, D. P., & Tayi, G. K. (1999). Enhancing data quality in data warehouse environments. *Communications of the ACM, 42*(1), 73–78.

Bell, J., & Pou, R. (2009). *Performance intelligence at work: The 5 essentials to achieving the mind of a champion*. New York, NY: McGraw-Hill.

Bossidy, L., & Charan, R. (2002). *Execution: The discipline of getting things done*. New York, NY: Crown Publishing.

Brandenburger, A. M., & Stuart, H. W. (1996). *Value-based business strategy (MIT Journal of Economics & Management Strategy, Vol. 5, No. 1, pp. 5–24)*. Retrieved November 01, 2010, from http://pages.stern.nyu.edu/~abranden/ValueBasedStrategy2.pdf

Bundesagentur für Arbeit. (2010). *About us*. Retrieved October 14, 2010, from http://www.arbeitsagentur.de/nn_426130/EN/Navigation/zentral/BA/BA-Nav.html

Buytendijk, F. (2009). *Performance leadership: The next practices to motivate your people, align stakeholders, and lead your industry*. New York: McGraw-Hill.

Buytendijk, F. (2010). *Dealing with dilemmas: Where business analytics fall short*. Hoboken, NJ: Wiley.

Candido, C. J., & Santos, S. P. (2008). *Strategy implementation: What is the failure rate*. Retrieved December 14, 2010, from http://www.casee.ricardoportela.com/workingpapers/CASEE_WP18_2008.pdf

Catalina Marketing. (2010). *About Catalina marketing*. Retrieved November 16, 2010, from http://www.catalinamarketing.com/company/

Chenoweth, T., Corral, K., & Demirkan, H. (2006). Seven key interventions for data warehouse success. *Communications of the ACM, 49*(1), 114–119.

Clifford, N. (2001). Strategic alignment between senior and middle managers in local government and health. *International Journal of Health Care Quality Assurance, 14*(2), 87–95.

Clifford, S. (2008). *New York Times: Web marketing that hopes to learn what attracts a click*. Retrieved November 16, 2010, from http://www.nytimes.com/2008/12/03/business/media/03adco.html

CNN. (2011, January 11). *Facebook likely to go public in 2012*. Retrieved February 15, 2011, from http://money.cnn.com/2011/01/06/technology/facebook_ipo_2012/index.htm

Codd, E. F., Codd, S. B., & Salley, C. T. (1993). In depth: Beyond decision support. *Computer world, 27*(30), 87–89.

Collins, J. (2001). *Good to great: Why some companies make the leap and others don't*. New York: Harper-Collins.

Collis, D. J., & Montgomery, C. A. (1995). Competing on resources. *Harvard Business Review, 73*(4), 118–128.

Commonwealth Scientific and Industrial Research Organisation. (2011). *CSIRO cane toad research*. Retrieved February 20, 2011, from http://www.csiro.au/resources/Cane-Toad-Research.html

Compamedia GmbH. (2010). *Die 100 innovativsten Unternehmen im Mittelstand [The 100 most innovative mid-sized companies]*. Retrieved August 07, 2010, from http://www.top100.de/die-top-100/uebersicht/maihiro-gmbh-.html?p=1

CompUSA Inc. (2011). *About us*. Retrieved March 30, 2011, from http://www.compusa.com/sectors/aboutus/index.asp

Cooper, J. C. (2003). *Price elasticity of demand for crude oil: Estimates for 23 countries*. Retrieved January 12, 2011, from http://15961.pbworks.com/f/Cooper.2003.OPECReview.PriceElasticityofDemandforCrudeOil.pdf

Covey, S. R. (1990). *The 7 habits of highly effective people: Restoring the character ethic*. New York: Fireside.

Covey, S. R. (2004). *The 8th habit: From effectiveness to greatness*. New York: Free Press.

Cwarel Isaf Institute. (2010). *How is effective order introduced into a complex system?* Retrieved January 22, 2010, from http://www.stafford-beer.com

Daimler AG. (2010). *Daimler: Pioneers of sustainable mobility – Annual report 2009*. Retrieved August 08, 2010, from http://www.daimler.com/Projects/c2c/channel/documents/1813321_DAI_2009_Annual_Report.pdf

Data Warehousing Institute. (2011). *tdwii: The premier source for business intelligence and data warehousing*. Retrieved February 09, 2011, from http://tdwi.org/

Davenport, T. H., & Harris, J. G. (2007). *Competing on analytics: The new science of winning*. Boston, MA: Harvard Business School Press.

Davenport, T. H., Harris, G. J., & Cantrell, S. (2003). *The return of enterprise solutions: The director's cut*. Retrieved August 05, 2010, from https://www.accenture.pl/NR/rdonlyres/78B7B1E9-C69E-4578-BDB2-D78F08944B94/0/Return_of_Enterprise_Solutions.pdf

Davis, J., Miller, G. J., & Russell, A. (2006). *Information revolution: Using the information evolution model to grow your business*. Hoboken, NJ: Wiley.

Day, G. S., Reibstein, D. J., & Gunther, R. E. (1997). *Wharton on dynamic competitive strategy*. Hoboken, NJ: Wiley.

de Geus, A. (1997). *The living company*. Retrieved November 05, 2010, from http://hbr.org/products/8202/8202p4.pdf

Diamond, J. (1997). *Discover magazine: The cures of QWERTY*. Retrieved February 15, 2011, from http://discovermagazine.com/1997/apr/thecurseofqwerty1099

Dickson, D., Ford, R. C., & Laval, B. (2005). Managing real and virtual waits in hospitality and service organizations. *Cornell Hotel and Restaurant Administration Quarterly, 46*(1), 52–68.

Dresner Advisory Services. (2011). *The business intelligence study*. Retrieved March 23, 2011, from http://business-intelligence-study.com/

Dresner, H. J., Buytendijk, F., Linden, A., Friedman, T., Strange, K. H., Knox, M., et al. (2002). *The Business Intelligence Competency Center: An essential business strategy (Gartner Research, ID R-15-2248)*. Retrieved March 23, 2011, from http://www.gartner.com/DisplayDocument?doc_cd=107134

Drucker, P. F. (2001). *The essential Drucker*. New York: Harper Collins.

Drucker, P. F. (2006a). *The practice of management* (2nd ed.). New York: Harper Collins.

Drucker, P. F. (2006b). What executives should remember. *Harvard Business Review, 84*(2), 144–152.

Eckerson, W. W. (2006). *Performance dashboards: Measuring, monitoring, and managing your business*. Hoboken, NJ: Wiley.

Eckerson, W. W. (2007). *Predictive analytics: Extending the value of your data warehousing investment (TDWI 2007 Q1 Best Practices Report)*. Retrieved November 19, 2010, from http://tdwi.org/research/2007/01/bpr-1q-predictive-analytics/bpr_1q07_report.aspx?tc=assetpg

Eckerson, W. W. (2009). *Beyond reporting: Delivering insights with next-generation analytics (TDWI 2009 Q3 Best Practices Report)*. Retrieved November 19, 2010, from http://tdwi.org/research/2009/07/bpr-3q-beyond-reporting/bpr_3q09_report.aspx?tc=assetpg&LCSKey=d80fe836-d926-435a-9266-ce9b43415712

Economist. (1997). *How to live long and prosper*. Retrieved November 05, 2010, from http://www.economist.com/node/149064

Entrepreneur Magazine. (2000). *Dun & Bradstreet and Entrepreneur's 6th annual Hot 100: America's fastest-growing new businesses*. Retrieved January 25, 2011, from http://www.profheesen.de/images/stories/Entrepreneur.pdf

Evans, P., & Wurster, T. (1997). Strategy and the new economics of information. *Harvard Business Review, 75*(5), 71–82.

Evelson, B. (2011). *Trends 2011 and beyond: Business intelligence*. Retrieved April 26, 2011, from http://www.forrester.com/rb/Research/trends_2011_and_beyond_business_intelligence/q/id/58854/t/2

Fair Isaac Corporation. (2009). *Optimization drives $19 million gains at Avis*. Retrieved November 17, 2010, from http://www.fico.com/en/FIResourcesLibrary/Avis_Success_2540CS.pdf

Favaro, K., Karlsson, P.-O., & Neilson, G. L. (2010). *CEO succession 2000–2009: A decade of convergence and compression*. Retrieved November 16, 2010, from http://www.booz.com/media/file/CEO_Succession_2010.pdf

Federal Express Corporation. (2011). *FedEx innovation*. Retrieved March 14, 2011, from http://about.fedex.designcdt.com/our_company/fedex_innovation

Fleisher, C. S., & Bensoussan, B. E. (2009). *Business and competitive analysis: Effective application of new and classic methods*. New York, NY: Financial Times.

Flottau, J. (2010). *Airbus: Verlustbringer A380 – Flug ins Ungewisse*. Retrieved September 16, 2010, from sueddeutsche.de: http://www.sueddeutsche.de/wirtschaft/airbus-verlustbringer-a-flug-ins-ungewisse-1.947454

Fortune. (2009). *Fortune 500: Our annual ranking of America's largest corporations 2009 – Top industries: Most profitable*. Retrieved September 16, 2010, from http://money.cnn.com/magazines/fortune/fortune500/2009/performers/industries/profits/equity.html

Fortune. (2010). *Fortune 500: Our annual ranking of America's largest corporations 2010 – Top companies: Most profitable*. Retrieved September 16, 2010, from http://money.cnn.com/magazines/fortune/fortune500/2010/performers/companies/profits/

Frankl, A. (2010). *Validated requirements from business use cases and the Rational Unified Process*. Retrieved September 10, 2010, from http://www.ibm.com/developerworks/rational/library/aug07/frankl/index.html

Freyburger, K., Gardiner, L., Hawking, P., Heesen, B., Jovanovic, R., & Lehmann, P. (2008). *SAP Community Network: University Alliances business intelligence curriculum materials*. Retrieved October 28, 2010, from http://www.sdn.sap.com/irj/uac/library-bi?rid=/webcontent/uuid/a01169ee-d539-2d10-dca3-a8e0020d1859#section2

Fung, K. (2010). *Numbers rule your world: The hidden influences of probability and statistics on everything you do*. New York: McGraw Hill.

Gartner. (2006). BI competency centers: From 'Should We?' to 'How Should We?' *Gartner Business Intelligence Summit*. Amsterdam.

Gartner. (2008a). *Gartner EXP worldwide survey of 1,500 CIOs shows 85 percent of CIOs expect significant change over next three years*. Retrieved August 05, 2010, from http://www.gartner.com/it/page.jsp?id=587309

Gartner. (2008b). *Gartner says worldwide Business Intelligence spending to grow 11 percent in 2008*. Retrieved August 05, 2010, from http://www.gartner.com/it/page.jsp?id=636310

Gartner. (2008c). *Gartner launches Business Intelligence Excellence Award for Asia Pacific region*. Retrieved August 05, 2010, from http://www.gartner.com/it/page.jsp?id=780912

Gartner. (2009a). *Gartner reveals five business intelligence predictions for 2009 and beyond (press release)*. Retrieved March 30, 2009, from http://www.gartner.com/it/page.jsp?id=856714

Gartner. (2009b). *Gartner announces Winner of Inaugural Business Intelligence Excellence Award for Asia Pacific*. Retrieved August 4, 2010, from http://www.gartner.com/it/page.jsp?id=901712

Gartner. (2011a). *Gartner says new relationships will change business intelligence and analytics*. Retrieved April 26, 2011, from http://www.gartner.com/it/page.jsp?id=1513714

Gartner. (2011b). *Gartner says worldwide business intelligence, analytics and performance management software market surpassed the $10 billion mark in 2010*. Retrieved April 26, 2011, from http://www.gartner.com/it/page.jsp?id=1642714

Giesecke & Devrient. (2010). Corporate Controlling.

Google. (2010). *Google milestones*. Retrieved November 16, 2010, from http://www.google.com/corporate/milestones.html

Grant, R. M. (2010). *Contemporary strategy analysis: Text and cases* (7th ed.). Chichester: Wiley.

Hackathorn, R. (2003). *Minimizing action distance*. Retrieved September 15, 2010, from http://www.tdan.com/view-articles/5132

Hamel, G. (2002). *Leading the revolution: How to thrive in turbulent times by making innovation a way of life*. New York: Plume Printing.

Hamel, G., & Phahalad, C. K. (1994). *Competing for the future*. Boston, MA: Harvard Business School Press.

Hamer, P. (2005). *De organisatie van Business Intelligence*. Den Haag: Academic Service.

Harris, J. G., & Davenport, T. H. (2006). *New growth from enterprise systems: Achieving high performance through distinctive capabilities*. Retrieved August 05, 2010, from http://www.accenture.com/NR/rdonlyres/243230F6-99AF-4361-B8F0-2E95510847E1/0/growth_systems.pdf

Harvard Business School. (2005). *Strategy: Create and implement the best strategy for your business*. Boston, MA: Harvard Business School Press.

Heesen, B. (2010). Business Intelligence: Correlating performance to communication. In R. Schuttler (Ed.), *Laws of communication: The intersection where leadership meets employee performance* (pp. 141–152). Hoboken, NJ: Wiley.

Henschen, D. (2010). *The big data era: How data strategy will change – from Barnes & Noble to Cabela's to Catalina Marketing, big companies are shifting their approaches*. Retrieved November 16, 2010, from http://www.informationweek.com/news/business_intelligence/warehouses/showArticle.jhtml?articleID=226600091

Hewlett-Packard. (2009). *The HP business intelligence maturity model: Describing the BI journey*. Retrieved August 05, 2010, from http://h20195.www2.hp.com/V2/GetPDF.aspx/4AA1-5467ENW.pdf

Hormby, S., Morrison, J., Meyers, M., Dave, P., & Tenca, T. (2010). *Marriott International increases revenue by implementing a group pricing optimizer*. Retrieved October 04, 2010, from http://revenue-mgt.section.informs.org/download/Marriott_Informs_RMP_Presentation.pdf

Hwang, H.-G., Ku, C.-Y., Yen, D. C., & Cheng, C. C. (2004). Critical factors influencing the adoption of data warehouse technology: A study of the banking industry in Taiwan. *Decision Support Systems, 37*(1), 1–21.

IBM. (2008). *7-Eleven finds SAP applications and IBM i provide the greatest convenience*. Retrieved August 05, 2010, from http://www-01.ibm.com/software/success/cssdb.nsf/CS/STRD-7M9J7A?OpenDocument&Site=default&cty=en_us

IBM. (2010a). *Capitalizing on complexity: Insights from the 2010 IBM Global CEO Study*. Retrieved November 16, 2010, from http://www-935.ibm.com/services/us/ceo/ceostudy2010/index.html

IBM. (2010b). *Informix product family*. Retrieved October 19, 2010, from http://www-01.ibm.com/software/data/informix/

Information Management and SourceMedia. (2003). *Cutter Consortium Report on corporate use of BI and Data Warehousing technologies*. Retrieved August 05, 2010, from http://www.information-management.com/news/6437-1.html

Information Week. (2008). *Bi at 50 turns back to the future*. Retrieved February 14, 2011, from http://www.informationweek.com/news/software/bi/showArticle.jhtml?articleID=211900005

INFORMS Revenue Management and Pricing Section. (2010). *News*. Retrieved October 04, 2010, from http://revenue-mgt.section.informs.org/news.html

Ittner, C. D., & Larcker, D. F. (2003). Coming up short on nonfinancial performance measurement. *Harvard Business Review, 81*(11), 88–95.

Jennings, J., & Haughton, L. (2002). *It's not the big that eat the small. It's the fast that eat the slow: How to use speed as a competitive tool in business*. New York, NY: Harper Collins.

Johnson, L. K. (2004). Strategies for data warehousing. *MIT Sloan Management Review, 45*(3), 9.

Kaplan, R. S., & Norton, D. P. (1992). The Balanced Scorecard: Measures that drive performance. *Harvard Business Review, 70*(1), 71–79.

Kaplan, R. S., & Norton, D. P. (1996). *The Balanced Scorecard: Translating strategy into action*. Boston, MA: Harvard Business School Press.

Kaplan, R. S., & Norton, D. P. (2001). *The strategy-focused organization: How balanced scorecard companies thrive in the new business environment*. Boston, MA: Harvard Business School Press.

Kaplan, R. S., & Norton, D. P. (2005). The office of strategy management. *Harvard Business Review, 83*(10), 72–80.

Kaplan, R. S., & Norton, D. P. (2008). *The execution premium: Linking strategy to operations for competitive advantage*. Boston, MA: Harvard Business.

Kim, W. C., & Mauborgne, R. (2009). How strategy shapes structure. *Harvard Business Review, 87*(9), 72–80.

Kugel, R. (2007). *Information technology is eevolutionizing management reporting*. Retrieved August 10, 2010, from http://businessfinancemag.com/print/6451

LaValle, S. (2009). *Business analytics and optimization for the intelligent enterprise (IBM Global Business Services Executive Report)*. Retrieved February 19, 2010, from http://www-05.ibm.com/de/services/bao/pdf/gbe03211-usen-00.pdf

Lendio. (2011). *FedEx Corporation*. Retrieved February 12, 2011, from http://www.fundinguniverse.com/company-histories/FedEx-Corporation-Company-History.html

Liker, J. K., & Meier, D. (2006). *The Toyota way fieldbook: A practical guide for implementing Toyota's 4Ps*. New York, NY: McGraw-Hill.

Lingle, J. H., & Schiemann, W. A. (1996). From balanced scorecard to strategic gauges: Is measurement worth it? *Management Review, 85*(3), 56–62.

Lorange, P. (2001). Strategic re-thinking in shipping companies. *Maritime Policy and Management, 28*(1), 23–32.

Loshin, D. (2003). *Business intelligence: The savvy manager's guide*. San Francisco, CA: Morgan Kaufmann.

Luhn, H. P. (1958). A business intelligence system. *IBM Journal*, pp. 314–319.

MacGregor Serven, L. B. (1999). Can your company actually execute its strategy? *Harvard Management Update, 4*(5), 10.

maihiro. (2010). *Welcome to maihiro*. Retrieved August 07, 2010, from http://www.maihiro.com/maihiro/en/home.php

May, T. (2009). *The new know: Innovation powered by analytics*. Hoboken, NJ: Wiley.

McNeilly, M. (2006). *The Sun Tzu strategy site: The six principles from Sun Tzu and the art of modern warfare*. Retrieved September 22, 2010, from http://www.suntzu1.com/content/six_principles_from_the_art_of_modern_warfare/

Microsoft. (2010). *Microsoft SQL Server*. Retrieved October 20, 2010, from http://www.microsoft.com/sqlserver/en/us/default.aspx

Microstrategy. (2010). *Business Intelligence products and services*. Retrieved October 19, 2010, from http://www.microstrategy.com/Products-Services/

MID. (2010). *Innovator modeling platform*. Retrieved October 19, 2010, from http://www.mid.de/en/products/innovator-modeling-platform.html

Mihailovich, S. (2005). Harrah's database grows with Ceasars deal. *Las Vegas Business Press, 22*(33), 1–10.

Millward Brown Optimor. (2010). *TOP100: Most valuable global brands 2010*. Retrieved September 17, 2010, from http://c1547732.cdn.cloudfiles.rackspacecloud.com/BrandZ_Top100_2010.pdf

Mintzberg, H., Ahlstrand, B., & Lampel, J. (1998). *Strategy safari: A guided tour through the wilds of strategic management*. New York: Free Press.

Moody, D., & Walsh, P. (1999). Measuring the value of information: An asset valuation approach. *Proceedings of the 7th European Conference on Information Systems (ECIS '99)*, 496–512. Copenhagen, Denmark.

Moss, T. L., & Atre, S. (2003). *Business Intelligence Roadmap: The complete project lifecycle for decision-support applications*. Boston, MA: Addison-Wesley.

Neely, A., & Bourne, M. (2000). Why measurement initiatives fail. *Measuring Business Excellence, 4*(4).

Neely, A., Adams, C., & Kennerley, M. (2002). *The performance prism: The scorecard for measuring and managing business success*. London: Prentice Hall Financial Times.

Ness Global Industries. (2010). *From expected to achieved: Four steps to making business intelligence work*. Retrieved October 01, 2010, from http://www.nessdownload.com/forms/NGI_WP_BIResearch_Final.pdf

New Economics Foundation. (2009). *The unhappy planet index 2.0: Why good lives don't have to cost the earth*. Retrieved February 20, 2011, from http://www.happyplanetindex.org/public-data/files/happy-planet-index-2-0.pdf

New Economics Foundation. (2011a). *Valuing what matters*. Retrieved February 20, 2011, from http://www.neweconomics.org/programmes/valuing-what-matters

New Economics Foundation. (2011b). *The unhappy planet index 2.0*. Retrieved February 20, 2011, from http://www.happyplanetindex.org/

New Economy Working Group. (2011). *Living wealth indicators*. Retrieved February 20, 2011, from http://www.neweconomyworkinggroup.org/visions/living-wealth-indicators

Nike. (2011). *Nike iD*. Retrieved February 11, 2011, from http://nikeid.nike.com/nikeid

Niven, P. R. (2002). *Balanced scorecard step-by-step: Maximizing performance and maintaining results*. Hoboken, NJ: Wiley.

NOAA. (2004). *NOAA and the Indian Ocean Tsunami (NOAA News Online – story 2358)*. Retrieved September 14, 2010, from http://www.noaanews.noaa.gov/stories2004/s2358.htm

Nobelprize.org. (2010). *The Nobel Prize in Chemistry 2010 – Scientific Background*. Retrieved October 23, 2010, from http://static.nobelprize.org/nobel_prizes/chemistry/laureates/2010/Sciback_2010.pdf

Nonaka, I. (1998). The knowledge-creating company. In H. B. School (Ed.), *Harvard Business Review on knowledge management* (pp. 21–45). Boston, MA: Harvard Business School Press.

Oracle. (2010). *Oracle outlines next major release of Oracle Solaris*. Retrieved October 20, 2010, from http://www.oracle.com/us/products/servers-storage/solaris/index.html

Palladium. (2010). *Kaplan & Norton's Palladium Execution Premium Community (XPC) is now the home of BSC Online*. Retrieved November 14, 2010, from http://www.thepalladiumgroup.com/communities/bsconline/Pages/xpc.aspx/

Panko, R. R. (2008). *What we know about spreadsheet errors*. Retrieved October 28, 2010, from http://panko.shidler.hawaii.edu/My%20Publications/Whatknow.htm

Panko, R. R., & Aurigemma, S. (2010). *Revising the Panko-Halverson taxonomy of spreadsheet errors (published in Decision Support Systems, May 2010, Vol. 49 Issue 2, p.235-244)*. Retrieved October 28, 2010, from http://panko.shidler.hawaii.edu/ssr/

Pearce, J. A., II, & Robinson, J. R. (2009). *Strategic management: Formulation, implementation, and control* (11th ed.). New York, NY: McGraw-Hill.

Pfeffer, J., & Sutton, R. I. (2000). *The knowing-doing gap: How smart companies turn knowledge into action*. Boston, MA: Harvard Business School Press.

Pfeffer, J., & Sutton, R. I. (2006). *Hard facts, dangerous half-truths, and total nonsense: Profiting from evidence-based management*. Boston: Harvard Business School Press.

Porter, M. E. (2004a). *Competitive advantage: Creating and sustaining superior performance*. New York, NY: Free Press.

Porter, M. E. (2004b). *Competitive strategy: Techniques for analyzing industries and competitors*. New York, NY: Free Press.

Prescient. (2011). *Prescient*. Retrieved January 25, 2011, from http://www.prescient.pro

Radcliff, D. (2000). *Aligning Marriott*. Retrieved November 03, 2010, from http://www.computerworld.com/s/article/44339/_Aligning_Marriott

Raynor, M. E. (2007). *The strategy paradox: Why committing to success leads to failure (and what to do about it)*. New York, NY: Currency Doubleday.

Rogers, E. M. (2003). *Diffusion of innovations* (5th ed.). New York: Free Press.

RYI Enterprises. (2010). *Fastpass*. Retrieved November 17, 2010, from http://allears.net/tp/fastpass.htm

SAP. (2010a). *SAP*. Retrieved August 05, 2010, from http://www.sap.com

SAP. (2010b). *SAP Netweaver business warehouse*. Retrieved August 05, 2010, from http://www.sap.com/platform/netweaver/components/businesswarehouse/index.epx

SAP. (2010c). *SAP Netweaver Business Warehouse Accelerator*. Retrieved August 05, 2010, from http://www.sap.com/platform/netweaver/components/businesswarehouse/bwa/index.epx

SAP. (2010d). Top 10 most influential people in SAP. *Inside SAP, 2010* (47), pp. 11–24.

SAP. (2010e). *Customer Relationship Management (CRM) software from SAP*. Retrieved August 07, 2010, from http://www.sap.com/solutions/business-suite/crm/index.epx

SAP. (2010f). *SAP Business Communication Management*. Retrieved August 07, 2010, from http://www.sap.com/solutions/business-suite/crm/businesscommunications/index.epx

SAP. (2010g). *SAP BusinessObjects portfolio*. Retrieved October 19, 2010, from http://www.sap.com/solutions/sapbusinessobjects/index.epx

SAP. (2011). *SAP crystal solutions*. Retrieved March 20, 2011, from http://www.sap.com/solutions/sap-crystal-solutions/index.epx

Schwaninger, M. (2009). *Intelligent organizations: Powerful models for systemic management* (2nd ed.). Berlin, Germany: Springer.

Souitaris, V. (2003). Determinants of technological innovation: Current research trends and future prospects. In L. V. Shavinina (Ed.), *The international handbook on innovation* (pp. 513–528). Boston, MA: Elsevier.

Stair, R., & Reynolds, G. (2006). *Principles of information systems* (7th ed.). Boston, MA: Thomson Course Technology.

Stern, C. W., & Deimler, M. S. (2006). *The Boston Consulting Group on strategy*. Hoboken, NJ: Wiley.

Stiglitz, J. E., Sen, A., & Fitoussi, J.-P. (2010). *Mismeasuring our lives: Why GDP doesn't add up*. New York: New Press.

Strong, D. M., Lee, Y. W., & Wang, R. Y. (1997). Data quality in context. *Communications of the ACM, 40*(5), 103–110.

Tetra Pak. (2010). *Tetra Pak*. Retrieved August 05, 2010, from http://www.tetrapak.com

The Economist Intelligence Unit. (2006). *Business intelligence: Putting information to work*. Retrieved October 28, 2010, from http://graphics.eiu.com/files/ad_pdfs/eiu_intel_sap_Business_intelligence_.pdf

Thinking Networks. (2010). *Custom planning solutions*. Retrieved October 19, 2010, from http://www.thinking-networks.com/index.html

UNESCO. (2005). *International coordination meeting for the development of a tsunami warning and mitigation system for the Indian Ocean within a global framework, Intergovernmental Oceanographic Commission (Workshop Report No. 196)*. Retrieved September 14, 2010, from http://www.ioc-tsunami.org/components/com_pdffarm/files/WR196.pdf

United Nations Development Programme. (2009). *Human development report 2009*. Retrieved February 20, 2011, from http://hdr.undp.org/en/media/HDR_2009_EN_Complete.pdf

United Nations Development Programme. (2011). *International human development indicators*. Retrieved February 20, 2011, from http://hdr.undp.org/en/statistics/

Victoria University. (2010). *Victoria University: A new school of thought*. Retrieved August 07, 2010, from http://www.vu.edu.au/

Vitale, M. R., & Mavrinac, S. C. (1995). How effective is your performance measurement system? *Management Accounting, 77*(2), 43–47.

Vitt, E., Luckevich, M., & Misner, S. (2002). *Business intelligence: Making better decisions faster*. Redmond, WA: Microsoft.

Volkswagen Group. (2011). *Experience d[r]iversity: Facts and figures navigator 2011*. Retrieved April 1, 2011, from http://www.volkswagenag.com/vwag/vwcorp/info_center/en/publications/2011/03/Navigator_2011_-_Facts_and_Figures.-bin.acq/qual-BinaryStorageItem.Single.File/NAVIGATOR_2011.WEB150dpi_englisch.pdf

Watson, H., Ariyachandra, T., & Matyska, R. J. (2001). Data warehousing stages of growth. *Information Systems Management, 18*(3), 42–50.

Watson, H., Wixom, B. H., Hoffer, J. A., Anderson-Lehman, R., & Reynolds, A. M. (2006). Real-time business intelligence: Best practices at Continental Airlines. *Information Systems Management, 23*(1), 7–18.

Weber, J., & Schäffer, U. (2008). *Einführung in das Controlling [Introduction in Controlling]* (11th ed.). Stuttgart: Schäffer Poeschel.

Webster's. (1996). *Webster's encylopedic unabridged dictionary of the english language*. New York: Random House.

Werner Technologies. (2010). *Theme parks: Disney FASTPASS information*. Retrieved November 17, 2010, from http://www.wdwinfo.com/wdwinfo/fastpass.htm

White, C. (2004). *Strategic management*. New York, NY: Palgrave Macmillan.

WHO. (2010). *Executive summary: The world health report*. Retrieved February 20, 2011, from http://www.who.int/whr/2010/10_summary_en.pdf

WHO. (2011). *About WHO*. Retrieved February 20, 2011, from http://www.who.int/about/en/

Wikipedia. (2010a). *Business Objects*. Retrieved August 05, 2010, from http://en.wikipedia.org/wiki/Business_Objects_(company)

Wikipedia. (2010b). *Indian Ocean Tsunami Warning System*. Retrieved September 14, 2010, from http://en.wikipedia.org/wiki/Indian_Ocean_Tsunami_Warning_System

Wikipedia. (2010c). *List of countries by GDP (nominal)*. Retrieved October 31, 2010, from http://en.wikipedia.org/wiki/List_of_countries_by_GDP_(nominal)

Wikipedia. (2010d). *Metacognition*. Retrieved November 15, 2010, from http://en.wikipedia.org/wiki/Metacognition

Wikipedia. (2011a). *Christopher Columbus*. Retrieved February 17, 2011, from http://en.wikipedia.org/wiki/Christopher_Columbus

Wikipedia. (2011b). *Dvorak simplified keyboard*. Retrieved February 14, 2011, from http://en.wikipedia.org/wiki/Dvorak_Simplified_Keyboard#cite_note-hurdling-15

Wikipedia. (2011c). *Human development index*. Retrieved February 20, 2011, from http://en.wikipedia.org/wiki/2010_Human_Development_Report#2010_report

Wikipedia. (2011d). *Management cybernetics*. Retrieved February 08, 2011, from http://en.wikipedia.org/wiki/Management_cybernetics#Organizational_cybernetics

Wood, D. (2011). *ABCD: A Basic course in Dvorak*. Retrieved February 14, 2011, from http://gigliwood.com/abcd/dvorak_links.html

World Bank. (2011a). *Gross domestic product 2009*. Retrieved April 28, 2011, from http://siteresources.worldbank.org/DATASTATISTICS/Resources/GDP.pdf

World Bank. (2011b). *Gross national income per capita 2009, Atlas method and PPP*. Retrieved April 28, 2011, from http://siteresources.worldbank.org/DATASTATISTICS/Resources/GNIPC.pdf

Zook, C., & Allen, J. (2010). *Profit from the core: A return to growth in turbulent times*. Boston, MA: Harvard Business.

About the Authors

Arndt Borgmeier, Dr. rer. pol. in Remote Services (Teleservices), is Professor for Sales, Marketing, Service Management and Supply Chain Management at the University of Applied Sciences Aalen, Germany. He is founder and CEO of the Steinbeis Institute of Technology, Marketing and Service Management (ITMS), Aalen, and specializes on management consulting, training, and coaching. In his career, he held different leading positions in the energy, utilities, manufacturing industry, and in business consulting as well as in Germany´s leading Engineering Association, VDMA. These positions allowed him to gain more than 10 years of profound management experience. Dr. Borgmeier analyzed and influenced remote services and remote solutions for about 15 years. Moreover, he is an expert in strategic management, business-to-business marketing, service engineering, complex change processes, and project management.

Bernd Heesen, D.M., is Professor of Management at the University of Applied Sciences in Ansbach and CEO of Prescient (2011), a management consultancy. He received his Doctor of Management in Organizational Leadership from the University of Phoenix in 2004 and a Master in Management Information Systems from the Technical University Darmstadt and has been teaching courses related to strategy, management information systems, project management, and consulting for many years. He was a member of SAP's Global University Alliance Curriculum Initiative for Business Intelligence (Freyburger, Gardiner, Hawking, Heesen, Jovanovic, & Lehmann, 2008). He has been invited to teach courses at leading business schools in Europe, USA, Asia, and Australia.

Professor Heesen also looks back on a career of more than 10 years in consulting, serving global customers such as Nike, Anheuser Busch, Coca-Cola, Eastman Chemicals, US Navy, and many others on all continents. Prior to his academic career Professor Heesen was management consultant at Price Waterhouse, founder and President of the International Consulting Group, cofounder and President of Prescient Consulting, and President of SAP SI America. In the year 2000, his company, Prescient Consulting, was recognized as one of the "HOT 100 – America's fastest growing new businesses" (Entrepreneur Magazine, 2000) by Entrepreneur Magazine and Dun & Bradstreet.

B. Heesen, *Effective Strategy Execution*, Management for Professionals,
DOI 10.1007/978-3-642-19205-0, © Springer-Verlag Berlin Heidelberg 2012

Catherine Fabbri is a graduate of Sceaux University and René Descartes University in Paris where she obtained bachelor's degrees, respectively, in law and in psychology. Officer in a legal department during 3 years, Catherine Fabbri has also worked on violence (interaction of violence between autistic children and facilities...). She then worked abroad and in France where she held various positions such as "Employment" Project Officer within ANPE (1992) and Chargée de mission RMI (social welfare) for the prefect of Savoy. She joined the city of Aix les Bains in 2005 as Director of the urban social policy. She is currently project manager at the office of general director and at the urban community of the CALB (community of agglomeration of the Bourget Lake).

Chris Roberts, Ph.D., is Professor and Director of the School of Hospitality Leadership at DePaul University in Chicago. He received his doctorate in Strategic Management from the University of Massachusetts-Amherst in 1995 and has been teaching strategy, lodging, resort, and casino related courses for 20+ years.

Professor Roberts has 8 years of hotel industry experience in both operations and reservation centers. In addition, he owned and/or operated a travel agency for another 8 years. He also has 11 years of corporate marketing and sales experience with the Bell Telephone System.

Dr. Roberts has published widely with more than 50 publications in various academic journals and industry publications and he has given more than 60 presentations at conferences and seminars. His research focus is centered on the strategic decision-making process, strategy implementation, and the composition of executive teams.

Christopher Rowley is a senior IT executive with more than 15 years of leadership experience for global leaders such as Tetra Pak and Silicon Graphics. His background includes business transformation, business-IT alignment and governance, IT planning and architecture, supply chain systems, and SAP program management.

During his time as Director Business Intelligence & e-Business Systems for Tetra Pak Global Information Management, Mr. Rowley contributed to shortening the financial close process by 50%, implemented an effective business intelligence strategy, and saved the company millions of Euros per year by establishing a Singapore-based information management group, migrating development and other IT responsibilities from Europe.

Christian Schneider, M.A., is principal consultant at the CRM consulting company maihiro. He has supported customers in the area of CRM (Customer Relationship Management) for 10 years. Besides, he is a communication trainer and mediator. As project manager, he is specialized in software implementations and accompanies Würth Handelsges.m.b.H. with their implementation since 2008.

Maihiro received the "TOP 100" seal of quality awarded to Germany's most innovative mid-sized companies in July 2010 by compamedia GmbH (Compamedia GmbH, 2010). They reward and champion companies that excel in the areas of innovation, personnel management, consulting, and value management.

Erich Maierhofer deals with questions related to the employment market and innovative IT solutions the last 15 years. A focus of his activities included his activity as project manager responsible to develop a system of KPIs for operative as well as strategic control at the Federal Employment Agency. Since 2007 he is Head of the Coordination Office for Business Intelligence Requirements.

Friedrich Saller started at Würth Handelsgesellschaftm.b.H. as a software developer for sales and distribution processes 20 years ago. Since 1999, he has taken over responsibility as the Chief Information Officer (CIO).

Michael Jungbauer is Manager for the After Sales Support at Daimler AG with more than 10 years leadership experience in the automotive industry. After a trainee program, he gained experience in controlling, business development, and project management before he became head of product management passenger cars in the Mercedes-Benz Bank. At the same time, he completed the 1-year Advanced Degree Program at the University of Southern California (Los Angeles/USA). Then he took over the project leadership to redesign the support-landscape for Global Service & Parts with the aim of the restructuring process and establishing a global support tool. Since 2007, he is working on a PhD on "use categories of remote service in the after sales area of the automotive industry" (Prof. Dr. Holzmüller, TU Dortmund).

Pascale Fressoz, MBA, graduated at the University of Geneva (HEC) and has been certified by the Balanced Scorecard Institute in Washington and the High College of Sustainable Development in Lyon. With 17 years of experience within a multicultural and international environment (Europe, Middle East, Africa.), she worked in Sales and Marketing, Project Management, and held a Deputy Director position before creating her consulting firm Millennium Enterprises in strategy and sustainable development for both the public and private sector.

She also created an international NGO, in 2006, the International Alliance for the Millennium Development Goals (AIODM, 2010), aiming at supporting the UN program, the Millennium Development Goals. On the other side, she is also elected in Haute-Savoie and has been nominated Honorous Citizen of the Village of Eri Makouguié I, in Africa (Ivory Coast), where she implemented an innovative program "AIODM Millennium Villages." Between 2002 and 2008, she strongly supported the cause of the 3,000 hostages in Colombia and Ingrid Betancourt, where she was Vice President in charge of Public and International Relations.

Paul Hawking is a Senior Lecturer in Information Systems at Victoria University, Australia (Victoria University, 2010). He is also a leading commentator on ERP systems and specifically SAP solutions. His knowledge is well respected in both industry and academia and accordingly he is often required to assist companies with their ERP strategies and understanding SAP solutions. He has presented at Sapphire, ASUG, and SAUG conferences and was a member of SAP's Global University Alliance Curriculum Initiative for Business Intelligence (Freyburger, Gardiner, Hawking, Heesen, Jovanovic, & Lehmann, 2008). He has been a committee member of the SAP Australian User Group for the past 9 years including the role of Chairman.

In 2009, Paul was voted by the SAP community as one of the Top Ten Most Influential People in SAP for Australia and New Zealand (SAP, 2010d, p. 15).

Paul is also one of Australia's best selling IT authors having written ten books which are sold throughout the world. His areas of teaching and research are ERP system strategy and implementation, and Business Intelligence.

Thomas Paal is engaged in software development for more than 20 years. He has designed transactional systems as well as performance management systems with responsibility as project manager or as general manager. Since September 2009 he works at the IT System House of the Federal Employment Agency where he has the responsibility for the data warehouse solution.

Ute Riemann is Business Process Architect at Giesecke & Devrient responsible for the design and implementation of new processes in the organization. Before joining she has worked in various positions as project manager with companies such as T-Systems, Kurt Salmon Associates, and SAP where she headed the SAP Process Office in the Board Unit Global Service and Support. She has built a key expertise in business process development/optimization and SAP. Based on her background in project and process management she lectures seminars at various universities. She holds a Master in Computer Science of the TU Dortmund and an MBA of the University of Cologne. She is member of the PMI.org – Project Management Institute.

Index

B. Heesen, *Effective Strategy Execution*, Management for Professionals,
DOI 10.1007/978-3-642-19205-0, © Springer-Verlag Berlin Heidelberg 2012

23346559R00136

Printed in Great Britain
by Amazon